THE HENRY L.
STIMSON CENTER

IRAQ AND AMERICA: CHOICES AND CONSEQUENCES

**Ellen Laipson and
Maureen S. Steinbruner, Editors**

July 2006

TABLE OF CONTENTS

ACKNOWLEDGEMENTS

This project would not have been possible without a generous grant from the Christopher Reynolds Foundation. We are grateful for their support. We also wish to recognize the important contributions made by the Stimson Center's staff, especially Research Associate Emile El-Hokayem, Scoville Peace Fellow Amy Buenning Sturm, Program Coordinator Marvin Lim, and interns Wael Al-Zayat and Michael Schoengold. They have played an important part in organizing our meetings, and in providing fine research and editorial support for this book.

LIST OF ACRONYMS

AIRP	Accelerated Iraq Reconstruction Program
ASEAN	Association of Southeast Asian Nations
CBO	Congressional Budget Office
CERP	Commander's Emergency Response Program
CD	Conference on Disarmament
CDA	Congressionally Directed Actions
CPA	Coalition Provisional Authority
CSCE	Conference for Security and Co-operation in Europe
DART	Disaster Assistance Response Team
DCM	Deputy Chief of Mission
DD	Defense Directive
DFI	Development Fund for Iraq
DoD	Department of Defense
EU	European Union
FBI	Federal Bureau of Investigation
FOB	Forward Operating Bases
FTA	Free Trade Argeement
FY	Fiscal Year
GCC	Gulf Cooperation Council
IAEA	International Atomic Energy Agency
IDA	International Development Agency
IG	Inspector General
IMF	International Monetary Fund
INL	International Narcotics and Law Enforcement Bureau
IRMO	Iraq Reconstruction Management Office
IRRF I	Iraq Relief and Reconstruction Fund I

IRRF II	Iraq Relief and Reconstruction Fund II
ISF	Iraqi Security Forces
ISAF	International Security Assistance Force
KDP	Kurdistan Democratic Party
KEDO	Korean Peninsula Energy Development Organization
LEU	Low Enriched Uranium
MNF	Multi-National Force
MNSTC-I	Multi-National Security and Transitional Command Iraq
NATO	North Atlantic Treaty Organization
NDU	National Defense University
NGO	Non-Governmental Organization
NPT	Treaty on the Non-Proliferation of Nuclear Weapons
NSC	National Security Council
NSPD	National Security Presidential Directive
NSS	National Security Strategy
OAS	Organization of American States
ODC	Office of Defense Cooperation
OIC	Organization of the Islamic Conference
OMB	Office of Management and Budget
ORHA	Office of Reconstruction and Humanitarian Assistance
OSCE	Organization for Security and Co-operation in Europe
PCO	Project and Contracting Office
PMO	Program Management Office
PRDC	Provincial Reconstruction and Development Councils
PRT	Provincial Reconstruction Teams
PUK	Patriotic Union of Kurdistan
S/CRS	State Department Office of the Coordinator for Stabilization and Reconstruction
S&R	Stabilization and Reconstruction

SCIRI	Supreme Council for the Islamic Revolution in Iraq
SIGIR	Special Inspector General for Iraq Reconstruction
TDA	Trade and Development Agency
UAE	United Arab Emirates
UN	United Nations
UNAMI	United Nations Assistance Mission for Iraq
UNDP	United Nations Development Programme
UNSCR	United Nations Security Council Resolution
ACE	United States Army Corps of Engineers
USAID	United States Agency for International Development
UNSC	United Nations Security Council
WMD	Weapons of Mass Destruction

POLITICAL MAP OF IRAQ

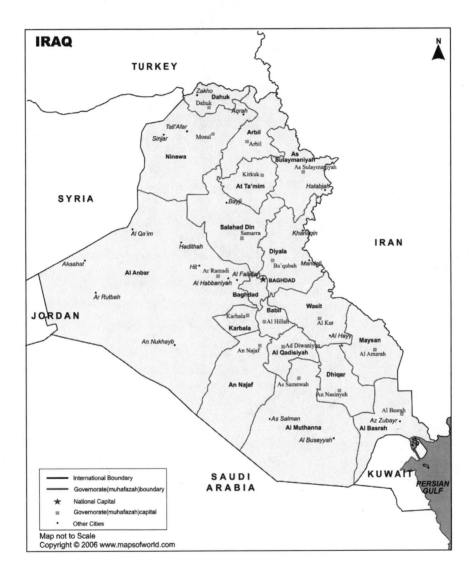

—1—
INTRODUCTION

Ellen Laipson and Maureen S. Steinbruner

America's engagement in Iraq will have profound consequences for US interests and American national security for the foreseeable future. The US-led invasion that deposed the regime of Saddam Hussein, the shifting priorities of the US occupation in attempting to restore security and establish a more representative government, and the reluctance of Iraq's neighbors and so much of the international community to become full partners in the endeavor will have lasting implications for Iraq, the region, international politics in general and US power and influence in particular. This volume of essays examines some of the consequences of US engagement in Iraq and considers choices for American policymakers that might contribute to more favorable outcomes in Iraq and beyond.

BACKGROUND

The Henry L. Stimson Center, over the first half of 2006, convened a group of former policy practitioners and academics to reflect on ways to achieve more favorable outcomes in Iraq and to begin to assess the impact of America's engagement there for other US foreign policy and national security objectives. Many in the group had extensive experience in Iraq and in the Middle East, while others looked at the topic through a wider-angle lens. The group was united in some key working assumptions:

Irrespective of our personal views on the Iraq war, we believe that what happens there matters for a range of US interests. Achieving better results is therefore critical, not only for Iraqis but for Americans too.

We agreed that our effort should be focused on the future; there is already some important literature assessing the decision to go to war, and the early implementation phase. We chose not to revisit all those issues, but to take today's reality as our baseline. We believe that decisions taken with respect to the timing of withdrawal, drawdown and/or repositioning should reflect a pragmatic, broad rethinking of U.S. policy, interests, and objectives. We recognize that an indefinite extension of the status quo in our policy will not bring stability to Iraq.

We also approached the task with humility, understanding that US leverage and ability to shape events in Iraq are sorely constrained. We wanted to concentrate on what may be achievable in practice, rather than what might be ideal in principle.

It is our hope that the judgments and analysis offered here will contribute to the national conversation on Iraq, and to the effort better understand the costs of this engagement on other critical US interests and concerns. We are well aware that Iraqi views of US policies would have added a valuable dimension to our work, but this exercise was structured to solicit the advice of US experts.

This volume focuses on choices for the United States, but it acknowledges that the policy decisions and actions of Iraq's leaders and its people will be the primary drivers and shapers of its future. That said, we nonetheless believe that the US has a unique responsibility, moral and political, for what happens there, even if our influence on events is diminishing.

SUMMARY

One recurrent theme of these essays is the importance of ensuring that Iraqis get the help they need from the international community. In achieving this, however, the US must be prepared to support Iraq's own efforts, not to dictate them. In general, we believe it is time for Iraq to set its agenda, and not rely on the US to set goals, timetables, and milestones. Second is the requirement for flexibility. There is a process underway that will evolve, posing different dilemmas and opportunities along the way. The US must be prepared to adapt to changing circumstances, to the point of adopting alternative objectives as well as different policies, as needed. Finally, but not least important, there are long-term implications to confront, even though they are not yet entirely understood. It is not yet possible to calculate the full impact of Iraq on US resources for other international engagements and commitments, on priorities for all other federal spending, and on how the nation budgets and plans for national security requirements in the future. But we believe it is time to start thinking about all of these issues.

While we did not push for consensus on policy options, there are some broad points of agreement on current US policy and the debate on troop withdrawal:

- We approach the troop withdrawal issue as a means, not an end. Decisions about deployments in Iraq cannot be considered in isolation but also cannot be made entirely contingent on specific facts on the ground, which are likely to remain problematic and uncertain for some time. We have avoided the simple slogans of "get out now" or "stay the course;"

- We believe there must be a better strategy for constructively involving the participation of other nations and international organizations. A number of the authors in this volume are skeptical about prospects for multilateral engagement at this stage, but all agree that stability in Iraq will require support from neighbors and donors, and that obtaining such support must be a US and Iraqi priority. As we go to print, some important progress is being made on this front; and

- We also recognize that Iraq's leaders need to take the initiative in engaging the international community on their behalf, and could well take positions that differ from those of the US. That is their right as well as their responsibility.

This volume begins with several chapters on **governance and legitimacy**. *Paul Pillar* argues for flexibility, not pushing the Iraqis for more centralization than the political market can bear, and scaling back ambitious US milestones for their political development. He suggests that we need to support processes rather than specific outcomes, and that we should support the grand bargain on the constitution that was reached in October 2005, calling for a parliamentary process of review, as a way to ensure Sunni participation and buy-in to the new political system. *Barbara Bodine* argues that an over-reliance on security as the dominant criterion for US withdrawal risks creating a house of cards if not balanced with an equal commitment to leave a viable and truly legitimate Iraqi state. The insurgency and sectarian violence can only be defeated politically, not destroyed militarily. To get there, she lays out a series of policy proposals, including the need to change our vocabulary and mindset from "troop withdrawal" to "political transition," to keep faith with the grand bargain of 2005 and to seek out nationalist forces within Iraq while building capacity at the regional level. *Robin Raphel* sets out a series of steps for the critical transition in the reconstruction and assistance relationship, calling for a dramatic streamlining of procedures and actors on the US side, and a more strategic focus on key sectors where US technical aid can make a difference: education, agriculture and health. She also encourages Iraq to invite the World Bank and other international players to take the lead on assistance, and proposes that it is time for a quite different approach to Iraqi reconstruction, and a transition to a more traditional aid relationship.

Two experts on security offered their analysis of **trends in the insurgency and in other security problems in Iraq**. *David Edelstein* looked conceptually at how a US withdrawal might affect the insurgency and other forms of strife in Iraq. He argues that withdrawal may be desirable and even necessary for US interests, but in and of itself will not have an immediate impact on levels of violence, unless there is a significant shift in politics in the country. He considers the relationship between the form of government and the state of unrest, raising the uncomfortable issue of whether Iraq's new parliamentary democracy will be capable of taking the hard decisions to get security under control. *Michael Eisenstadt* proposes a number of concrete steps the US could take that would address Iraq's troubled situation, including resisting the temptation to shelter our forces in large bases, finding employment for internally displaced Iraqis, addressing the war economy that has diverted Iraq's oil wealth to support militias and insurgents, and lending strong support to efforts aimed at cleaning out the Ministry of Interior, some of whose forces have been complicit in Iraq's domestic strife.

The third set of essays deals with the **multilateral dimensions of Iraq**. *Avis Bohlen* describes the damage Iraq has done to US standing in the world, and how US influence even in Iraq itself has eroded. She identifies America's greatest leverage as the US military presence in Iraq, not in terms of its ability to impose order, but rather the political leverage it wields by threatening to leave. She argues that other countries, despite their disapproval, will calculate their own engagement in Iraq and relations with the United States on the basis of their own interests. *Dan Poneman* reminds us of the core logic of multilateralism, as an enabler or enhancer of American power, rather than as a phenomenon that diminishes US power and influence. He believes that a decision to bring new international involvement in Iraq would now have to come from Iraq, not as a US policy initiative. He also reflects on the world after Iraq, and suggests that there are practical ways to promote multilateral approaches in the future, in order to increase chances of success in addressing the challenges of an interdependent world. *Nancy Soderberg* proposes new multilateral efforts for Iraq, including a contact group of neighbors and stronger roles for the United Nations, the European Union, and the Arab League. She also proposes that the United States shift its focus from Iraq's internal political process, which must be owned by the Iraqis, and instead use its leverage and power to secure broader international involvement in Iraq.

Two authors looked at **regional issues**. *Michael Kraig* offers a strategic analysis of the failure to achieve more durable security for the Middle East, arguing that Iraq has become a pawn in a struggle between two regional hegemons, the United States and Iran. Kraig believes the United States needs to fundamentally restructure its approach to the region, and to now focus on preventing Iraq from becoming a failed state. He thinks the US needs to look for a balance of interests in the region and inside Iraq, rather than seeing winners and losers. The goal should be the creation of a sovereign order in the region, not a strategic competition with Iran. *Ellen Laipson* looks more narrowly at the dilemma of active US policies toward Iraq and Iran that can adversely affect each other. The United States also has to adjust to evolving Iraq-Iran relations, and to recognize that it cannot unilaterally shape or set limits for Iraq, even though it continues to fear excessive Iranian influence on Shia politics inside Iraq. The United States needs to have a positive agenda for its relations with both countries and avoid playing them off each other.

Iraq and the US policy process is the focus of two essays on how engagement in Iraq has revealed some enduring structural weaknesses in national security policymaking and budgeting. *Gordon Adams* looks at stabilization and reconstruction (S&R) and at a range of near-term and more strategic budget issues. He explains how the ad hoc approach to funding our engagement in Iraq undermined the formal mechanisms for budgeting and planning and dramatically reduced the normal oversight mechanisms. He proposes greater integration of strategic planning and budgeting, and ways to enhance US capacity to manage S&R for contingencies beyond Iraq. *Denis McDonough* focuses on Congress and the historic pattern of Congressional support for overseas military commitments. He recommends that the Executive branch return to more routine budgeting for Iraq, and that Congress restore its oversight function.

These essays were produced in the spring and early summer of 2006. We realize that changing conditions in Iraq will affect our analysis and our policy recommendations, and we recognize that the Administration is making many course corrections that may render some of our ideas no longer relevant. This exercise has been an effort to capture the thinking of some experienced policy experts, and to share that thinking with diverse American audiences as concerned citizens reflect on the way forward in Iraq.

— 2 —
GOVERNANCE AND NATIONAL UNITY

Paul Pillar

Any assessment of, or recommendation about, Iraq's political future must start by acknowledging that most of the hopes and dreams that inspired Operation Iraqi Freedom will not be realized. Iraq will not be—within any time frame that is politically or psychologically meaningful for most people—anything close to a unified, liberal democracy. This acknowledgement is important not as a judgment about the past but as a necessary frame of mind for considering how best to influence the future.

Three corollaries follow. First, policy toward Iraq and its political reconstruction must focus at least as much on avoiding the worst possible outcomes as on trying to attain the best. Pursuit of the ideal would be likely, in this case, to be the enemy not only of the good but also of the merely acceptable. Second, although Iraqi leaders and their outside supporters need to keep an eye on the long-term evolution of the Iraqi polity, much of their attention must be on the short-term because unless Iraq survives the short-term its long-term possibilities are irrelevant. Third, the geopolitical realities that explain most of the troubles that have beset Iraq for three years will continue to impose severe limits on its political future. The most appropriate attitude for anyone who cares about that future is less that of an engineer constructing a new political edifice than that of an ecologist looking for ways to survive in a harsh political environment.

> *Any assessment of, or recommendation about, Iraq's political future must start by acknowledging that most of the hopes and dreams that inspired Operation Iraqi Freedom will not be realized.*

Within the limits imposed by that environment, the range of possible Iraqi political futures is nonetheless broad. Prognostication is hazardous.

Numerous domestic and external variables will influence the story of Iraqi governance in the months and years ahead.

Iraq will not be—within any time frame that is politically or psychologically meaningful for most people—anything close to a unified, liberal democracy.

Two domestic variables that already are affecting Iraqi politics in critical ways are especially difficult to anticipate or predict. One is leadership. A generation of would-be Iraqi leaders was crippled under Saddam's dictatorship. Those who were not either co-opted or killed went into exile, and some returned three years ago with a deficit of legitimacy for having been out of the country, out of touch, and not having shared the suffering of their countrymen inside. The squabbling and ineffectiveness that have characterized the first several iterations of post-Saddam governing authorities reflect in part this leadership deficit. And yet, there also have been acts of statesmanship and even courage.

In addition to the overall prospects for good versus bad leadership, even more unpredictable is the possibility of the emergence of a single great, transformational figure—an Iraqi incarnation of Ataturk, Tito, or Nasser—with larger-than-life skills and charisma capable of overcoming even the severe divisions of the Iraqi polity. That no candidate for such a role is in sight does not mean it is impossible for one to surface. If one were to surface, the United States should feel relief over the advent of such a figure as offering the most direct route out of the current disorder. Washington would have to be willing to live with his less appealing—from a US standpoint—attributes, including a probable Nasser-like proclivity for standing up to the United States.

The second variable is the possibility of inflammatory incidents, similar to the destruction of the Shia mosque in Samarra in February 2006, capable of derailing even the most carefully prepared political reconstruction initiatives. The basis for such incidents can easily be analyzed and understood; the prediction of specific incidents is impossible. Possible events include further dramatic, large-scale terrorist attacks with a sectarian flavor, such as the one in Samarra. Another possibility is overreaction by Iraqi security forces, such as firing into protesting crowds. Yet another is the death, especially by assassination, of one or more key leaders. The current leader whose death would be most disruptive—bearing in mind the leadership deficit among politicians—is Grand Ayatollah Ali al-Sistani, who has more influence than anyone else among Iraqi Shia. One should assume that more inflammatory incidents will occur. A priority for American advice and influence should be to encourage Iraqi leaders in the wake of such incidents to exercise restraint, quash rumors and dampen popular emotions.

Part of governance is the provision of services that any public sector must furnish to make daily life bearable and economic activity feasible. This means making the trains—and the electrical, water, and sewer systems, among other things—run on time. The serious and well-known problems plaguing Iraqi infrastructure since the invasion are a constant reminder of how far Iraq has to go on this score. But good governance entails not just making things run but doing so in a modern, fair, and efficient manner. This means not using brute force—which the current Iraqi authorities are incapable of doing anyway. It also means not using graft and corruption as lubricants for making the machinery of the public sector operate. Unfortunately, corruption is a major part of public life in today's Iraq—so major that reducing it to what most westerners would consider insignificant levels probably is impossible within the next few years. Meanwhile, corruption will be a drain on economic performance and an additional reason for Iraqis to regard their government with cynicism and distrust, thereby undermining every other aspect of governance. Making at least some headway in combating corruption should be a priority for outside players as they seek to influence Iraqis. Placing this task under the umbrella of the World Bank's anticorruption efforts might be useful.

There is no quick or obvious fix to the problems besetting this particular aspect. Improvement can come only slowly and will depend on a combination of outside assistance with things such as rehabilitation of infrastructure and a fuller application of Iraqis' own expertise. Meanwhile, a major impediment to progress in furnishing public services is the inability of the Iraqi government and the foreign coalition to provide the most important public service of all: security.

Another aspect of governance is what political scientists call the articulation and aggregation of interests—the voicing of different views and their conversion, through a peaceful political process, into public policy. The articulation of the diverse interests of Iraqis has blossomed since Saddam's fall. The aggregation of these interests is not working well, however, largely for reasons rooted in Iraqi political culture. Iraqis have not developed a sense of a loyal opposition—of being out of power but still a relevant and respected part of a political process. The years under the Ba'athists led Iraqis to associate losing power more with losing one's life. Iraqis express support for the idea of democracy, but it is not clear that for most of them it means anything more than majority rule.

The transitional period to date has aggravated some of these unfavorable aspects of Iraqi political culture. Elections (including to the current legislature) and negotiations have largely reflected ethnic and sectarian divisions and, because of this, have tended to accentuate those same divisions. Discontent with political outcomes has been amplified by the belief of many Iraqis that their own communities constitute larger proportions of Iraq's population than they really do. Animosity toward, and distrust of, communities other than one's own have been further amplified by the sectarian violence that has been a constant and bloody backdrop to the politicking. All of this has tended to offset or even undo the more promising indications of a "Sushi" mentality that crosses communal lines.

Iraq also clearly is a long way from exhibiting the most fundamental attribute of a sovereign state: exercising a monopoly of violence on its own territory. The preponderance of armed power in most of Iraq rests with militias, whose role has, if anything, increased over the past three years. Much of the mosaic of political power in Iraq mirrors the mosaic of armed power in the streets.

All of this leads to the biggest question about governance in Iraq: can a central government evolve and strengthen to the point that it effectively rules as the sovereign over all of Iraq? Iraq was three separate provinces under the Ottomans, but after independence it had the opportunity to develop some degree of Iraqi nationalism. Which of these elements in Iraqi history will shape the Iraqi mindset in the next few years, and will Iraqis be able to overcome the more divisive aspects of the first three years of transition?

To understand one major limit to central rule, one need look no further than the Kurds of northern Iraq, who since 1991 have enjoyed something close to de facto independence in the form of mini-states governed by the Kurdistan Democratic Party (KDP) and Patriotic Union of Kurdistan (PUK). "Enjoy" is the right word, for post-1991 Iraqi Kurdistan has exhibited a degree of prosperity and (despite some intramural KDP-PUK fighting during the 1990s) peace exceeding what Iraqi Arabs experienced during Saddam's last years, or have seen amid the disorder since his ouster. The Kurds use their cohesion to play the Iraqi political game adroitly, and PUK leader Jalal Talibani is the incumbent Iraqi president, but the less attractive the mess to the south appears, the more the Kurdish inclination will be to find fulfillment in its bastion in the north. The Kurds will continue to negotiate, but they would be crazy to settle for less than what they have now.

The Kurdish position alone therefore appears to put out of reach a central Iraqi government whose writ, in fact as well as name, would run throughout all of Iraq. The Kurdish position encourages similar postures elsewhere, especially among Shia leadership in southern Iraq. Supreme Council for the Islamic Revolution in Iraq (SCIRI) leader Abdul Aziz Hakim has spoken of an autonomous region in the south. The power of militias lends credibility and clout to such talk.

These realities may make an open and complete break-up of Iraq along communal lines appear to be the most stable and least undesirable political outcome, but the major and possibly fatal flaw in that idea is that the lines, at least for now, are not clear. In Baghdad and other cities there is neighborhood-by-neighborhood intermingling. In areas such as Kirkuk there would be intense conflict over where the lines should be drawn, with the stakes heightened by oil resources and emotions heightened by a prior history of ethnic cleansing under Saddam. Oil resources underlie another major problem, which is that Sunni Arabs in the west and center of Iraq would have little if any of them. Instability in an impoverished and unhappy rump Sunni state—in an area that already is the center of an insurgency—could not be walled off from the other fragments of Iraq, or from other neighboring states.

For these reasons, there will be—and should be—an effort, admittedly arduous, to keep all of Iraq as one color on the map and to develop a central Iraqi government that has enough acceptance by the major Iraqi communities to be worthy of that name, even if its actual span of control were seriously limited. What would it take to achieve that goal? Most of all, time. The task should be thought of in generational terms, both in changing attitudes and in developing governmental effectiveness. In the meantime, official US rhetoric should continue to be couched in terms of the goal of a unified Iraq, despite being at variance with facts on the ground. Early talk from Washington of a permanent division of Iraq would risk becoming a self-fulfilling prophecy.

The time required would be lessened (but still long by most measures) by the emergence of an Iraqi leader with leadership skills significantly surpassing those demonstrated to date by Baghdad politicians. Such a leader need not have the historical stature of the larger-than-life figures mentioned earlier, but would have to be a source of hope to most Iraqi ethnic and sectarian groups as someone who could restore a modicum of stability and security.

Stability is what such a leader would offer—not liberalism or democracy. Such a mid-term political formula, however, would not preclude later evolution to a more liberal and democratic order. Any such eventual evolution would be more likely to grow in top-down fashion out of this kind of reasonably stable but authoritarian system than to emerge bottom-up from the grass roots of Iraqi politics. The dominant feature of those roots will remain, for the foreseeable future, militias rather than town meetings.

Such a model could, in the meantime, have the form of a representative democracy while lacking much of the substance—rather like the Egypt of Hosni Mubarak or the Pakistan of Pervez Musharraf. Although undoubtedly there would be numerous human rights issues to be raised with such a regime, it would be unlikely to exhibit the brutality of Saddam, which would exceed the tolerance both of the overwhelming majority of Iraqis and of the international community. The dearth of genuine democracy certainly would be an issue, as it is today with Egypt and Pakistan. The United States could and probably should be more vocal about this issue regarding Iraq than it has been with those other two countries, given its enormous investment in Iraq and perceived responsibility for leaving it a better place than it was at the time of the invasion. But such a pseudo-democracy would be a credible enough interlocutor that the United States could deal with it constructively and, with a straight face, portray it as an embodiment of "success" of Operation Iraqi Freedom, however patently short it would fall from the original hopes for that expedition. This political outcome probably would be the best, by most measures, that can be expected in Iraq by the end of this decade. Compared with the current disorder, even getting this far would be a remarkable accomplishment.

The authority of such a regime, especially beyond Baghdad, would be limited and defined by bargains and understandings it would reach with centers of power elsewhere in the country. Kurdish leaders probably would be satisfied with continuation of de facto independence in return for disavowal of any attempt to make it de jure and the reaching of some compromise regarding disposition of northern oil revenues. The Kurds, mindful of the sensitivities of Ankara in particular, might be content to continue this fiction indefinitely, as the Taiwan of the Middle East. Similar but less salient understandings would have to be reached with power brokers elsewhere in the country, such as the leadership of SCIRI. In some respects the political system would resemble Lebanon, with apportionment of political power the result less of national elections than of inter-communal negotiations. This would continue a pattern of current Iraqi politicking, in which leadership positions are apportioned first to particular ethnic and sectarian groups, and only secondarily are filled with specific individuals.

Indeed, Lebanon is a model for a variant—probably a more likely variant—of this mid-term political scenario, in which the most salient feature of Iraqi politics would be not a single figure with even as much power as a Musharraf or a Mubarak but instead the ethnic/sectarian mosaic itself. The main measure of success in this model would be whether the inter-communal bargains being struck would have enough clarity and legitimacy to make the system more like the Lebanon of the 1990s than the Lebanon of the 1970s and 1980s.

The political evolution of Iraq into even an acceptable way-station of the sort described above—let alone into something more liberal and democratic—probably will outlast American patience for continued heavy involvement in Iraq, including patience for maintaining a substantial troop presence. Bearing that in mind, the goals of the United States and other concerned outsiders should be less the completion of any particular Iraqi political project than the encouragement of constructive attitudes and behaviors and the limitation of damage while the generation-long process of Iraqi political evolution into a hoped-for brighter future continues. In particular, a high priority should be the limitation of the sorts of distrust-exacerbating behaviors that have been all too prevalent during the transitional period (such as Shia and Kurdish negotiators in effect telling Sunni Arabs to take a hike during some of the constitutional deliberations in 2005).

In this regard, it would be a mistake to push Iraqis harder and faster toward a centralization of power than so many of them are obviously unprepared to go, however desirable the construction of a strong central government may be for other reasons. Not only is all politics ultimately local; for a frightened and distrustful people, one's own sect, town, party, or militia is a refuge from fear. Keeping power close at hand is the default solution in a situation as disorderly as present-day Iraq. For reasons having to do with political geography, culture, and history (both distant and very recent), Iraq is going to have a decentralized political order, with almost any of the several possible outcomes along the spectrum of possibilities during the next several years. It would require emergence of a truly great, transforming Iraqi leader to change that any time soon.

Given this reality, useful US influence during the next stages of the transition may be as much a matter of restraining leaders of the central Iraqi government as of bucking them up. While retaining the concept of a unified Iraq as at least a nominal or distant goal, the United States should encourage accommodation and compromise with centers of power outside the capital. The United States has much to offer in this regard as an exemplar. It is, after all, not just a powerful democracy but also a successful federal state—one that demonstrates how dispersal of political power need not equate with national weakness.

Regardless of the size of the coalition troop presence, outside diplomatic and economic help will be important in easing Iraq's near-term political evolution. Continued mediation efforts by the energetic US ambassador, Zalmay Khalilzad, are worthwhile, despite the periodic and inevitable accusations of favoritism by one side or the other. That help—bearing in mind the preceding points about limiting damage and encouraging constructive attitudes—should focus at least as much on what are called in other contexts interim arrangements rather than final solutions. Another useful comparison is with Bosnia, where a decade ago the head-cracking US negotiator Richard Holbrooke led a successful effort to end a communal civil war. The Dayton settlement was seen as an interim arrangement that would buy Bosnia perhaps a decade's time. A decade later, it is still seen that way, which is why further political evolution in Bosnia is a renewed issue. Anything that would buy that kind of time for Iraq would be a major plus.

In exerting influence on the constitutional process, Americans also should focus on the process more than on the product. No single formula will placate, let alone please, all the Iraqi communities with interests at stake. Keeping open the prospect of further adjustments in the new Iraqi political order, however, will maintain the incentive for even dissatisfied communities to remain part of constitutional negotiations. The United States should support the principle that important constitutional issues were not fully resolved by the constituent assembly in 2005 and that the current legislature will have to readdress them.

The United States needs to calibrate carefully its own role in this process. It must use what leverage it has to keep the process alive while scrupulously avoiding any impression of dictating the result. This means eschewing, especially publicly, any statements that could be seen as imposing on Iraq a made-in-Washington political structure. It also means reminding Iraqi politicians, especially privately, that the American military presence will not provide an indefinite cover for their own disagreements and dithering.

As the international community contemplates the less-than-optimum, less-than-liberal-democracy possibilities it faces in Iraq, it needs to stay flexible. To a large extent it needs to go with the flow of political events inside Iraq. Fighting that flow would mean incurring the resentment of many Iraqis over what they would perceive as outside interference, and perhaps forcing Iraqis to deal with each other in ways that would exacerbate their mutual animosity. Going with the flow means being sensitive to which acceptable political outcomes are becoming relatively more feasible and which less so. Events on the ground are likely to foreclose some possibilities and to open others. Developments such as population movements associated with intensified civil strife, for example, may make even a formal division of Iraq—at least on an interim basis, along the lines of the Dayton accord—more worthy of consideration than it appears to be now.

The United States needs to keep its principal security interests in the region uppermost in mind, of course, and in particular to worry about the outcomes in Iraq that would be least favorable and most threatening to those interests. One possible threat would be the recovery and rise of an Iraq that could become, as an aggressor, a future threat to regional peace. This threat would be less of a worry to the extent that Iraq remained divided or weak rather than unified and strong. Saddam Hussein could not have initiated two regional wars if he had been president of a much weaker Iraq, and there is no reason to assume that Iraq never will have another leader with similar aggressive designs on his neighbors. A weak Iraq also would be less able to develop weapons of mass destruction. This certainly does not mean a weak or divided Iraq would be on balance beneficial to regional security interests. Among other things, it would preclude Iraq playing certain constructive roles—such as acting as a counterweight to Iran—as well as destructive ones. It is a reminder, however, that not all advantages from the US point of view lie in the direction of a strong central government in Baghdad.

Two other distinctly unfavorable outcomes ought to be greater worries, one of which would be an intensified Iraqi civil war that draws in neighboring states. Such a development would carry the risk of unrestrained escalation in terms of intensity, number of participants and geographic scope. The specter of an expanded war certainly would not argue in favor of keeping Iraq weak and divided, but neither does it imply that the best political course would be to push for a rapid accretion of power by a central government. The risk of an expanded civil war might be heightened either by a paucity of power at the center or by conflicts arising from the very effort to move power to the center—or from the higher stakes that such a move would place on how power is apportioned at the center. Which political strategy, for Iraqis and for outsiders advising them, would minimize the chance of civil war spiraling out of control would depend on the state of play at any given moment and is impossible to encapsulate in a general rule. The risk of a wider war will depend not only on the political state of play but also on the state of security forces. This is related to the separate issue (not addressed in this chapter) of the coalition troop presence, and perhaps also to the contribution of regional or other international forces to take their place.

The other major worry (not mutually exclusive with the first one) would be that Iraq slides farther in the direction of a failed state and assumes a larger role as a haven for global jihadists and terrorists. Although Iraq is unlikely to approach the nadir of governance exhibited by a prototypical failed state such as Somalia, the disorder of the last three years and its exploitation by foreign extremists have shown some of the same symptoms. Here the most relevant lessons might be drawn from Afghanistan. Most self-respecting Iraqis probably would resent this comparison; Afghanistan's economic and social development has always lagged far behind that of Iraq. But most recently, its political development has not. Afghanistan has, despite the enormous turmoil and destruction to which it had been subjected over the previous quarter century, accomplished political reconstruction over the last couple of years. In Iraq, should comparable progress occur there over the next couple of years, it would widely be considered a success.

Despite the obvious and significant differences between the two situations, it is the similarities that are more germane to avoiding the danger of sinking into an extremist abyss. In each country there is a history of jihadist use of the territory, recovery from the rule of a repulsive regime, and an effort to construct a new political order in the face of ethnic and sectarian differences. Not least, there are the militias, and the centers of power associated with them. What has worked so far in Afghanistan is a process of near-term acquiescence in the local rule of those other centers of power and a very slow increase in the central government's authority through bargains with, co-optation of, and occasional well-planned power plays against individual warlords. The United States, holding its nose, has dealt with warlords as legitimate political players.

Applying the Afghan lesson to Iraq implies (besides the hope that a leader with at least the skill set of a Hamid Karzai will emerge) a recognition of where most power in most Iraqi towns and cities resides, and an acceptance of the principal political implication of an inevitable fact: that Iraq in the near term will be a very decentralized polity, with effective power in many parts of the country residing with those politicians most closely linked to the men with guns in the streets. This means, for example, not only a continuation of Kurdish local rule as backed up by the Kurdish pesh merga but also effective rule, perhaps, by SCIRI in places where the main law and order is provided by its associated militia, the Badr Organization.

Long-term development of the central government's power must be a constant goal, but with the emphasis on "long-term." If that goal eventually is achieved it more likely will be through a long succession of deals that are struck individually with local power brokers than through constitutional fiat emerging from large conclaves in Baghdad.

Working with, rather than against, local centers of power in no way ensures that there will be no further slide into extremist-exploitable chaos. Afghanistan, after all, has a continuing—and over the past year, worsening—security problem with the Taliban. In Iraq, a jihadist haven that existed even before Saddam's overthrow was located in a corner of Kurdistan that otherwise was controlled by the PUK. To provide security in the near- to mid-term requires using what security forces are available, and that requires certain political compromises.

Development of a strong and effective central government will eventually be the best insurance against the eventualities most damaging to US security interests in Iraq. Development of such a government, however, will entail its own risks to those interests. Pushing that development too hard and too fast could be more damaging than not pushing it at all. In the meantime, US policy toward the next stages of the political experiment in Iraq will require a keen sense of the Iraqi political environment and the possibilities within it and the agility to adapt to changes in those possibilities.

There are no good options for achieving in Iraq, any time soon, what most westerners would consider good governance. That is a statement of reality, not despair. Recognition of reality will at least increase the odds of attaining better rather than worse outcomes and in particular of avoiding the very worst outcomes.

— 3 —
SETTING PRIORITIES:
SECURITY OR LEGITIMACY IN IRAQ?

Barbara Bodine

Judgments on criteria for the withdrawal of US forces from Iraq reflect judgments on what constitutes success. Success in Iraq can no longer be defined by what is optimal; policies must now focus on which end states are acceptable. At what point and on what basis can and should we declare victory and go home? Is it security (victory) or legitimacy (success)? Can one prioritize or sequence these two interrelated and interdependent objectives?

Such judgments reflect assumptions about the motivation and makeup of the insurgents and/or terrorists. To what extent do they represent a finite number of "dead-enders," a nationalist/anti-occupation insurgency, foreign jihadists, or sectarian factions in a nascent civil war? Such judgments also reflect assumptions on what Iraqi political structure is reasonably attainable, and on how much control the US has over either the security or the legitimacy of the state.

In the US public debate, security has become the prime, sometimes sole criterion. The reality of mounting American casualties, the financial burden of the continuing war, and the war's impact on our ability to pursue other national security issues, most notably Iran, registers with the American public. Questions of sustainable stability and political legitimacy do not. The standoff over Prime Minister Jaafari shifted the spotlight to the political arena, but much like the focus on the constitutional process, the issue was the speed, or lack thereof, of the process. The completion of the Iraqi cabinet with Prime Minister al-Maliki's appointment of broadly acceptable ministers of defense, interior and national security was swamped by the news of Zarqawi's death, even as most observers cautioned that the latter was not the end of jihadist violence. The Prime Minister's comprehensive National Reconciliation and Dialogue Project has received scant attention beyond the issue of amnesties.

Some observers explicitly discount legitimacy as a valid measure of progress in Iraq, dismissing the notion of a credible governing structure in the near term, or at least anything which approximates our notion of a western-style liberal democracy. Their argument is that Iraq is inherently violent, irreparably divisive and eternally undemocratic. It can, they conclude, only be governed effectively by an authoritarian government, something of Saddam-lite. At the other end, there are those who remain convinced that Iraq can be the beacon of democracy in the Middle East, that it has a democratic past on which to build and a pre-Saddam history of sectarian and ethnic coexistence and accommodation from which to work.

Iraq will not spring forth as a mature democracy anytime soon, but it is a disservice to believe that the Iraqis can aspire to no more than a benign but strong leader. This is the imposed democracy model that sees the failure to install a government-in-exile as the great lost opportunity of the early occupation. Reasonable political outcomes are probably somewhere in between the optimism of a reborn utopian past and cynicism from the legacy of the near past.

SECURITY: CONFRONTING THE IMMEDIATE AND THE OBVIOUS

Prudence and good sense dictate that security must be the first priority and the key determinant. It is difficult to imagine a legitimate government absent an acceptable level of security and stability within and provided by the state. A basic function of the state is to provide a reasonable measure of personal and communal security. One reason Iraqi security forces are brutally targeted is in order to deny the Iraqi state the tools and the personnel to provide security, i.e. to delegitimize the Iraqi government in the eyes of the citizens. Therefore, before legitimacy can be established, Iraq needs security.

As a criterion for withdrawal, security seemingly has the advantage that it can be measured. As the US military mission shifted to training, the debate centered on how many Iraqi troops should be trained, to what level of competence, and at what ratio of Iraqi troops to US troops. What is not always factored into this discussion is the question whether Iraqi troops will face the same security challenges we do. If a measure of the insurgency is anti-occupation, then our withdrawal should lessen the intensity of the insurgency and therefore the same number and competence of Iraqi troops may not be required. Despite how objective this criterion appears, however, agreement on the number of existing forces already trained, the number of those in training, and their capability varies widely even among the Administration and its supporters.

Like those who dismiss the notion that Iraq can forge a truly legitimate state, there is the subtle assumption by some that the Iraqis can never match US troops, that training an indigenous force is politically required, but operationally suspect. History indicates that counterinsurgency operations are more effective if undertaken by local forces and, to the degree that the deployment of Iraqi forces reduces American casualties, it can relieve American domestic political opposition to the war. The fact that April 2006 was the deadliest month since November invites the question of how valid this line of reasoning is. The decision to train Iraqi forces is sometimes explained with a reference to the TE Lawrence phrase, "it is better the Arabs do it tolerably than you do it perfectly."[1] The combination of the soft bigotry of low expectations and the stunning arrogance of the quote says a great deal about our approach, and our problem. President Bush's repeated statements that US troops will remain in Iraq for years to guarantee the success of the new Iraqi government further implies that we believe the Iraqis may never be able to stand on their own.

However uneven the training of Iraqi armed forces has been, the US military's mission was expanded to include the police. Questions of mandate, doctrine, expertise and appropriateness seem to have figured inadequately in the decision to turn over a civilian function to train a civilian police force to military trainers.

Others who argue for security first assert that a US decision to pull troops precipitously from a still highly insecure and unstable environment, be it through a timetable for withdrawal or "cut and run" strategy, would signal defeat. The insurgents and the jihadists could claim credit for having driven us out, as we were driven from Beirut and Somalia, and the Israelis from southern Lebanon and Gaza. In the Global War on Terrorism this will only embolden our enemies. Proponents of this view counter that nothing short of unequivocal military victory is acceptable; to accept anything less is defeatist.

---

[1] T.E. Lawrence, "The 27 Articles of T.E. Lawrence," *Arab Bulletin*, August 20, 1917. The full quote is instructive: "Do not try to do too much with your own hands. Better the Arabs do it tolerably than that you do it perfectly. It is their war, and you are to help them, not to win it for them. Actually, also under the very odd conditions of Arabia, your practical work will not be as good as, perhaps, you think it is."

Conversely, a US decision to withdraw troops while Iraq is gripped by an insurgency and jihadists pushing it to the brink of a full-out civil war could be seen by Iraqis as The Second Betrayal. Zbigniew Brzezinski's Darwinian proposal to withdraw and let the Iraqis sort it out for themselves assumes that the combined forces of the Shia and the Kurds could overwhelm the Sunni Arabs and to reinforces the apprehension of abandonment.[2] A US decision to withdraw troops under these conditions, leaving an intensely corrupt, divided, dysfunctional and/or authoritarian regime, would be as callous and short-sighted as was the decision to let the looting run its course in the spring of 2003. Further, the chaos, the sorting out process that would follow would not be confined to Iraq and could not be ignored by Iraq's neighbors.

Finally, there is the argument that we are in some good measure responsible for the violence, both insurgent and jihadist. The occupation fuels the insurgency and our presence validates the jihad. We thus are accountable in some good measure to resolve it. General Batiste and others believe the decision to demobilize the Iraqi army in May 2003 was a critical mistake and one we are obligated to redress.[3]

A HOUSE OF CARDS

Taken together, the conventional criteria for the withdrawal of US troops thus come down to the capacity of US-trained Iraqis to impose, enforce and maintain security. In this formula, the benchmark is a competent, skilled, equipped security-making and security-keeping Iraqi force. The US must stay until security, defined most commonly as entailing the destruction, not just the defeat, of the insurgents and the jihadis, has been assured, either directly or by US-trained Iraqi units.

> *To be considered a success, an occupation must ensure the occupying power's political and strategic interests well after the occupation concludes.*

But security and stability as ends in themselves are short-term goals, reactive and potentially counterproductive, and not a sufficient measure of occupation success. To be considered a success, an occupation must

---

[2] Zbigniew Brzezinski, "Iraq: Next Steps for US Policy" (lecture, Center for American Progress, Washington DC, March 16, 2006).

[3] Eric Schmitt, "The Struggle for Iraq: Reconstruction; US Generals Fault Ban on Hussein's Party," New York Times, April 21, 2004, A11.

ensure the occupying power's political and strategic interests well after the occupation concludes–typically meaning to put in place a functioning, legitimate government with which the occupier has a constructive relationship. The more complex challenge therefore is to leave behind an Iraq that is a viable, sustainable state that provides for its citizens and is not a threat to its neighbors.

The issue, therefore, is not the size of the Iraqi military or police force. The issue is the legitimacy, not just the legality, of the Iraqi government. Creating an army or a police force absent not just a functioning state but a legitimate one is to create a house of cards, a hollow structure unable to stand.

An understanding of the difference between short-term security and long-term sustainable legitimacy is reflected in the new US Army Field Manual section on counterinsurgency operations. The Field Manual recognizes the importance of legitimacy as the main goal, accepts the primacy of political objectives, and recognizes that security can only be established under the rule of law. It describes legitimacy as: (a) the selection of leaders in a manner considered just and fair by a substantial majority of the population; (b) popular participation in or support for the political process; (c) a low level of corruption; and (d) a high degree of regime acceptance.[4] This goes beyond "hearts and minds," which often defaults to building schools and painting clinics, or the establishment of village councils of elders.

To date both the US occupation and successive Iraqi post-invasion governments have manifestly failed the legitimacy test as well as the security test. Over a period of three years, sustainable economic investment and sustainable political and economic development have been delayed or derailed for immediate and urgent requirements of security, stop-gap construction projects and a frog-marched political calendar. In dismissing the validity of the Reconciliation Project, Secretary Rumsfeld stated "the goal is not to trade something off for something else to make somebody happy. The goal is to succeed."[5]

Millions, if not billions, have been allocated to army and police training, and reconstruction funds have been diverted to security needs. There has been a demonstrated unwillingness to invest a fraction of these funds in

---

[4] US Department of the Army, *Counterinsurgency* FM 3-24 (Washington, DC: June 2006), http://www.fas.org/irp/doddir/army/fm3-24fd.pdf (accessed July 14, 2006).

[5] Donald Rumsfeld, "Iraqi Insurgents Propose Cease-Fire," *CBS News Online*, June 28, 2006, http://www.cbsnews.com/stories/2006/06/29/iraq/main1763114.shtml (accessed July 14, 2006).

institution building, even before the insurgency demanded the diversion of resources. A $12 million US Agency for International Development (USAID) project that was supposed to create 12 law schools completed only three. The rest of the funds went to cover security requirements for other projects.

WHAT IS LEGITIMACY?

What legitimacy is not is a predetermined set of events and entities—ticks to "check off" various boxes called democracy. It is not elections, a written constitution or a parliament, or at least it is not those solely. These are the hallmarks of a legitimate government if they reflect a social contract between the rulers, the government, and the ruled, the citizens. There are more than enough hollow elections, impotent parliaments, and dusty, unread constitutions right in Iraq's immediate neighborhood. Under Saddam there were elections, a parliament and a constitution. In a post-conflict environment, elections, even free and fair, can be divisive rather than unifying and parliaments can reinforce rather than transcend subnational loyalties. Without a political framework that reflects consensual governing principles, armies and police can become instruments of oppressive majoritarianism, or of parochial self-interest and defense.

Legitimacy has been described as: when the articulate members of a population are by and large satisfied with the government's actions in the areas of identity, participation, distribution, equality and sovereignty according to the norms they believe in. Legitimacy includes accountability, transparency, participation, equality and rule of law, with rule of law perhaps the first among equals. Rule of law is a governing principle that reflects, enshrines, enables and guarantees the elements of legitimacy.

If security is the capacity to impose, maintain and enforce order, legitimacy is the capacity to engender compliance. It is what the Army Field Manual calls "regime acceptance."[6] Legitimacy explains why rules are followed and rulers are accepted without constant coercion. Legitimacy of any given rule or rule-setting body is based on the perception of citizens that it is valid. Legitimate consensus is achieved because the dominated believe in the appropriateness of those who dominate. If the rules, and the process through which they are created, are believed to be proper, then the rules have legitimacy. Police authority

---

[6] US Department of the Army, *Counterinsurgency*, 25.

comes from acceptance of the idea that the rules they enforce are legitimate, and fairly and equitably applied.

Conversely, when the perception of the ruled is that the police or the army reflect and enforce a structure and a process that are neither fair nor equitable, that they are loyal first and only to a particular person, sect or ethnic group, then compliance must be forced. If the state is in control as it was under Saddam, compliance can be guaranteed through fear. In fractured societies, parallel security structures, (i.e. militias and paramilitary organizations), may fill the void.

Another element of legitimacy is outcome. When the perception and acceptance exist that there is fairness, equality, and justice in the distribution of goods and services, then the rules and the rulers are accepted as legitimate. The converse is corruption and cronyism.[7]

CAN LEGITIMACY BE MEASURED?

As a basis for a decision on when to withdraw US troops from Iraq, legitimacy is problematic. It cannot be quantified and, in and of itself, it cannot be taught. It is not finite or concrete, and cannot be imposed or granted. It derives from subjective judgments based on a totality of factors. But a number of the elements that make up legitimacy can be supported, encouraged, and fostered. Public confidence in a credible process conducing to legitimate state behavior can itself be a satisfactory indication of long-term sustainability if seen to be matched by resources, both financial and human. For example:

- The need for fairly and equitably provided services, including security services, an education system, health system and basic infrastructure requires allocation of resources, the training of technocrats and the creation of a professional civil service.

- The need for rule of law, including a criminal code and independent judiciary, not just a police force, requires training of justices, lawyers, court clerks and the rest of the support system. Rule of law has been described as the most critical factor in the return to a sense of normalcy in a post-conflict environment.

---

[7] There also is a practical reason to support a process leading toward legitimacy—the need for foreign direct investment. Corporate leaders look to the stability of the government, rather than the immediate security conditions, short of anarchy, in deliberations on where to invest. They want to know whether there is a legal regime that will protect their investments.

- The need for accountability, transparency and public integrity can be supported through tough anti-corruption legislation, creation of watch-dog organizations, both internal and citizen-based, and a viable and independent press. Transparency and accountability are also fundamental to a process of rule-making that is accepted as legitimate.
- The need for participation can be supported through the development of civil society, not just electoral mechanisms.

CHANGING THE US APPROACH

If support for the development of a legitimate and a viable Iraq is as important to US interests as dealing with security, then shifts in US policy and priorities are required. These are not resource intensive, certainly not compared to security.

FROM WITHDRAWAL TO TRANSITION

The US should change the rhetoric from withdrawal to transition, and not just transition from the US military to the Iraqi military. The perception of Americans and Iraqis should not be that when the troops go, so goes the money and with it the political commitment. There has been more emphasis recently on the Iraqi political process, but with a time urgency that still suggests, despite overheated rhetoric on the perfidy of "timetables," that we are heading for the exit. The transition should be toward a more normal bilateral relationship, one in which we cease our role as enablers of the political process.

With this comes the need to change our profile from pro-active and publicly participatory to pro-active, but discreetly participatory. We need to recognize that our highly visible involvement in the process, including withholding or granting endorsement of key political leaders, however much our views align with prevailing Iraqi political sentiment, is inappropriate and unhelpful.

When we were preparing to hand over formal sovereignty, the US military made clear that US officers would remain in charge of security. We continue to assert that whatever drawdowns there may be, we intend to stay in Anbar governorate. We have resisted disclaiming any intention to secure permanent base rights, and coalition forces continue to operate under extraordinary privileges and immunities, granted by outgoing Coalition Provisional Authority (CPA) director Paul Bremer, that will "not terminate until the departure of the last element" of the Multi-National Force (MNF).[8]

We need to avoid the appearance that even after Iraq's transition to its first permanent government we remain in change of the politics. Given our expenditure of treasure and blood, US Secretary of State Condoleeza Rice and Britain's Foreign Minister Jack Straw were well within bounds when they expressed in clear terms concern over the stalemated prime ministry debate. What was outside the bounds was the high theater with which those views were conveyed, and the subsequent presidential laying of hands on Nouri al-Maliki.

SUPPORT THE PROCESS; STAY AWAY FROM THE PROVISIONS

It is important to support the constitutional review process actively, but avoid public involvement in or identification with specific provisions. The grand bargain of October 2005, to open the constitution to review, should be honored. It is the basis upon which the Sunnis engaged in the political process and was a critical first step toward deflating the insurgency.

The constitutional drafting process was artificially truncated, resulting in a document that was deeply flawed in content as well as process. The review process is an avenue to redress this. Time and political space are needed to craft a social contract that will allow the constitution to be a living document that looks forward, and not just a badly cobbled together recitation of past inequities, abuses and remedies. The process needs to be allowed to work.

Proposals to delay the review and address the constitution's shortcomings via legislation or executive order could very well be seen as a breach of faith by the Sunni community and exploited by those who are skeptical of any chance of a meaningful role for Sunnis in the political evolution of the state. It would not be in the US interest or Iraq's for us to waffle on our commitment or tacitly support efforts to delay or deflect the review process. This is not the time to play a political game of "gotcha." Many of the document's shortcomings, such as the oil revenue provisions, are too fundamental to the nature and structure of the

---

[8] Andrea Carcano, "End of the Occupation in 2004? The Status of the Multinational Force in Iraq After the Transfer of Sovereignty to the Interim Iraqi Government," *Journal of Conflict and Security Law* 11, no. 1 (January 20, 2006): 41-66.

state to be tweaked through legislation, much less by executive order, or addressed only at some ill-defined better time in the future.

The constitutional review process has every expectation of being long, drawn out, frustrating and conducted via the media. We need to resist the temptation to insert ourselves into the process, to take public positions on provisions as they are debated, to kibitz on Sunday morning talk shows, to display increasing irritation as it drags on and on, or to be drawn into those debates by parties seeking either to gain an advantage, or to embarrass their foes. This has to work on an Iraqi timeline not on one keyed to the American political calendar.

WORK WITH THE PROVINCES; SPEAK TO THE CENTER

There is some confusion in the debate between the understandable wariness of a strong central authority and the need for a strong Iraq state. A strong state and a functioning albeit asymmetrical federal structure can coexist. But, the institutional capacity and political credibility problems that the central government has are magnified at the provincial level, except perhaps in the Kurdish region. Therefore, efforts to decentralize power and authority to the provincial level when the institutional capacity at that level may be even weaker than at the national level, could undermine the viability of the state. Efforts at civil and political institution-building have to be as aggressive in the provinces as in Baghdad if either is to be effective.

While recognizing regional, sectarian and ethnic differences, it also is important to speak to the national identity. Many Iraqis bristle at the American obsession with sectarian and ethnic labels and the related presumption that Iraq, created artificially, remains an artificial state with no national identity. Iraqis can and do manage multiple identities. More emphasis should be placed on identifying and working with the country's centripetal forces as well as countering the centrifugal forces.

COMMIT THE FUNDS, AND THE POLITICAL WILL

A change in policy from withdrawal to transition has to be backed up with commitments to fund transitional and institution-building programs, the political sustainability programs. Congress is generally reluctant to fund "nation-building." These efforts do not have the immediacy of security-related tasks, are harder to quantify and may take years to produce measurable results. More cynically, these programs do not provide good photo ops with troops from back home. This is compounded by the lingering belief that Iraqi reconstruction should be self-financing and that institution-building cannot be supported from the outside. The Administration has to be as firmly and clearly behind funding this stage of the US involvement as it was for the occupation.

INTERNATIONALIZE THE TRANSITION

One senior US general with a better grasp of the criticality of legitimacy, and a certain impatience with the troop-training paradigm, recently talked about the need for State Department advisors in each of the civilian ministries as counterparts to military advisors with the army and police. This is in addition to civilian staffing requirements for provincial-level teams. Beyond State's very real resource constraints, an element in regime legitimacy is perceived sovereignty and independence. Lowering the American profile needs to happen across the board. Internationalizing not only relieves the burden on the American taxpayer, but also underscores the commitment to withdraw militarily but not abandon Iraq politically.

SECURITY VS. LEGITIMACY: TO PUSH OR TO PULL?

It is not a choice between security and legitimacy. The issue is the degree to which they are coincident or sequential. Security alone will consist of short-term stop gap measures, not unlike some of the non-sustainable reconstruction projects. It is difficult to imagine how a security only or even security first approach avoids a withdrawal that does not look like a defeat or at least a failure. Legitimacy, however, cannot exist in a vacuum, or in anarchy. The criteria for the withdrawal of US troops should therefore be taken in a broader context than troops trained or police stations opened. A process that is evident and credible to the Iraqis, resourced adequately over the long term, is needed to create an environment within which political accommodation and regime acceptance can effectively counteract the root causes of instability. US policy should be pushed by the goal of defeating the insurgency, rather than pulled by the need to destroy it.

Prime Minister al-Maliki's National Reconciliation and Dialogue Project, a compilation of initiatives that address security, electricity, detainees, economic development, an international compact for reconstruction, political reintegration of elements of the insurgency and possibly a reconsideration of the de-Ba'athification Commission, was unveiled at the end of June. As designed it is a comprehensive effort to confront many of the failings of the government's interim predecessors and offers a process, a dialogue, and a goal—national reconciliation—that get at the very fundamentals of a legitimate, viable Iraqi state. It is too early to judge whether he, his cabinet and the Council of Representatives will be able to credibly and effectively reverse the downward spiral that has Iraq at the edge of an abyss.

Our challenge will be whether we are prepared for and capable of changing our approach—to transition, to support for the process, to political will and financial commitment, and to internationalization—in order to allow this Iraqi effort to go forward.

— 4 —

US ECONOMIC AND RECONSTRUCTION ASSISTANCE TO IRAQ: PRINCIPLES FOR THE NEXT PHASE

Robin Raphel

Significant changes in the US posture in Iraq have been underway for some time now. During the next 18-24 months, US military forces will most likely be reduced from the present 130,000 to 40-50,000 troops, consolidated in a small number of bases and charged primarily with providing logistics and combat support for military contingences in Iraq and the neighborhood, as well as providing more focused, sophisticated training for Iraqi officers. The US mission will decamp from its sprawling and cumbersome occupation of Iraqi properties in the International Zone, and re-establish itself in the new 100-acre compound on the Tigris. US consulates will likely be operating in Basrah, Mosul, Kirkuk, and Hilla, but the military Forward Operating Bases (FOBs) that currently house the nascent Provincial Reconstruction Teams (PRTs) are likely to have been absorbed into the remaining bases as the US military consolidates.

The assumption underlying these changes is that the insurgents will have begun to lose the critical mass of material and local support, and that their activity will be confined more and more to isolated regions in the Sunni heartland. The Iraqi government, while still struggling with inefficiency, corruption and ethnic tensions, will exert real authority over ministries and resources. This scenario would also accelerate the return to Iraq now underway, of more expatriate staff, simplifying donor coordination, and easing the freedom of movement of US assistance staff.

On the threshold of these changes, it is worthwhile to consider what sort of US assistance program would be most appropriate for Iraq in the five-year period after coalition forces have been drawn down, heavy construction projects have been largely completed, and the Iraqi government has had the opportunity to find its rhythm. The goal will remain enhanced overall stability in an increasingly democratic context; the question is how to best promote that goal. Based on the experience of the first three years of reconstruction, and a realistic assessment of the Iraqi environment, six basic principles stand out as being important to this next phase of US assistance. Should the insurgency and sectarian violence persist at current levels, the US posture will shift more slowly, and reconstruction will be more constrained, but the basic principles discussed here will still hold.

An active and appropriately focused US economic engagement in Iraq is unlikely to displace the bilateral security dialogue in the foreseeable future, especially given continued security challenges inside Iraq and with its neighbors. However, a more expansive and sophisticated focus on the twin themes of economic reform and capacity development will help prepare the way for a time when Iraq's inherent economic strengths will dominate its external relations in the region and beyond.

PEOPLE VS. CONCRETE

HISTORY

The original Iraq Relief and Reconstruction Fund (IRRF) II spending plan was fundamentally a physical infrastructure rehabilitation plan. It was driven by the twin views that the greatest need in Iraq at the time was electricity and other essential services, and that the US Congress would be willing to appropriate large sums for immediate physical infrastructure needs, but not for longer term development programs for capacity development and policy reform, which in any case were assumed to be the preferred sectors for other donors. It was also believed that major infrastructure projects would enable more rapid obligation and expenditure of the reconstruction funds. Although the original plan has been adjusted several times to accommodate growing security and political requirements, it has remained focused on infrastructure. By the end of FY 2006 over $14 billion of grant assistance will have been disbursed toward that purpose, with the remainder to follow by early 2008. Implementation efforts have often been heroic, but overall results disappointing.

REMEDIES

With new funding in the FY2006 supplemental and subsequent budgets, the US should focus on programs that develop human capital—technical assistance for capacity building at all levels of the Iraqi government and with civil society. This effort to enhance "democratic capacity" would include institutions of governance such as the national and provincial assemblies, and the Prime Minister's and Governors' immediate offices. Such a program could easily absorb $1 billion per year for the 2008-2013 period. The capacity development efforts would include a component of further community police training, building on the basic and other training conducted under the Multinational Security Transitional Command-Iraq (MNSTC-I) .

The US should engage deeply in a handful of sectors where it has an internationally recognized comparative advantage, and let other donors take the lead in other areas, in accordance with an overall agreement with the Iraqis on a division of labor. Education, health and agriculture would be likely candidates for a US lead. Activities in relevant ministries should include: developing and applying modern personnel management, budgeting and procurement techniques; strategic sector planning; incorporating market principles in economic decision-making; crisis management techniques; and decentralization of government. Curriculum development, university exchanges, vocational education, and media training should be part of educational activity; public health policy reform, training primary health workers and crisis management techniques part of the health sector; and water management, improving livestock and crop varieties and extension services part of agriculture.

The US should continue supporting civil society, helping the new government raise awareness among the population of the responsibilities of the citizenry in a democracy, and promoting anti-corruption and human rights. Programs for women will remain a priority, especially given the surge in conservative Islam. This is particularly true in southern Iraq. Technical assistance on economic policy reforms, on tax and tariff policy, privatization, subsidy reduction, creating a social safety net, and improving the investment climate would continue an important dialogue with economic officials begun in 2003. Policy reform should also bring renewed focus on how to promote both short and long term employment, a problem that has thus far stymied Iraqi economists and their myriad advisors. Cultural and educational exchange of all types should be constrained only by Iraqi capacity. Programs to support local community associations and promote local decision-making should continue, especially in ethnically and religiously mixed communities. The labor intensity of some of these programs, especially on the Washington end, needs to be recognized and supported by additions to staff where necessary.

The oil sector continues to under-perform despite substantial US and Iraqi expenditures. The formula for moving the oil sector forward—

some combination of further rehabilitation of fields and infrastructure, more effective infrastructure protection, a check on rampant corruption, and a legal environment that encourages private investment—has not yet congealed. The US has certainly been the greatest foreign influence in the sector since the war. Other donors tend to believe that the US has a proprietary interest in the oil sector and does not welcome consultations. In fact, there is an emerging US willingness to engage the international community to put more effective pressure on the Iraqis to persuade them of the need to take urgent steps to tackle this crucial sector.

As the US shifts its focus to capacity building, international institutions should be poised to take over infrastructure rehabilitation with major loan programs. The World Bank, for example, is already programming $500 million in International Development Assistance (IDA) loans.

ELIMINATE THE AD HOCRACY

HISTORY

The construction-heavy IRRF II program has been implemented largely by the temporary and ad hoc Project and Contracting Office (PCO), successor to the similarly ad hoc Program Management Office (PMO), established by the Department of Defense (DoD) as part of the Coalition Provisional Authority (CPA), in mid 2003. This succession of temporary organizations has been supported by the Department of the Army, and staffed by a collection of active duty military, Army Corps of Engineers personnel and contract-hire civilians with varied professional backgrounds. The PCO is now run by the Gulf Region Division of the Army Corps of Engineers (ACE), but is still manned by a collection of staff who do not all have similar contracting and program management backgrounds.

The Iraq Reconstruction Management Office (IRMO), another temporary organization, was created in 2004 by the Department of State when it took over the US mission in Iraq, to coordinate and oversee US Agency for International Development (USAID) and PCO project implementation and to determine overall reconstruction priorities. IRMO also assumed responsibility for the ministerial advisory system established during the CPA era. These advisors, recruited through an ad hoc office set up at DoD, and transferred to the Department of State in mid-2004, compete with PCO contract managers, design-build and program management contract experts, and with USAID sector experts; for the ear of Iraqi officials and Washington agencies interested in the status of various sectors from electricity to education. The result is often conflicting perspectives and advice on how to approach development of a particular sector.

REMEDIES

The next phase of reconstruction assistance to Iraq needs to simplify the organizational structure, allowing multiple layers of advisors and program managers to be conflated. As more IRRF money is disbursed and projects completed, PCO and IRMO should be allowed to shrink and finally disappear, consistent with the three to five-year life of temporary government organizations. If there are any further US construction projects, USAID or ACE, both experienced and in country, should do the contracting and program management. The responsibility for planning and implementing the assistance program also needs to return to traditional implementing agencies with established contracting, managing and monitoring procedures. Under this reorganization, USAID would maintain a staff of 100 or more direct-hire personnel in Baghdad to manage the lion's share of a roughly $1 billion per year grant assistance program. The program would be implemented largely by the major USAID contractors, some of whom have been working in Iraq over the last three years with reasonable success.

The Department of State would regain the police training function run by the International Narcotics and Law Enforcement Bureau (INL). INL has managed US participation in civilian police training programs in more than a dozen countries over the last 12 years. The INL program concentrates on civilian and community policing, with training that incorporates a large human rights awareness component and standards for emergency situations, such as riot control. In the rush to stand up Iraqi police in the numbers and with the skills to deal with the growing insurgency in Iraq, INL's traditional post-conflict approach was quickly overwhelmed. The early focus was on large-scale, rapid processing of recruits to a basic competency level, and specialization in counterinsurgency techniques. With this basic training now nearing completion and the Iraqi police able to take on increasing responsibility, the need for civilian-led training in community policing, human rights, and the solving of law enforcement problems without recourse to force will re-emerge.

While US infrastructure rehabilitation will have been largely completed, there will be an ongoing need for engineering and construction advice, both for the Iraqi civilian projects and for the bases that US forces continue to use. The Army Corps of Engineers, which has been involved in civil engineering projects in many countries since the 1950s, and which is currently running the PCO in Iraq, should maintain a presence in Baghdad with a cadre of engineering and contracting specialists that can be on called on for technical advice and program management.

The Treasury Department's Office of Technical Assistance was active in the immediate aftermath of the war re-establishing Iraq's banking system and helping the Ministry of Finance and line ministries prepare their first budgets. With International Monetary Fund (IMF) and other technical assistance now underway, Treasury should ensure that its attaché office in the embassy is able to draw on experts from the Office of Technical Assistance to assist Iraq with specialized banking and budget questions.

An increasingly important part of US assistance is in creating opportunities for private sector partnerships between US and Iraqi firms. The US Trade and Development Agency (TDA) has had a modest Iraq program involving training for the oil sector and orientation visits in sectors such as civil aviation. TDA will likely have ample opportunity to expand its programs in Iraq and increase the chances of US private sector engagement there. The Department of Commerce should continue its efforts to keep both US and Iraqi business communities aware of the opportunities, and to provide match-making services through business centers in Iraq.

Military assistance to the new Iraqi security forces will be an ongoing effort through the next decade. As US forces drawdown, this function will shift from the current temporary MNSTC-I to a large Office of Defense Cooperation (ODC) in the new US mission compound in Baghdad. Part of the ODC mission should be continuing the capacity development of the Ministry of Defense. To be effective, this will likely require the services of a major contractor that can provide an organized package of capacity-building, training and services to the ministry.

GIVE IRAQIS A VOICE UP FRONT

HISTORY

Giving voice to Iraqi ideas about the reconstruction of their economy and up to this point has been a challenging task. With the government changing every year, many ministries have faced serial wholesale changes in senior staff, often more motivated by the politics of new ministers than technical qualifications. This has made it extremely difficult to have a consistent and continuing dialogue with Iraqis on the national level on what reconstruction path makes sense. The distraction of de-Ba'athification and the growing violence compounded the problem. The post-war collapse of communication and authority between the center and the provincial authorities further added to the difficulty.

In addition, in early consultations, Iraqis themselves had not had the opportunity to think through what would be the best use of donor funding, and even when asked, often gave ill-considered opinions. When the proposal for the IRRF II supplemental was put together, ministries took project proposals off the shelf, many of which had languished for years waiting for funding from the cash-strapped Iraqi government. Iraqi officials, like bureaucrats around the world, tended to favor concrete facilities that would please their constituents over less visible capacity-building. Many of the proposed projects had not been vetted in recent years and little was known about the actual cost to build or sustain them. This method of project selection led to major cost overruns and perpetuated the systemic lack of capacity among Iraqis to sustain US-built structures and programs. Finally, the scale and administrative/logistical complexity of the US effort has remained beyond the grasp of most Iraqi officials, creating an unhealthy feeling of impotence and dependency on US advisors.

REMEDIES

In the next phase of assistance, negotiating with the Iraqis on the nature and content of the program should be easier. A permanent government is now in place, and will have had the chance to establish procedure in dealing with international donors. The US assistance structure should be simpler and easier to navigate (see section on coordination below). With few if any new US-funded infrastructure projects, the problem of budgeting for future operations and maintenance will be minimal. Nonetheless, Iraqis need to be intimately involved in program priorities. They need to decide whether assistance to elementary education is more important than university exchanges, agricultural extension services more urgent than agricultural engineering training courses, and so forth.

Engagement with the Iraqis needs to take place at the provincial as well as the national level. Whatever degree of federalism is enshrined in the final Iraqi Constitution, the centralized system that existed under Saddam Hussein is not meant to be restored. Provincial officials need to learn to plan and implement reconstruction and development projects, and to coordinate their activities and budgets with the national government. The Ministry of Planning and Development Cooperation is already engaging provincial officials in its planning process. The Provincial Reconstruction and Development Councils (PRDCs), representing all elements of the community, have been active in most provinces for some months and are responsible for determining local development priorities. Provincial Reconstruction Teams, consisting of representatives from a number of US assistance implementing agencies and military civil affairs officers, have been meeting with the PRDCs to help them develop their priorities and coordinate US-funded projects. Sustaining the PRTs, once the majority are created, is likely to prove too costly when US forces withdraw and "free" perimeter security is no longer available. However, there will still be projects in the provinces which require engagement and coordination with the PRDCs. Additionally, there should be continued assistance to local communities similar to the USAID Community Action Program, where local communities put up a portion of the cost and are expected to take some responsibility for planning and execution of a project.

The next phase of US assistance also needs to include conditionality, to help the Iraqis discipline themselves to do their part in a particular development activity. Iraq needs to share local costs of programs, commit to providing jobs to newly trained officials, and accept programs that promote better humans rights practice or subsidy reforms even when they are not politically convenient. Iraqi officials in Baghdad need to understand and accept that the US wants to fund programs which promote some decision-making authority and autonomy in provincial governments.

All of this negotiation with the Iraqis takes time, and the temptation is to skip over these essential engagements in the interest of getting projects started, allowing imperfect Iraqi understanding and support to linger. US implementers succumbed to this temptation with IRRF I and II, and the Iraqi voice, not strong in any case, was drowned out in the frenetic haste to move money, create jobs, and show progress on the ground. In the end, the lack of Iraqi buy-in led to projects and programs that were difficult to sustain.

ACTIVELY ENGAGE INTERNATIONAL DONORS

HISTORY

The international donor community, including the US, was active in the run-up to the war in Iraq, responding to appeals by UN agencies and non-governmental organizations (NGOs) to support their preparations for humanitarian disaster relief. The Office of Reconstruction and Humanitarian Assistance's (ORHA) planning was also largely focused on humanitarian relief, and the ORHA humanitarian section initiated discussions with UN offices in Cyprus and Amman before their final deployment to Baghdad. US military planners had also contacted the United Nations Development Programme (UNDP) seeking information on key infrastructure to help determine what targets to avoid in the US air war. The first donors' meeting in New York in June 2003 was organized and sponsored largely by the United Nations (UN) and World Bank, and it was there that the decision was made to have an international donors' conference in Madrid in October. The preparations for the conference—including planning details for the UN and World Bank Trust Funds for Iraq—were chaired by the UN and World Bank. The UN and World Bank together produced the 2003 sector-by-sector needs assessment in preparation for the Madrid conference. International donors have held several meetings since, but the multilateral donor effort as envisaged at Madrid and implied by the $13.5 billion in non-US pledges has been slow to be realized.

A major reason for this was the August 2003 attack on UN headquarters. This attack tragically decapitated the UN mission, dealing a severe blow to UN programs in Iraq, and ensuring that the World Bank, following the UN's security guidance, did not open a regular office in Baghdad. The UN has since implemented projects through local Iraqi staff, with a small expatriate humanitarian assistance staff rotating in and out of Baghdad from Amman. Earlier this year the UN established small regional offices in Erbil and Basra. Similarly, the World Bank works through Iraqi staff, with an expatriate representative in Baghdad. While UN and World Bank staffs have both been very creative in their Iraq programming, there is no substitute for a regular mission on the ground that works closely with the largest donor to date, the United States. Plans are currently underway to augment the World Bank contractor presence with a small office led by a direct-hire country director for Iraq. This is expected to simplify decision-making and enable more direct communication with Iraqi ministers.

Besides security concerns, which have constrained international donors, some donors, particularly the neighboring Arab states who made large pledges, were uncomfortable in principle with the Coalition Provisional Authority, the US-run occupation government. They were inclined to sit back and wait to see how the situation evolved, both politically and militarily. Smaller donors simply deposited money in the trust funds for the UN and World Bank to manage. With the new government settling in, some donors are beginning to reconsider their prospective role.

One of the most difficult problems for other donors was the overwhelming scale of the $21 billion US reconstruction effort. The US was involved in every sector, sometimes with more than one agency. It was difficult for other donors—let alone the Iraqis—to get a good sense of US programs, and to determine where they might bring distinct and identifiable value-added. The Iraqi officials capable of interacting with donors were few, and monopolized by US counterparts. Many of the US personnel were not accustomed to working with other donors, and, while toiling for long hours in difficult working conditions, had simply to ignore the intermittent pleas for more information.

REMEDIES

In recent months, the US has begun to recognize that, with IRRF funds nearing full obligation and much left to do in the reconstruction effort, there is a need to engage other donors more actively. A larger donor presence is very much in the US interest as the broader the fabric of assistance and engagement, the more quickly Iraq can become anchored in mainstream economic principles and organizations. The projected drawdown of US troops and the waning of the insurgency should make it easier both politically and logistically for both international organizations and bilateral donors to be present in Iraq. However, a deliberate strategy is still needed to entice donors into Iraq on an accelerated timetable.

The movement of the US mission to the new embassy compound should free up some space in the International Zone, which will ease one of the biggest obstacles for donors—lack of secure office space. The US should remind the Iraqi government that in the scramble for space in the International Zone precipitated by the US departure, they would be wise to reserve appropriately for other donors.

The US needs to redress the complaint that with its massive presence and influence, it intends to continue to dominate the reconstruction effort, monopolize key Iraqi officials and sectors (e.g. oil) and relegate others to projects of lesser importance or interest. Whether it is true or not, this is a widespread perception among donors. One way to ameliorate this problem is to encourage the Iraqis to invite the World Bank to assume its traditional role in organizing a consultative group of donors. The World Bank would assist the Iraqis in organizing donors and determining who would take the lead with their Iraqi counterparts in which sector. The US has resisted this system, in part because there have been too few donors on the ground, but in this new phase it will be important to have at least the perception of a more objective and balanced division of labor and responsibility among donors.

Of course, a major reason for engaging other donors is the prospect of new funding for the reconstruction effort. In June 2006, President Bush announced a high-level US effort to help develop a "compact" between the Iraqis and the international community in which Iraq would undertake various reforms in exchange for political and reconstruction support. In this context, another pledging conference—a "Madrid II"— is likely by the end of the year. It will be important at this conference for the Iraqi government to take the lead in articulating its reconstruction needs. Further, the US needs to recognize that significant additional support from other donors is likely to be contingent upon a continued US commitment to Iraq's reconstruction and development. In this context, the additional $3.2 billion in the FY 2006 supplemental and the FY 2007 foreign assistance budget and further indications of a sustained US financial commitment will be crucial. Given the reluctance of Congress to provide further reconstruction assistance for Iraq, the Administration needs to commit to an aggressive strategy to secure further funding.

The proposed compact would not obviate the need for more deliberate and structured US engagement with other donors. This re-engagement might begin in the oil sector, with the US supporting and facilitating an oil and gas investment seminar, led by the Iraqis. Topics of discussion could be: elusive security for the oil infrastructure, anti-corruption measures, investment regulations, and potential private investment opportunities in the oil sector.

COORDINATE, COORDINATE, COORDINATE

HISTORY

The US needs to intensify its coordination among US agencies and with other donors in the next phase of assistance. A bewildering array of implementers have been operating in Iraq since the CPA period. Some, the most significant being USAID, were well-established and experienced in post-conflict reconstruction, while the temporary organizations PMO, PCO and Iraq Reconstruction Management Office all suffered from the same limitation—no established professional cadre or practice. The results were:

1) duplication of effort where more than one agency had responsibility for the same sector (e.g., schools being repaired twice by two sets of contractors working for different agencies);
2) lack of an agreed set of priorities for which projects should be done first;

3) inconsistent contracting and personnel policies;
4) different procedures for consulting Iraqis;
5) different standards for construction work; and
6) different metrics, measuring systems, and data bases.

Some sectors had several advisors—the prime contractor, program management contractor, PCO, USAID, USAID contractor and IRMO—each often believing he or she was the senior US expert advising the US mission and a given ministry. This was very confusing to all, particularly to the Iraqis, especially since advisors in the same sector (e.g. electricity and oil) often had contradictory views as to reconstruction priorities and approaches.

REMEDIES

In the next phase this multi-layered structure needs to be simplified. The US needs to institute a tightly coordinated assistance structure both in Baghdad and Washington. The current IRMO function of measurement and reporting discipline is a crucial one. In Baghdad, where a dual Deputy Chief of Mission (DCM) model is under consideration, the DCM responsible for economic and development issues should be responsible for ensuring coordination, high standards of program management, and standardized reporting from all implementing agencies. This would include coordinating any new military assistance programs like Foreign Military Sales or International Military Education and Training, as well as managing the ongoing Commander's Military Support Program with civilian reconstruction efforts. Further, at least the leadership of all implementing organizations need to be co-located at the new embassy chancery to enhance communication and coordination. In Washington, the related coordinating responsibility should fall to the new dual-hatted USAID Director/Deputy Secretary of State, drawing on regional and budget offices in other organizations.

Baghdad would need a sub-group of the country team, comprised of all economic agencies and implementing agencies, to maintain a close watch over the reconstruction and development program. It would be chaired by the appropriate DCM. Even at $1 billion/year this would be a considerable undertaking. This group would develop a basic consensus on what programs are working and which are not, and if and how funds should be reprogrammed. It would also determine whether metrics and reporting methods meet the standards set by Washington and also adequately convey to Congress and taxpayers what US assistance funds are accomplishing.

US technical advisors will likely remain a valuable tool for Iraq for the next decade. However, this function needs to be more regularized and coordinated, and targeted at Iraqi needs. Again, a return to a more traditional division of labor is in order. The economic minister, under the appropriate DCM, should coordinate the economic policy dialogue with Iraqi ministries, relying on heads of various agencies such as USAID, Treasury, Agriculture and Commerce to take the lead with their counterparts. Implementing agencies will have technical advisors in various ministries, either attached to specific projects such as health system reform, or, if the minister desires, in a more generalized advisory capacity. Where more than one advisor is required, they should be deployed as a coherent team, not as a collection of individuals. All of these advisors should be specifically requested by the Iraqi organization to which they are assigned, and be part of a formal agreement between the implementing agency and the appropriate Iraqi authority. Each advisor needs to know how to walk the fine line between being a US government employee and advising an Iraqi minister with an agenda that could be somewhat at variance with US interests.

Given the importance of the oil and electricity sectors in Iraq, the embassy might want to recruit technical experts in these fields to help senior leadership in the embassy and Washington understand the technical issues involved in these key sectors. In such cases, guidelines for the recruitment, responsibilities, and the reporting chain need to be clearly drawn so that the advisor remains close to the embassy leadership and does not confuse his or her mission with advisers whose job it is to assist the Iraqis. With that distinction clear, all experts in a given sector should of course communicate regularly with each other.

USAID and other implementers are likely to retain personnel in Mosul, Basrah, Kirkuk and Hilla, working on provincial programs even as the Provincial Reconstruction Teams phase out or relocate. They need to be subject to the same coordination and reporting guidelines as their counterparts in Baghdad to ensure that provincial initiatives remain consistent with overall policy and are part of the picture developed in Baghdad to represent the totality of US assistance efforts in Iraq.

Coordination among international donors also needs to be re-energized. With the likelihood of more donors on the ground, donors' meetings can focus more on policy and program issues, and less on gathering information about what is going on in Iraq, as more donors will have their own sources of information. An Iraqi request to the World Bank or the UN to coordinate donors would also help stimulate more regular and constructive exchanges among donors.

MAINTAIN STRONG OVERSIGHT

HISTORY

The US reconstruction effort has been plagued from the beginning by allegations and instances of fraud and mismanagement. A comptroller arrived at CPA in July 2003 almost as an afterthought to help get a handle on the CPA budget and lay down a prioritization process for projects to be funded with Iraqi assets. This process remained problematic throughout CPA's tenure and might still result in legal action by the government of Iraq. The Congress established the CPA Inspector General (IG) in November 2003 to provide oversight of the CPA and IRRF II reconstruction program. When authority over the US mission reverted to the Department of State, the inspection function transferred over to the Special Inspector General for Iraq Reconstruction (SIGIR). Its mandate will expire only when 80 percent of the IRRF II funds are disbursed. This is likely to be well into 2007.

A strategic and selective approach to the next phase will lessen the burden on the taxpayer, enable broader participation by international donors and thus more firmly anchor Iraqis into the broader international community, and lay the groundwork for more productive and effective post-conflict assistance in the future.

The individual Inspectors General of the implementing agencies were slow to engage given the legal ambiguities of the CPA, the general confusion and logistical constraints on the ground, and the paucity of resources to engage in such a costly arena as Iraq. Only USAID had the foresight to deploy auditors with its original staff. However, they were looking solely at individual USAID projects and programs, and not at the larger portion of IRRF II being implemented by the PCO or other agencies. A small team of DoD auditors arrived in Baghdad in the summer of 2003, but they were quickly overwhelmed. State's IG began to consider elements of the IRRF program that State offices managed (e.g., police training, democracy programs) as the US mission reverted to the State Department in mid-2004. DoD's IG established an office in Qatar in spring 2006 that will focus primarily on the security forces training functions managed by MNSTC-I. Only SIGIR has been sufficiently well funded (a total of nearly $100 million) to begin to answer the fundamental question of why so much effort and money seems to have produced such a modest result.

REMEDIES

Given this history, strong oversight should be a central element of the next phase of the US reconstruction program in Iraq. While it should not be necessary to maintain an independent Inspector General such as SIGIR, the implementing agency IGs should consider replicating some of the SIGIR practices, such as reporting regularly on the overall progress of each sector of a particular program.[1] This provides an informative picture of what the program is accomplishing and encourages the development of more widely accepted metrics by which to measure progress, and therefore better help inform the Congress and the public.

U.S leadership remains crucial to the further reconstruction and development of Iraq. Indications are that other donors believe the US, despite the billions of dollars it has already spent to rebuild Iraq, has not yet earned the right to pass the torch to others. To convince others to pledge, the US must commit more funds as well. US leadership, however, should not mean US dominance in every sector. A strategic and selective approach to the next phase will lessen the burden on the taxpayer, enable broader participation by international donors and thus more firmly anchor Iraqis into the broader international community, and lay the groundwork for more productive and effective post-conflict assistance in the future.

---

[1] Special Inspector General for Iraq Reconstruction, *Message from the Special Inspector General For Iraq Reconstruction*, October 30, 2006.

—5—
THE DESIRABILITY AND DOWNSIDES OF WITHDRAWAL: THE EFFECT OF US WITHDRAWAL ON THE INSURGENCY IN IRAQ

David Edelstein

The basic debate over whether the United States should withdraw from Iraq is familiar. Those advocating withdrawal argue that the United States is more of an irritant than a salve for the violence in Iraq. Those advocating a continued US presence fear the eruption of a civil war in the aftermath of a precipitous US withdrawal. Rather than rehashing this often simplistic debate, this chapter looks beyond at the likely consequences of withdrawal for the insurgency in Iraq. Would a substantial US withdrawal significantly reduce the amount of violence in Iraq, or on the other hand, would those nationalist Iraqis who have battled the United States for the last three years simply find another target for their violence? What regional consequences might a US withdrawal have?

I divide my analysis into three parts. The first section delves further into the nature of the problem being examined here. That is, what effect would withdrawal have on the continuing violence in Iraq and the broader Middle East? The second section examines potential scenarios that might influence the reaction to a US withdrawal. Third and finally, I offer some suggestions for how the United States and the emergent Iraqi government might best manage the challenge of withdrawal so as to lessen the likelihood of the most dangerous post-withdrawal scenarios.

THE PROBLEM

The issue of what is likely to happen to the insurgency after US withdrawal turns on the question of at whom the insurgency has been directed to this point. As many have noted, the insurgency in Iraq has actually been several different insurgencies, each with different targets, though evidence suggests a convergence among some of these different insurgent groups.[1] Disgruntled Saddam loyalists and other Sunni Arabs have targeted both the US occupation forces and the Shia majority that they fear will be in control of a democratic Iraq. These Sunni groups have often been joined by foreign jihadists who have infiltrated Iraq with similar purposes: simultaneously preventing the United States occupation from succeeding in Iraq and impeding the Shia majority from dominating a post-war Iraq. Shia militia violence has largely been driven by impatience at a continuing occupation that only seems to deprive the Shia majority of what it views as its legitimate control over a post-Saddam Iraq.

> *This is one of the great, unanswered puzzles of the Iraqi insurgency: just how much of this violence is motivated by resentment at the US occupation of the country, and just how much of the violence stems from the tension between the various ethnic and religious groups within Iraq?*

The motivations of these different groups are critical for understanding their likely development after the United States withdraws. If these groups have been acting primarily out of unhappiness with the continuing US presence in Iraq, then presumably a US withdrawal would assuage their concerns and, thus, alleviate the violence. This is one of the great, unanswered puzzles of the Iraqi insurgency: just how much of this violence is motivated by resentment at the US occupation of the country, and just how much of the violence stems from the tension between the various ethnic and religious groups within Iraq? What is likely to happen in Iraq after US withdrawal depends heavily on the answer to this puzzle.

The best guess as to the answer suggests that Iraqi insurgents have, in fact, been motivated by both factors and have been able fairly easily to retarget their attacks. Insurgent violence in Iraq has been driven by community-based nationalism—the desire of identified groups to govern themselves within a sovereign state. The goals of this nationalism need not be isolated to expunging the US presence from Iraq. Instead, as we have vividly observed, the goals of these types of nationalist groups can fairly easily be transformed from anti-US in nature to anti-Sunni or anti-

---

[1] *In Their Own Words: Reading the Iraqi Insurgency,* Middle East Report no. 50 (Washington, DC: International Crisis Group, February 15, 2006).

Shia in nature. Nationalist violence directed at American occupation forces that deprives the occupied population of self-determination can be readily transformed into violence directed at other Iraqi groups that are perceived to be depriving certain groups of political self-determination.

This line of argument suggests that violence is likely to continue—and perhaps even grow—in the aftermath of a US withdrawal. For disgruntled nationalists, enemies are highly substitutable. Post-withdrawal violence could, however, play out in a number of different ways. In the next section, I delineate three potential scenarios for what Iraq could look like after US withdrawal and assess the probability of each outcome.

SCENARIOS

Unfortunately, discussions of what Iraq is likely to look like after a US withdrawal have too often been painted in simple dichotomies: either it is a civil war or no civil war; either it is a functioning democracy or it is an anarchic failed state. The brevity of this chapter precludes discussing all the nuanced differences among possible scenarios in a post-withdrawal Iraq, but I will examine three possibilities. The scenarios focus on the consequences of withdrawal in terms of the level of violence for Iraq itself, for the broader Middle East and for the United States. Of course, violence is not the only indicator of the effect of withdrawal on Iraq, but it is one indicator to which many are likely to look. In addition, extreme violence, as would occur in civil war, has the possibility for affecting not just Iraq, but also the Middle East more generally.

INTENSE LARGE-SCALE VIOLENCE

Many observers expect that that probability of a large-scale civil war will be high in the aftermath of a US withdrawal from Iraq. Insurgency becomes civil war when the magnitude of the violence increases and when the two (or more sides) fighting organize themselves into effective fighting forces with distinct political goals. American withdrawal, it is thought, will simply take off whatever lid the current American presence in Iraq might be keeping on the violence. In the absence of an effectively trained Iraqi military, insurgent groups will easily be able to turn their dissatisfaction with the state of affairs in Iraq against the emergent Iraqi government. Such violence would most likely be dominated by violence between Sunni Arabs and Shia, though internecine Shia violence is a distinct possibility. The role of the northern Kurdish population in such a civil war remains unclear. Even before the American-led invasion of Iraq in 2003, the Kurds had established an enclave of de facto self-governance in northern Iraq. How and on whose side the Kurdish population would be drawn into an Iraqi civil war is somewhat unclear.

One of the great dangers of an Iraqi civil war is that it would not be possible to contain such a conflict to Iraq. Instead, other neighboring states are likely to become involved. Some, like Turkey, might become involved for fear of the destabilizing effects of such a conflict. Others, like Iran, might become involved in an opportunistic attempt to take advantage of the chaos and disorganization that is likely to attend an Iraqi civil war. Just how contagious an Iraqi civil war would be is also an uncertainty. While the reasons for other states potentially to become involved in an Iraqi civil war are logical and understandable, one could also imagine a situation in which states neighboring on Iraq prefer to sit this one out and avoid entangling themselves in a bloody and vicious fight.

The implications of a civil war for the future of Iraq are also a matter of some debate. An Iraqi civil war introduces the possibility of comprehensive state failure, which could potentially turn Iraq into a haven for jihadists resembling pre-9/11 Afghanistan. Thus, some insist that such a civil war would necessitate reintervention by the United States, by other states, or by the United Nations in order to stop the violence. The potential scale of such a struggle and the possible contagion to other states in the region would mandate that the war be stopped before it could reach its most malign conclusion. On the other hand, others are more optimistic that an Iraqi civil war could essentially be confined to Iraq. While a civil war is certainly not a desirable outcome, it is also not clear to these analysts that an Iraqi civil war poses any great threat to the region or to American interests in the region or elsewhere. In other words, despite the potential costs to the United States' reputation, an Iraqi civil war is something the United States can live with as long as the US is not stuck in the middle of it.

PERSISTENT MID-LEVEL VIOLENCE

As an alternative to a full-fledged, large-scale civil war, it is conceivable that Iraq after US withdrawal could continue to see persistent mid-level violence (fewer than 10,000 deaths per year). Insurgent groups might calculate that they will be better able to achieve their interests by simply preventing the consolidation of an effective Iraqi government without necessarily provoking a civil war. If, for example, Sunni Arab insurgents were to attempt to escalate the current level of violence to more extreme violence characteristic of a civil war, then it is likely that the Iraqi central government might respond with commensurate violence. Such a conflict may not be in the interests of insurgent groups who may not be able to defeat the Iraqi military supported by US resources.

Rather than provoking such a civil war, insurgents might continue to use violence in more limited, tactical ways in order to prevent the consolidation of a strong central Iraqi government. The project of a majority-controlled democratic Iraq would consequently fail without the insurgents having to pay the potential costs of an intense and lengthy full-scale civil war.

Persistent mid-level violence might appear to be in the short-term interests of the United States. It would allow the United States to withdraw without an immediate outbreak of civil war and the potential regional consequences of such a war. In the long term, however, it is unclear how sustainable Iraq would be if such mid-level violence persists. At some point, if the central Iraqi government is unable to deliver basic human services to their people and if the continuing violence prevents the economy from functioning effectively, then Iraq may become a failed state and chaos may overwhelm the fledgling government. In the face of such chaos, it may be incumbent upon the United States and its allies to ensure that Iraq does not become prey to its neighbors, such as Iran, nor that it becomes an ungoverned safe haven for the training of jihadists who hope to target the United States or its interests. Thus, while persistent mid-level violence may appear more attractive in the short-term, it is likely to constitute "death by a thousand cuts" to any emerging Iraqi government.

PERIODIC LOW-LEVEL VIOLENCE

Periodic low level violence (fewer than 1000 deaths per year) is possible in Iraq under two opposite post-withdrawal circumstances. In one possible development, a post-withdrawal Iraq would witness the emergence of an Iraqi central government that is both willing and able to employ coercion to control opposition. To achieve this outcome, the United States and its coalition partners may have to be willing to look the other way as the Iraqi government asserts its authority in ways that may not be consistent with the stated goals of achieving a liberal democracy. Defeating insurgency, however, often requires the ruthless use of force, and if the Iraqi government is to succeed, it may have to employ such force.

Like the previous scenario, however, this scenario too poses difficult long-term challenges. While an assertive and ruthless government may be able to suppress violence in the short-term, this is unlikely to be a sustainable policy for the Iraqi government in the long-term. At some point, those groups that have been subject to repression by a new Iraqi government will again rise up and devise new strategies for undermining it. Ultimately, successful counterinsurgency is likely to require not only the ruthless use of force, but also an effective political strategy that addresses the desires of different groups within society to have their rights, identities, and futures protected.

For the United States, the prospect of emboldening and empowering the Iraqi government and military promises a mixed bag. Such a policy may lessen the immediate likelihood of a full-fledged civil war, but at the risk of completely undermining the goals of the invasion in the first place. Replacing Saddam Hussein with simply another form of strongman government could hardly be pointed to as a rousing success. In addition, this scenario would be completely dependent on the establishment of a competent and reliable Iraqi military. The establishment of such a military obviously remains a difficult task for the coalition.

Alternatively, low-level violence might also attend a more federalist solution to Iraq's political challenges. In this scenario, the major communities within Iraq might be permitted self-governance under a loose federalist constitution. Such a solution might satisfy the political aspirations of different groups, but it simultaneously introduces other problems. Most notably, a system for dividing Iraq's oil revenues would have to be devised. A federalist solution might also make Iraq more vulnerable to predatory states who might seek to lop off sections of the country in the absence of a unified Iraqi state and military. For the United States, a federalist Iraq would introduce the challenge of maintaining a delicate balance between disparate political forces. Devising an effective federal system is likely to be quite difficult, but if created, such a system might be a sustainable long-term solution to the political challenges confronting Iraq.

The lowest level of violence, then, can be expected to accompany two opposite types of political solutions. One solution would envision a strong and perhaps illiberal central government able to control violence through the effective use of military force. Another solution would reduce the level of violence by dispersing power among the different ethnic and religious communities in Iraq.

POLICY OPTIONS

All three of the scenarios painted above suggest that violence is likely to persist in the wake of a US withdrawal. Is there any conceivable situation in which a US withdrawal is attended by a cessation of violence? For this to be achieved, a solution would have to be found to the underlying political problem that Iraq confronts as a country. Fundamentally misunderstood before and throughout the occupation has been the importance of nationalism to explaining this continuing conflict. Part of the intensity would be assuaged by a US withdrawal, but the alternative nationalist and communalist visions of different groups within Iraq will remain. More resources alone cannot address this problem; instead, it requires a political solution that has historically been elusive in cases where multinational societies have been occupied. If, however, a political solution can be negotiated that satisfies the demands of each of the many interests competing in Iraq and if that solution is deemed to be sustainable by those same parties, then the US presence would come to be seen as the last remaining impediment to Iraqis reclaiming full sovereignty over their territory. Locating such a political solution is, however, fraught with difficulties, not the least of which is determining with whom one should negotiate. Given the fits and starts with which the Iraqi political process has moved along, it is unclear whether such a political solution is likely to be reached before the pressure for withdrawal in Washington is irresistible.

If the prospects for a violence-free Iraq after US withdrawal are relatively slim, then does it follow that the policy trajectory toward withdrawal should be rethought? In the face of a possible civil war or even lesser violence, should the US reconsider withdrawal and continue to make the necessary commitment to provide security (as much as it can) for Iraq? Sustaining a longer US presence in Iraq only makes sense under two conditions. First, abandoning plans for withdrawal is sensible if one believes that the continued US presence will eventually lead to an abatement in the level of violence in Iraq over both the short- and long-term. Second, withdrawal is nonsensical if the presence of the United States in Iraq is welcomed, rather than rejected, by the population. On neither issue does the evidence suggest that the United States should plan on a lengthier stay in Iraq. On the first issue, the presence of the United States in Iraq may be keeping a lid on to some extent, but it is unclear that the United States can effectively eliminate the desire for violence among the insurgents. Instead, a continued US presence would probably see a continuation of the current level of violence, directed against both Iraqi and American targets. On the second issue, there are certainly significant elements of the Iraqi population that hope that the United

States will remain until the country is secure, but other significant segments of the population continue to resent an American presence that they view as an impediment to self-determination. A continued US presence is unlikely to win this population over to more cooperative strategies for the future. In the end, withdrawal ultimately promises the best hope of resolving at least part of the nationalism problem that has plagued the US mission in Iraq from the outset, and it promises to do so at a lesser cost in life, money, and reputation to the United States.

If withdrawal remains the best possible option, what should the United States do to prepare itself for the eventuality of withdrawal in order to ensure the most stable possible Iraq after American troops leave? First, the United States should attempt to enroll Iraq's neighbors in the difficult project of rebuilding stability and peace. An unstable or failed Iraq, plagued by a civil war, is in the interest of no country in the region. Such a war could eventually spread across international borders and wind up costing an enormous amount in lives and productive capacity across a wide area. The nations of the Gulf region and the Middle East, more generally, should be encouraged to commit to policies that will contain any violence in Iraq after the United States leaves.

Second, the United States needs to devise a political, economic, and military strategy for continuing to assist the Iraqi government in the wake of withdrawal. The difficulties in Iraq will not end with the withdrawal of US forces, so it is incumbent upon the US to be prepared for that post-withdrawal reality. The survivability of the emergent Iraqi government is going to depend, in part, on the support that the United States and other countries offer it. The US must implement a strategy that supports this government without making it seem that the government is acting at the behest of the United States. Sovereignty and independence must be real, or the nationalist instincts of the Iraqi population are likely to be rekindled shortly after the withdrawal.

Third and perhaps most importantly, Washington must consider the type of government it is willing to accept in Iraq. The best hope of quashing the insurgency and allowing Iraq to move forward probably does not lie in the American vision of a liberal democratic Iraq. In the short term, at least, defeating the insurgency is likely to require an assertive, forceful, and sometimes ruthless Iraqi central government and military. To accept this type of government may undermine America's very purpose in Iraq. To reject this type of government may only guarantee a continuation or even exacerbation of the violence. Similarly, loose federalism may alleviate much of the political pressure that is generating violence, but also runs contrary to initial US goals and introduces a host of other problems, including resource allocation.

Each of these policy prescriptions would shift the emphasis in current US policy toward Iraq. Making the future of Iraq a priority concern for all of Iraq's neighbors must become a larger priority for US policy. A regional summit to discuss the future of Iraq including all relevant parties should be called in the near future. At the same time, the United States should soon publicly offer a comprehensive plan for its involvement in Iraq after a substantial military withdrawal from the country. Publicly revealing such a plan would both make US intentions more credible and reassure those in Iraq who worry about potential abandonment. The plan should include specific programs for economic development, political institutions, and internal and external security that will enhance the sincerity of the US commitment.

Finally, the US has begun to recognize that "the perfect is the enemy of the good" when it comes to the emergent Iraqi government, but Washington must prepare itself to negotiate and support a government that may be less than the ideal that some had envisioned. The government that is best for stability may not be a centralized, democratic government. Instead, the US must continue to prepare for a post-withdrawal Iraq that is likely to be quite fractured and violent.

Ultimately, the future of Iraq and the direction it is likely to take rest with finding a solution to the political problems that afflict Iraq as a country. Internecine fighting and the Shia and Sunni confrontations are rooted, after all, in the political aspirations of these different groups. An American withdrawal is likely to remove one source of opposition within Iraq, but sectarian rifts are already taking the place of opposition to the US presence. Until a political solution is found to these problems in Iraq—liberal democratic or not, unified country or not—violence is likely to persist.

— 6 —
SECURING IRAQ: THE WAY AHEAD

Michael Eisenstadt

Much of the current public debate about US policy in Iraq is based on a flawed reading of Iraqi society and politics, an inadequate appreciation of the political, economic, and military constraints that limit US options, and misconceptions about the likely path to "victory." The result is a plethora of proposals that fail to address adequately the extraordinarily complex political realities and policy challenges that confront the US in Iraq.

Critics of American policy say that the US presence fuels the Sunni Arab insurgency and widespread anti-occupation sentiment, and that the withdrawal of US forces is a necessary first step toward stemming the violence and forcing the Iraqi Security Forces (ISF) to assume responsibility for the security of the country. This leads them to conclude that US forces should leave Iraq—the sooner the better.[1]

While some of these assumptions may be true, this prescription ignores several factors:

1) the insurgency has entrenched itself throughout the Sunni triangle and will try to influence, infiltrate, and overthrow the Iraqi government, whether or not US forces remain in Iraq;
2) the US has adjusted its force footprint and rules of engagement to greatly reduce friction with the population, though some friction is inevitable in areas where US forces have the lead in providing security;

---

[1] John P. Murtha,"War in Iraq," press release, November 17, 2005,
http://www.house.gov/apps/list/press/pa12_murtha/pr051117iraq.html (accessed July 13, 2006);
Barry Posen, "Exit Strategy: How to Disengage from Iraq in 18 Months," *Boston Review* 30
(January/February 2006), http://www.bostonreview.net/BR31.1/posen.html (accessed July 13, 2006);
Nir Rosen, "If America Left Iraq: The Case for Cutting and Running," *Atlantic Monthly* 296, no. 5
(December 2005), http://www.theatlantic.com/doc/200512/iraq-withdrawal (accessed July 13, 2006).

3) although most Iraqis want the US gone, they do not want the US to leave until a modicum of stability has been achieved; and

4) some Sunnis believe that the US presence, though onerous, constrains Shia revanchism and limits Iranian influence; this provides the US with a degree of leverage in Sunni circles.

Seen in this light, the rationale for a rapid withdrawal is much less compelling. In fact, the US effort in Iraq has, almost from the start, been hamstrung by a mismatch between means and ends, and a variety of military, economic and political constraints. The US neither has sufficient forces in-country, nor the right kind of forces. In particular, it lacks linguists, intelligence and civil affairs specialists, and military police to properly prosecute its counterinsurgency strategy or to sustain the significant long-term presence required to see through its transformational agenda in Iraq. Human and material resources devoted to reconstruction have likewise been inadequate. Iraq's foreign aid has mostly been spent on security and not reconstruction. The Commanders' Emergency Response Program (CERP) was under-funded and commanders were not given enough leeway to use these funds as they saw fit and the initial emphasis on large, multi-year projects was misguided. Iraqi resentment of the occupation, flagging American domestic support for the war effort, as well as concerns that repeated deployments to Iraq could gut the volunteer Army, make a US drawdown, sooner or later, a political and military necessity. Paradoxically, such a drawdown may be the only way to sustain a long-term American commitment to Iraq, though too rapid a drawdown could greatly reduce prospects for success.

In any event, it is not at all clear that the *National Strategy for Victory in Iraq* provides a formula for success against the insurgents and terrorists, or for a durable, lasting peace.[2] A more likely outcome may be a military stalemate, leading to a negotiated settlement and an imperfect peace. It is also not possible to rule out the possibility of a protracted civil war, or the collapse of the central government and the breakup of the country into numerous semi-autonomous fiefdoms ruled by tribal and party militias and local warlords.

The implementation of US strategy in Iraq has thus far been less than optimal. But given the aforementioned military, economic, and political

[2] US National Security Council, *National Strategy for Victory in Iraq* (Washington, DC: November 2005), http://www.whitehouse.gov/infocus/iraq/iraq_national_strategy_20051130.pdf (accessed July 13, 2006).

constraints, the current US approach probably represents the best use of the limited means available to coalition commanders on the ground in Iraq. It remains to be seen whether US policy objectives—the defeat of the terrorists, the co-optation or defeat of divergent strands of the insurgency, the revitalization of the economy, and the creation of a stable, democratic Iraq—can be achieved with the means available to the US and Iraqi governments.

A number of important decisions will likely be made in the coming year concerning the management of a US drawdown, Iraq's escalating sectarian violence, and the potential "end game." These decisions will occur in an extremely challenging policy environment, with the US seeking to make the most of its waning influence—as the last of its $21.9 billion in reconstruction monies is spent—and it starts drawing down its forces. Finally, in considering US options, it should be kept in mind that even the simplest of things are difficult in Iraq. Accordingly, policy recommendations should be practical and expectations modest.

MANAGING THE DRAWDOWN

The question is not whether the US should stay or go; the US is committed to lower, more sustainable force levels—a move dictated by a desire to minimize friction with the Iraqi population, American domestic politics, and US military requirements. The vital questions pertain to the timing, pace, and sequence of the drawdown, and how best to reposition US forces to support the ISF and to contain insurgent and/or sectarian violence in areas where the ISF is unable to take the lead. Accordingly, a rapid build-up of the ISF is a political and military necessity. This task cannot be deferred pending negotiation of a constitutional compromise, neutralization of the insurgency, or conclusion of a pact of national reconciliation, even if a rapid buildup results in an unrepresentative force that makes these goals more difficult to achieve in the near-term.[3]

That said, it will be important to retain significant numbers of US ground and air forces in Iraq, probably numbering in the tens of thousands, for years to come, or at least as long as their presence is tolerated by the Iraqi government. Their role will be to reassure and support the ISF by providing combat enablers and capabilities the ISF lacks; to deter or prevent atrocities by government "death squads;" and to provide quick-reaction forces to assist the ISF and contain a major escalation of

---

[3] Stephen Biddle, "Seeing Baghdad, Thinking Saigon: The Perils of Refighting Vietnam in Iraq," *Foreign Affairs* 85, no. 2 (March/April 2006), http://www.foreignaffairs.org/20060301faessay85201/stephen-biddle/seeing-baghdad-thinking-saigon.html (accessed July 13, 2006).

sectarian violence. Thus, as the ISF stands up, US forces should stand aside and continue to support the ISF, when and where necessary.

US forces, moreover, must avoid the temptation of hunkering down in super-FOBs (Forward Operating Bases) as they drawdown. A key lesson of Iraq and Afghanistan is that the proactive engagement of civil society by US military forces is, by and large, the best way to protect the force. Engagement creates opportunities for interaction with Iraqis that yield actionable intelligence, and provides the population with a stake in the protection of coalition forces when the latter are able to shield them from insurgent intimidation, or where the coalition is perceived as the lesser of two evils relative to the more extreme or violent insurgent groups. The challenge, as US forces drawdown, is ensuring that the ISF assimilates this lesson and engages the Iraqi civilian population in order to build the rapport and trust needed to succeed against the insurgents. Given the sectarian and ethnic composition of many ISF units, endemic police corruption, and the penetration of Ministry of Interior units by militias, this will be a major challenge.

> *The challenge, as US forces drawdown, is ensuring that the ISF assimilates this lesson and engages the Iraqi civilian population in order to build the rapport and trust needed to succeed against the insurgents.*

IMPLEMENTING "CLEAR, HOLD, AND BUILD"

Although the US has notched up a number of important counterinsurgency successes—clearing, holding, and rebuilding Falluja, Mosul, Tal Afar, and a number of smaller towns in the western Euphrates River valley—it has not consistently applied this counterinsurgency strategy throughout the Sunni Arab regions of Iraq. There are several possible reasons for the lack of consistent implementation. The first is the fact that there are not sufficient Iraqi and US forces on the ground to clear and hold additional areas without ceding previously pacified villages and towns to the insurgents. The second is a belief held by some that only Iraqi forces can ultimately defeat the insurgents (as they are better able to connect with the population and to gather intelligence, without engendering the kind of resentment caused by the coalition military presence), leading US commanders to defer additional major operations until more Iraqi forces become available. Finally, a desire on the part of Washington to avoid a series of major operations in the midst of a polarizing domestic political debate about the war, and in the run-up to November 2006 mid-term elections, precludes an effective strategy.

In the meantime, US forces have labored to prevent the insurgents from establishing a secure foothold in the Sunni triangle and to dislodge them from their safehavens (a strategy that some critics have derisively labeled "whack-a-mole"). Simultaneously, the ISF continues its rapid buildup and approaches the critical mass necessary to implement the type of "clear, hold, and build" strategy employed successfully by the British in Malaya and by the US in South Vietnam. It remains to be seen whether Iraqi forces can (with US assistance) defeat the insurgents, or set the conditions for a negotiated settlement.

REINING IN THE MILITIAS

Tribal and party militias have proliferated in post-Saddam Iraq, filling the security vacuum created by the collapse of the Iraqi state, and providing muscle to tribes and political parties. Militias are a source of concern because they contribute to the atmosphere of lawlessness that pervades post-Saddam Iraq, undermine central government authority, and are, in the words of US Ambassador to Baghdad Zalmay Khalilzad, "the infrastructure of civil war, and the basis of warlordism."[4]

It is unlikely that any of the major militias will disband as long as the overall security situation remains tenuous. Moreover, the lesson of numerous post-conflict experiences (e.g., Nicaragua, El Salvador, Lebanon) is that militias are most effectively disarmed, demobilized, and reintegrated into society as part of a negotiated settlement that leads to a process of national reconciliation. For this reason, resolution of Iraq's militia problem will probably have to await a negotiated settlement of Iraq's civil war and the emergence of effective central and local government institutions in Iraq. Nonetheless, something must be done in the meanwhile to deal with this problem. The best that can probably be hoped for is to limit the capabilities of the militias by clamping down on black market activities that provide them with a steady income stream, such as the smuggling of oil, and limiting their access to more capable weapons (such as anti-tank guided missiles, heavy mortars, and rockets) by interdicting weapons smuggling routes from Iran.

---

[4] Nelson Hernandez, "Diplomacy Helped To Calm the Chaos," *Washington Post,* February 28, 2006, A11.

Dealing with this issue is likely to become more difficult with the passage of time, as the problem of insurgent and militia violence becomes increasingly intertwined. In particular, the recent emergence of a nascent Shia resistance movement engaged in attacks on coalition forces in areas of southern Iraq where militias had previously been the dominant security concern is problematic. The emergence of Sunni militias in areas of the Sunni triangle where shadowy insurgent organizations had previously operated exclusively will only complicate efforts to rein in the militias.

CONTAINING SECTARIAN VIOLENCE

One of the key challenges facing the United States in Iraq is quelling the escalating sectarian violence that threatens to derail that country's troubled political transition, erode flagging US domestic support for the war effort, and heighten communal tensions throughout the Middle East. Because the Sunni Arab insurgency and the sectarian violence it has spawned are, at their core, politically motivated, the formation of a broad-based national unity government is an important first step toward halting the bloodshed.

But it is only a first step, and it will not bring about an end to a low grade civil war that shows no sign of abating—at least not yet. Moreover, a dramatic increase in sectarian violence could further undermine dwindling US domestic support for the war, stress an already overstretched force, and jeopardize the tacit US alliance with the Shia that has underpinned US policy in post-Saddam Iraq.

For this reason, there is a need for interim measures to deal with this problem. Identifying the factors that give rise to and perpetuate this civil conflict, and proposing practical steps for dealing with them, will be critical to US and Iraqi government efforts to contain, if not reduce sectarian violence there. So what can be done?

CONTAIN THE INSURGENCY, TO CONTAIN SECTARIAN VIOLENCE

The insurgency is the driving force behind Iraq's sectarian violence; containing the insurgency is therefore a prerequisite for curbing the sectarian bloodletting. The Sunni Arab insurgency, however, has mobilized only a fraction of the hundreds of thousands of aggrieved Sunnis with military or paramilitary training, and has little appeal beyond the Sunni community. Should the insurgency successfully exploit this untapped potential, or forge tactical alliances with aggrieved members of other communities, it could greatly increase its capacity for violence. This is why it is so important to offer Sunni Arabs a political alternative to violence and to avoid pushing the Sunni insurgents into the arms of extremist Shia elements, such as the followers of the radical Shia cleric Muqtada al-Sadr (a much less likely possibility today than it was in the recent past, given Iraq's current sectarian polarization). It remains to be seen, however, whether Ambassador Khalilzad can co-opt the Sunnis without turning the Shias into open enemies of the United States.

MITIGATE THE CONSEQUENCES OF ETHNIC CLEANSING

Victims of ethnic cleansing in civil war-torn countries (e.g., Lebanon, Bosnia) who are forced to relocate to a different part of the country often find employment with communal militias and parties in their new places of residence. This provides many of these victims with the means to act on their desire for revenge, further fueling the conflict. To avert such a dynamic in Iraq, it would be highly desirable to find legitimate employment for the tens of thousands of newly displaced Iraqis so that they do not contribute to the growth of the militias and radical Islamist movements and parties. However, even such a focused and limited job creation effort will likely prove extremely difficult to implement under prevailing circumstances.

PROTECT AT-RISK POPULATIONS

While much of the violence visited upon civilians during civil wars is random in nature, it is not without its own cruel logic, and is often perpetrated as part of a deliberate strategy. Atrocities and massacres, for instance, are most common in contested areas, and are conducted to secure these areas through ethnic cleansing (e.g., again, Lebanon and Bosnia) or to deter civilians from cooperating with "the enemy" (e.g., Algeria). In Iraq, mixed neighborhoods and villages and those close to ethnic or sectarian fault-lines have been hardest hit by sectarian and ethnic violence and the forced displacement of populations, and thus are at greatest risk. Much of the current violence, however, is low level and covert, occurring "under the radar" of coalition forces, so to speak, and thus is very hard to prevent.

If, however, violence were to escalate to involve larger groups of insurgents, militiamen, or government security forces, it might be possible for US forces to intervene with ground forces, attack helicopters, or gunships. At the very least, a clear willingness to use such means could keep the violence below a certain threshold. It might also be possible, in certain places, to prevent attacks on civilians by using traffic and population control measures (e.g., checkpoints and roadblocks) to interdict the movement of violent mobs and militia convoys. For instance, the Mahdi Army frequently buses its militiamen from one place to another. In this way, coalition forces might create "firebreaks" to contain or slow the spread of violence.

PREVENT THE BREAKUP OF THE ISF

The disintegration or neutralization of Iraq's security forces under the pressure of spreading sectarian violence would probably mark the death knell of US efforts to transform Iraq into a viable, functioning state. Such an eventuality must be averted at all costs.

In Iraq, most ISF units consist largely of Shia or Kurdish personnel, with a small but significant number of Sunni Arab commissioned and noncommissioned officers. The ISF is therefore unlikely to disintegrate should Sunni-Shia or Arab-Kurdish violence intensify, though some individuals might desert in order to fight with sectarian or ethnic militias. Desertions of key personnel could significantly diminish the capacity of some units.

The ISF is much more likely to disintegrate in the event of intra-communal violence among Shia or Kurdish groups. Intra-communal conflict among former allies has been a fairly common feature of civil war settlements (e.g., General Michel Aoun's 1990 uprising in Lebanon).[5] In Iraq, intra-communal violence could have fatal consequences for the ISF. The implication here is that US diplomats need to not only focus on resolving or managing the dominant communal conflict between Sunnis and Shias—but also on managing or resolving various latent conflicts among Kurds and Shias. While the United States may be well positioned to mediate among the major Kurdish factions, regional actors such as Iran may be better suited to mediate among the Shias, although it is not clear that Tehran would have an interest in doing so.

HALT THE DRIFT TOWARD FRAGMENTATION AND "CHAOS"

The fragmentation of political and religious authority in the course of civil conflicts (as occurred during the Lebanese civil war and the second Palestinian intifada) often complicates efforts to resolve these conflicts.

---

[5] Pierre M. Atlas and Roy Licklider, "Conflict Among Former Allies After Civil War Settlement: Sudan, Zimbabwe, Chad, Lebanon," *Journal of Peace Research* 36, no. 1 (1999): 35-54.

The rise of Shia militias operating within or independent of the ISF (such as the Mahdi Army and the Badr Brigades), the formation of Shia death squads comprised of Ministry of Interior employees, and the emergence of a new generation of younger, more radical Shia clerics unresponsive to the authority of the traditional Shia religious establishment, all portend a fragmentation of political and religious authority in Iraq that could accelerate the trend toward chaos and violence.

To counter this trend, the United States should try to identify members of Interior Ministry death squads and press the Iraqi government to punish them (the embedding of US police transition teams in Interior Ministry units should help, as the Iraqis tend to behave better when Americans are present). The US should also deny resources (e.g., funds disbursed by Provincial Reconstruction Teams) to individuals and entities associated with militias and radical clerics and clamp down on illegal financial activities that benefit the militias (such as the diversion and sale of oil and refined petroleum products).

A good first step toward dismantling Iraq's conflict economy would be a crackdown on kidnapping rackets, and the diversion of oil and refined products by militias and insurgent groups.

While a descent into chaos should rightly be feared, it should also be kept in mind that in even the most horrific civil wars (e.g., Lebanon, Algeria, Rwanda, Yugoslavia), violence has not taken the form of a general struggle involving every man against his neighbor. Rather, the carnage tends to be the work of bands of often poorly trained but well organized criminals, thugs, and militiamen (sometimes supported by local police and conventional military forces) who victimize civilians with the tacit or open encouragement and sanction of hostile neighbors, cynical politicians, extremist parties, or warlords.[6] This seems to be the case in Iraq as well.

Though challenges of humanitarian intervention in civil wars are not trivial, they should not be exaggerated either. Dealing with criminals, thugs, and militias is nothing that a well-equipped, professional military should not be able to handle—provided that it has an adequate number of

---

[6] John Mueller, "The Banality of Ethnic War," *International Security* 25, no. 1 (Summer 2000): 42-70.

troops on the ground and that it has prepared for this particular type of conflict environment. In fact, the US military has operated successfully against militias in Iraq on several occasions (most notably the Mahdi Army of Muqtada Sadr in April and August 2004), although the requirement for humanitarian intervention would greatly tax already overstretched American forces. Moreover, intervening on behalf of civilian victims on both sides of the Sunni-Shia sectarian divide could severely strain relations between the US and key Shia politicians and parties.

DISMANTLE THE CONFLICT ECONOMY

Civil conflicts often give rise to economic activities that are undertaken in order to finance arms purchases and pay the salaries of combatants. This creates a vested interest in the perpetuation of the conflict among those who benefit economically (e.g., drug cultivation in Lebanon and Afghanistan and the trade in conflict diamonds in Angola, Sierra Leone, and the Democratic Republic of the Congo). In Iraq, criminal elements, many with ties to militias and insurgent groups, are involved in the kidnapping of Iraqis and foreigners, the smuggling of oil, and the funding of the activities of these groups with the proceeds. A good first step toward dismantling Iraq's conflict economy would be a crackdown on kidnapping rackets, and the diversion of oil and refined products by militias and insurgent groups, which costs the Iraqi government billions of dollars a year in lost income.

HALT FOREIGN ASSISTANCE

Civil wars often have a transnational dimension, in that neighboring states may provide political, economic, and military support to one or more warring parties. Iraq is no exception; the insurgency and escalating sectarian violence is being fueled, at least in part, by some of its neighbors. Because Syria and Iran would probably like to see violence in Iraq continue to simmer in order to keep the United States tied down there, coalition and Iraqi efforts to halt foreign assistance to the combatants are likely to continue to emphasize unilateral measures that do not require the cooperation of its neighbors, such as enhanced security measures on the Iraqi side of its borders.

Efforts by the coalition and the Iraqi government to interdict the flow of foreign jihadists through Syria to the Sunni Triangle have apparently been somewhat successful, but a similar effort to interdict insurgent smuggling routes and "ratlines" along the border with Iran should likewise be undertaken. The length of the border and the paucity of Iraqi border security personnel and coalition troops will greatly complicate this task. It remains to be seen if proposed talks with Iran—currently on hold—will produce positive results in this area.

TOWARD THE END GAME: SETTING THE CONDITIONS FOR AN ACCEPTABLE OUTCOME

How do insurgencies end, and what are the implications for Iraq? Insurgencies may end in several ways: 1) an insurgent victory that results in the overthrow of the government; 2) the defeat of the insurgents through harsh repressive measures, and brute force; 3) the neutralization or defeat of the insurgents through a traditional counterinsurgency campaign that relies more on political, economic, and informational measures than on military force ("clear, hold, and build"), or; 4) a military stalemate that leads to a negotiated settlement, and the incorporation of the insurgents into the political process.

The Sunni Arab insurgents lack the means to overthrow the Iraqi government, and at any rate, US forces would almost certainly act to prevent such an eventuality. Conversely, the ISF lacks the means—tanks, artillery, attack helicopters—to crush the insurgents, using the methods employed by the Syrian Army to crush an Islamist uprising in the Syrian city of Hama in 1982 (killing up to 20,000 civilians in the process). At any rate, playing by "Hama rules" is neither an option for the United States or its close allies, nor the way to build a durable, lasting peace in Iraq.

Iraqi and US forces will face major challenges implementing their counterinsurgency strategy. They lack the numbers required to clear and hold large swathes of Iraq's Sunni Arab regions, and with the impending cutoff in US reconstruction assistance and the loss of much of Baghdad's oil income to corruption and smuggling, Iraq will lack the financial resources to make rapid progress in meeting its massive reconstruction needs (estimated at $50-100 billion). For these reasons, US and Iraqi forces are unlikely to quell the insurgency.

In tandem with these actions in the field, however, Iraqi and US government officials in Baghdad are engaged in ongoing efforts to draw Sunni Arab personalities, politicians, and insurgents into the political process—efforts that could divide and weaken the insurgency and set the stage for a negotiated settlement.[7] For now, this option offers the best hope for an acceptable outcome in Iraq.

> *It is probably too soon for the insurgents to conclude that the military option has run its course. For them, the impending US drawdown and mid-term elections in November 2006 mean that a window of opportunity may be opening, not closing.*

What are the necessary conditions for a negotiated settlement? Experience elsewhere indicates that they include: 1) a military stalemate that leads both sides to conclude that they cannot achieve their objectives by military means; 2) an emerging consensus over the contours of a settlement, and; 3) authoritative leaders capable of speaking and negotiating on behalf of their respective constituencies.[8] It is not clear, however, whether any of these conditions currently exist in Iraq.

It is probably too soon for the insurgents to conclude that the military option has run its course. For them, the impending US drawdown and mid-term elections in November 2006 mean that a window of opportunity may be opening, not closing. Moreover, forthcoming negotiations over Iraq's constitution will be a major test of whether there is sufficient common ground for a compromise settlement. At any rate, even if the answer is positive, the insurgents are not likely to abandon the military option. Rather, they are likely to keep up the pressure on the Iraqi government by pursuing a strategy of talking while fighting. Finally, it is not clear that the diverse entities that make up the Sunni Arab insurgency speak with a single voice or are capable of pursuing a common negotiating strategy in talks with the Iraqi government, although the fragmentation of the insurgency might allow it to be co-opted in a piecemeal fashion.

Several other factors have played a part in decisions by belligerents elsewhere to pursue negotiated settlements: 1) the perception that time is

---

[7] David Ignatius, "A Road Map Home," *Washington Post*, June 28, 2006, A25.

[8] This formulation of the prerequisites for a negotiated end to insurgencies and civil wars is based on the works of I. William Zartman, "Dynamics and Constraints in Negotiations in Internal Conflicts," in *Elusive Peace: Negotiating an End to Civil Wars*, ed. I. William Zartman (Washington, DC: Brookings, 1995): 3-29; "Ripeness: The Hurting Stalemate and Beyond" in *International Conflict Resolution After the Cold War*, ed. Paul Stern & Daniel Druckman (Washington, DC: National Academy Press, 2000): 225-250.

working against them, and that it is better to settle now and secure their position against rivals within their own camp or vis-à-vis the enemy, than to defer a settlement and possibly risk all; 2) geopolitical realignments that eliminate external factors that previously served to perpetuate regional conflicts (e.g., the end of the Cold War and of superpower competition for influence in the third world), and; 3) pressure by neighboring countries and key allies on both insurgent and government leaders to sue for peace. Some or all of these factors played a role in bringing about an end to insurgencies and civil wars in Rhodesia, Nicaragua, El Salvador, Lebanon, and the former Yugoslavia.

To set the conditions for a negotiated settlement, Washington must keep up the military pressure on the insurgents and convince them that military victory for them is unattainable; that the United States will stand by the Iraqi government come what may; that it will retain a potent (if somewhat diminished) military presence in Iraq for years to come in order to preclude an insurgent victory; and that such a US presence is also a major constraint on Shia revanchist violence and Iranian influence in Iraq, and is therefore in their interest. None of this will be an easy sell. Washington must also convince the insurgents that by passing up on a negotiated settlement, they risk missing a historical opportunity to ensure that Sunni Arab equities are protected in forthcoming negotiations to amend the constitution, and risk alienating erstwhile supporters in the Sunni Arab community who are increasingly weary of violence and fearful of a sectarian civil war.

Finally, the US should seek a commitment from each of Iraq's neighbors to do their part in putting an end to the violence, by securing their borders and reining in Iraqi client parties, militias and insurgent groups. Such an effort would face a major obstacle in the form of Syrian and Iranian satisfaction with the status quo in Iraq and their opposition to US regional policies. Success here may have to await a change in the tenor of relations between Washington, Tehran, and Damascus.

For these reasons, a negotiated settlement is neither imminent nor inevitable. The conflict in Iraq could grind on for years to come. Moreover, a negotiated settlement would pose challenges of its own: recalcitrant elements in the Sunni Arab community, believing that they have (once again) not been defeated, might try to obstruct a settlement, or join the security forces and the government in order to seize power in a coup or by other means. The outcome of a negotiated settlement is therefore liable to be a flawed peace that could be a source of domestic and regional instability for years to come.

The key to making a negotiated settlement stick and to averting such an outcome, then, may well be a small but significant long-term US military presence to monitor, verify, and if necessary, enforce compliance with such an agreement. It is not too early to start preparing American public opinion for such a possibility, and to start thinking out loud about what that might entail. But first, the American public has to recognize that there are no quick or easy fixes to the violence in Iraq, and that one way or another, the United States is likely to be involved on the ground in Iraq for years to come.

— 7 —

THE CONSEQUENCES OF IRAQ FOR US INFLUENCE AND POWER

Avis Bohlen

INTRODUCTION AND SUMMARY

At this juncture we have few options in Iraq and will probably be hard pressed to achieve even a minimally acceptable outcome. The US military presence provides limited leverage but is an unwieldy instrument for trying to shape political arrangements inside Iraq. It may be more profitable to use it to seek stabilization of Iraq by involving and working with the other regional powers.

Even a minimally acceptable outcome will fall far short of our original ambitious goals and is likely to be judged—to a greater or lesser degree—a failure by the rest of the world. The consequences of the Iraq war will resonate for a long time to come; almost nothing about it— whether the maneuvering and hype that preceded it, the assumptions that underpinned it, the mistakes of the post-invasion period, or the abuses that were an incidental consequence—will enhance America's reputation in the world. It has created widespread suspicion of our motives, with negative results for our influence and our ability to lead across a wide range of issues. It has propelled anti-Americanism into a real force in international affairs not only in the Middle East, but increasingly also in Europe. While the accumulated resentments, anger and grievances which make up anti-Americanism long predate the Iraq war and the Bush administration, Iraq has given them a new intensity and risks casting us as a permanent enemy of Islam. We should neither underestimate the damage this does to our standing in the world nor overestimate the impact on the behavior of governments. The interest of states is remarkably enduring. Others need to work with us and we with them. We have to some degree reknit the ties with the Europeans that were so badly damaged in the run up to Iraq. But our moral authority and our credibility have been tarnished and in many places the perceived interest of governments is sharply at odds with the sentiment of public opinion.

WHAT LEVERAGE DO WE HAVE IN IRAQ?

Today, our leverage to affect outcomes in Iraq and to influence its future has dwindled to a fraction of what it was in the immediate aftermath of the invasion. The impressive speed and decisiveness of our military victory gave us options in 2003 both in Iraq and in the region which we failed to exploit. As a result, outcomes that might have been available to us then— establishing the monopoly of force that would have provided stability and the security needed for large-scale reconstruction, exploiting the initial goodwill of the population, enlisting help from allies, establishing a commanding position in the region—are no longer possible.

Three years later, our choices are more restricted. Our military presence has not only failed to bring about the peaceful and democratic Iraq we aimed for, but seems powerless to stop a worsening of the insurgency and an increasingly violent sectarian struggle. We have made incontestable gains in forming a national army and police and in helping shape—four months after the election—a government which although weak is at least nominally supported by the three communities, but widely regarded as corrupt. The Sunni insurgency shows no signs of letting up. The anti-Sunni violence of Shia militias inside and outside the Iraqi police force is on the rise. There are well-founded fears of a downward spiral toward a Lebanese-style civil war. Remedies that at an earlier moment were urged on the

> *Our presence—and the growing possibility that it might be withdrawn or reduced in response to domestic pressures— constitutes our leverage.*

Administration such as bringing in the UN seem both beside the point and, under current security conditions, infeasible. Allied help is not available and at this point probably could not do much to stop the violence. Many of the allies who did send contingents in the early period of the war have now withdrawn them. Finally, the initially generous US funding for reconstruction—much of it never used because of security conditions—is being cut back. And of course public and Congressional support for the war in the United States is on the decline.

What leverage we have today is of a negative character—not the ability of our troops to apply force to achieve a desired security outcome but the fact that our military presence is viewed by many—and not only within Iraq—as the final bulwark against civil war and chaos. Our presence—

and the growing possibility that it might be withdrawn or reduced in response to domestic pressures—constitutes our leverage. In the long term, just about everyone would like us to leave; in the short term, just about everyone wants us to stay. The Sunni insurgents and some of the Shia militias are obvious exceptions. Indeed, there is widespread concern that domestic pressures in the US may lead to a premature departure. As deeply unpopular as the American occupation is with all Iraqis, it is judged by many to be preferable to the alternatives. We have not been able to impose order or to halt the growing drift into sectarian conflict, but our departure could well, in the view of most Iraqis, lead to even worse disorder. The Shia dominated government does not yet feel itself strong enough to deal with the insurgency alone and thus has no desire to see us leave until they do, a sentiment shared by the mainstream Shia. Even many Sunnis—our most bitter opponents in Iraq and the big losers from the war—have come to regard us as their only protection against vengeful Shia militias or Shia dominated police. Finally, whatever their differences, it appears that a majority of Iraqis in all three communities prefer, at least in theory, an arrangement that will keep the country together, a government based on a communal compromise rather than the alternative of splitting. It is of course true that sizeable minorities prefer other outcomes.

Iraq's neighbors similarly have no desire to see a permanent US military presence in Iraq, but in the short term, find it vastly preferable to the instability and chaos that might ensue following US withdrawal. Our Arab friends, some of whom have sizeable Shia minorities, fear the fighting in Iraq could lead to a broader Mideast conflict along sectarian lines, which would have negative consequences for their own internal stability. Despite growing tensions over the nuclear issue, Iran has—at least up to now—been generally acquiescent in our role in Iraq (and may indeed be the greatest long-term beneficiary) which it has accepted as a preferable alternative to either Saddam Hussein or chaos on its doorstep. The present governmental arrangement, since it ensures a dominant status for the Shias, very much accords with Iran's interest. Turkey, similarly, has no wish to see a civil war in Iraq which might push the Kurds over the brink towards an independent state.

Such sentiments are not limited to the immediate neighborhood. Our European allies, as much as some of them may have opposed the invasion, believe our departure at this juncture would worsen the violence and instability and feel some anxiety at the growing domestic pressures within the US for withdrawal. Though not unhappy to see us taken down a peg, they have no interest in an outcome that would leave the region in turmoil or could be seen as a US defeat. The Chinese and the Russians, similarly, do not believe chaos in Iraq is in any way in their interest. They are quite content to see us humbled and bogged down in Iraq, but would not welcome our speedy departure, especially if the consequence is increased violence and possibly civil war. For the Russians in particular, a perceived victory of the jihadists would not be welcome news, concerned as they are with the threat of Islamic extremism on their own borders.

Because it has broad support from all the principal players, at least in the short term, our continued military presence should, in theory, give us leverage in the situation. But can we exploit this and to what end? A military presence is a blunt instrument and not easily manipulated in pursuit of a political goal. A threat to withdraw if we do not mean it will not be credible and may be risky. Moreover, against the background of US domestic pressures to withdraw, the US military presence must be regarded to some degree as a wasting asset. Once started, reductions cannot be reversed or turned on and off like a faucet. In this respect, if not in most others, the lessons of Vietnam are applicable to Iraq.

Moreover, to what end should the leverage be used? Our present strategy comprises a security objective intended to build up an Iraqi army and police force and a political objective aimed at putting in place a minimally functioning government inclusive of all three communities. We have made some progress towards these goals. Some believe that this remains the most prudent course and the quickest route to an honorable exit and that we should therefore stick to it. Others argue that it has been and will continue to be ineffective in stemming the insurgency, the growing violence of the Shia militias and the sectarian conflicts. Without a different strategy, they maintain, there is no guarantee that our military presence will not simply produce more of the same, taking us farther from our goal. As to what the new strategy should be, some have argued for the adoption of lessons learned from the counterinsurgency in Vietnam: a "hearts and minds" campaign focused on protecting and winning over local populations, "providing security and opportunities to the Iraqi people in certain key areas."[1]

Another school of thought argues persuasively that Iraq has more in common with Bosnia than Vietnam and that different remedies are called for. The infiltration of the police by either Shia or insurgents nullifies the effort of Iraqization. We should, therefore, slow down the Iraqization

---

[1] Andrew Krepinevich, Jr., "How to Win in Iraq," *Foreign Affairs* 84, no. 5 (September/October 2005), http://www.foreignaffairs.org/20050901faessay84508/andrew-f-krepinevich-jr/how-to-win-in-iraq.html (accessed July 18, 2006).

of the security forces to catch up with a political arrangement based on a broad communal enterprise, or more specifically, "threaten to manipulate the military balance of power among Sunnis, Shias and Kurds in order to force them come to a durable compromise."[2] This school and others argue that we should use the threat of our withdrawal to persuade the parties to negotiate.[3] This seems a risky business, since withdrawal at this juncture is still seen as a last resort and the threat will hardly seem credible.

Yet another approach urges increased autonomy for each region: "maintaining a united Iraq by decentralizing it, giving each ethno-religious group—Kurd, Sunni Arab, and Shia Arab—room to run its own affairs."[4] Some have argued for outright partition.[5]

Each of these solutions has its own problems; none offers any guarantee of success. Using the threat of withdrawal to compel inter-community negotiation in particular seems a tricky business. We may overestimate the degree of our influence on different groups within Iraq and our ability to direct their behavior. There is a terrible inner dynamic to what is happening in Iraq today, to the increasingly sectarian violence in particular, that we may not really understand and are probably powerless to change.

More compelling are the arguments in favor of a regional approach.[6] Zalmay Khalilzad wrote of his experience of nation-building in Afghanistan: "If neighboring countries can help or harm our effort, the United States should engage them and shape their conduct to the extent

---

[2] Stephen Biddle, "Seeing Baghad, Thinking Saigon." *Foreign Affairs* 85, no. 4 (March/April 2006), http://www.foreignaffairs.org/20060301faessay85201/stephen-biddle/seeing-baghdad-thinking-saigon.html (accessed July 19, 2006).

[3] Carl M. Levin, "Iraq: The Way Forward, Session 2--A View From the Hill" (lecture, Council on Foreign Relations, Washington DC, October 21, 2005).

[4] Joseph R Biden Jr. and Leslie H Gelb, "Unity Through Autonomy in Iraq," *New York Times*, May 1, 2006, A19.

[5] Peter Galbraith, "How to Get Out of Iraq," *New York Review of Books* 51, no. 8 (May 13, 2004), http://www.nybooks.com/articles/article-preview?article_id=17103 (accessed July 19, 2006).

[6] Larry Diamond, James Dobbins, Chaim Kaufmann, Leslie H. Gelb, and Stephen Biddle, "What to Do in Iraq: A Roundtable," *Foreign Affairs* 85, no. 4 (July/August 2006), http://www.foreignaffairs.org/20060701faresponse85412/larry-diamond-james-dobbins-chaim-kaufmann-leslie-h-gelb-stephen-biddle/what-to-do-in-iraq-a-roundtable.html (accessed July 21, 2006).

possible, even if we have deep differences with those countries."[7] Proponents of this approach point out that Iraq is not a more divided society than Bosnia and Afghanistan and that the conflicts in those two countries were ended only by involving all the interested powers in the region in the negotiation of a settlement. This seems a more promising approach. Since a continued US presence is seen by most of Iraq's neighbors as a necessary, if not desirable, alternative to instability and civil war, we should use this leverage to work towards a regional agreement on the stabilization of Iraq.

Of course, the regional approach presents its own difficulties. The optimal time to involve the regional powers was in the immediate aftermath of the invasion, when we were at the peak of our power. Now it will seem less credible and risks being seen as a slightly desperate effort to devise a US exit strategy. Each of the regional powers has its own agenda in Iraq which, of course, they will seek to advance; it is not clear how much they actually control the behavior of different groups and factions within Iraq, though they no doubt have more influence with particular groups than the United States. Finally, it would mean subordinating our democratization agenda in Iraq and the Middle East to the more urgent goal of stabilizing Iraq. Nonetheless, providing a regional context for the Iraq problem and building on a common regional interest in stabilization seems a more promising and realistic approach than anything else on offer.

Are there ways in which European allies or the international community can help? At this juncture, probably not many. The military forces which would have been welcome at the beginning of the conflict would not materially change the situation now. European resources and expertise might be helpful in other areas, but those who are disposed to be helpful are probably already doing as much as they are prepared to do in the way of police training and the like. European contributions to economic reconstruction would certainly be welcome but under present security conditions, few countries will feel inclined to commit sizeable resources to this challenging task. Similar difficulties hinder the work of the international financial institutions. Moreover, though not wanting to see Iraq slide into chaos, some of our allies are wary of becoming identified with the Anglo-American effort—seen by many in the Middle East as an anti-Islamic crusade—and are happy to keep their distance.

---

[7] Zalmay Khalilzad, "How to Nation-Build" *National Interest* 80 (Summer 2005), http://www.keepmedia.com/pubs/NationalInterest/2005/06/01/908212?ba=m&bi=13&bp=24 (accessed July 19, 2006).

However, the Europeans generally would probably welcome the idea of a regional conference and might even be helpful.

RECOMMENDATIONS

Policy recommendations at this juncture are not easy. There are no obvious paths to follow that have not already been explored. Effects of the deadly combination of the Sunni/Al-Qaeda insurgency, the brutal violence perpetuated by sectarian militias, sectarian infiltration of the police and ethnic cleansing continue apace, undermining our goal of a stable and democratic Iraq. In the end, only the Iraqis themselves can halt this spiral. Many Iraqis—probably a majority—share our objective of a unified, democratic Iraq embracing all three communities. But many others of course do not. And it remains to be seen whether the first group—currently represented by the Maliki government—will be strong enough both to establish its credibility with all Iraqis, but in particular the Sunnis, and also to face down its challengers. Our current policy— building up an indigenous Iraqi army and police force, establishing and supporting a government based on the three communities (and to that end pressuring the Shia, as we have done, to bring in the Sunnis) and providing the default military force to back up the Iraqis until they are ready to hold their own—is certainly the logical one to pursue. However, it does not appear to be working. Every day the violence, insecurity and number of Iraqi casualties increase and it is far from certain that the strategy will be more successful with time.

So long as the security situation continues to deteriorate, we will find it hard to enlist our European allies or international institutions to provide more practical support than they are already doing. As noted above, until they are persuaded that we have found a winning strategy to achieve our goal of a unified, stabile and democratic Iraq—a goal which they support—they will not be prepared to invest in a deteriorating situation.

The regional approach has not been tried. It may be that trying to build on a common regional and international interest in stabilization offers some promise. There are various ways this could be done—and ways it should not be done. A US proposal would immediately generate suspicion; any initiative should come from the Iraqi government. It could take many forms: one possibility would be to build a conference around oil and invite all interested parties: Russia, China and the Europeans as well as the regional oil powers. A much bolder and more problematic step would be to deal with Iraq in the context of a regional security conference, again involving major extra-regional powers (China, Russia, and Europe). The difficulties with a regional approach are of course legion. The regional powers have more competing than common interests, other than not wanting to see civil war or chaos in a neighboring state. A weak Iraq may suit most of them very well. None of them has any interest in making life easier for the US. The three Iraqi communities may react with suspicion to the involvement of a particular regional power (i.e. the Sunni to giving a role to Iran, or the Kurds to Turkey). Moreover, by involving external powers, we will surrender control of the agenda, to the extent that we have it now. Nonetheless, a regional approach would probably garner strong support from extra-regional powers (proposals for a regional conference have long been a hardy perennial of Russian and French diplomacy). Despite all the objections and difficulties, we should seriously explore this option.

HOW WILL IRAQ AFFECT OUR POWER AND INFLUENCE IN THE WORLD?

On the long-term consequences for US influence, definitive judgments are difficult without knowing final outcomes, that is, whether we achieve a minimal acceptable outcome or must in the end settle for something less satisfactory (e.g. a premature US withdrawal that leaves Iraq in the throes of civil war). Nevertheless, the war in Iraq to date has already profoundly affected how the rest of the world views us. Two main messages emerge: after Iraq, US power seems less impressive and is less feared than before; and US leadership is regarded with deep suspicion and mistrust by much of the world, which damages our ability to lead.

> *After Iraq, US power seems less impressive and is less feared than before; US leadership is regarded with deep suspicion and mistrust by much of the world, which damages our ability to lead.*

It is hard, at this moment, to imagine an outcome in Iraq that will not be judged a failure of US policy in terms of our original ambitions and objectives. By much of the world, it will be seen as a huge strategic blunder—a conceptually flawed enterprise based on shallow assumptions about how societies are transformed, made worse by the mistakes of the post-invasion phase. Even those non-Americans who share the Administration's view that the invasion was necessary and justified have been appalled by the opportunities squandered during the early months of the occupation.

US military power will seem less daunting and will be less feared because of Iraq. In the short term, our involvement in Iraq precludes any large-scale engagement elsewhere.   In the short term also, the war has taken a heavy toll on our forces, particularly active duty Army and reserves, and their equipment has been battered by the war. Over time of course, these losses will be recouped and in terms of our capabilities, we will remain the world's only military superpower, far ahead of any other country. Our military machine will be as impressive as ever.   The problem lies elsewhere. It might be summed up as follows:

1) US military power is formidable and invincible in an initial, combat phase;
2) it can be neutralized in a second phase by asymmetric means (insurgency); and
3) in the long term, it is likely that it will be further neutralized or even reversed by inevitable domestic pressures to withdraw or drawdown if significant casualties are involved.

The experience of Iraq is reducing public support in the United States for large-scale military engagements. At least for the immediate future Iraq will raise anew for our friends and allies perennial questions about America's willingness to "stay the course." On a more general level, Iraq has made abundantly clear the limitations of using force to achieve broad policy goals.

Trust in US leadership has been severely eroded by the Iraq experience. The damage is across the board: to our credibility and reputation, to our moral authority, to confidence in our judgment and competence. As a British journalist put it, "suspicion of US intentions has become one of the most powerful facts of geopolitics."[8] On problematic issues, other countries are visibly more reluctant to give us the benefit of the doubt. Even our allies are anxious about our next move. This is evident in the ongoing United Nations (UN) debate over Iran, which—rightly or wrongly—for many has disquieting echoes of the 2002 debate that preceded the Iraq invasion. The resistance to including any reference to Chapter VII in a United Nations Security Council (UNSC) resolution clearly reflects mistrust of our intentions and reluctance to give us any tool that will allow us to justify the use of military force. Suspicions that this is our ultimate objective have been strengthened by the authorized leaks about military options (including the President's insistence about

---

[8] Philip Stephens, "World's Suspicions Bedevil US," *Financial Times*, March 17, 2006, http://198.62.75.1/www1/news/ft-3-17-06a.html (accessed July 14, 2006).

keeping open a nuclear option) that have appeared in the *New Yorker* and *Washington Post*.[9] The British have felt it necessary to publicly distance themselves from the use of force.

Our documented willingness to fix the facts and intelligence to fit the policy[10] in the run-up to the war, coupled with the failure to find any weapons of mass destruction (WMD) in Iraq, has compromised our credibility and reputation for honesty. Inevitably, intelligence we put forward to justify future policies will be viewed with skepticism and cynicism. In the future, we will find it harder to make our case.

> *The experience of Iraq is lessening public support in the United States for large-scale military engagement.*

Our moral authority is another casualty. US leadership has always been based on more than sheer power. Historically, we have been able to lead because we were generally (though not universally) believed to stand for certain values; the sense of shared values were a critical underpinning of the transatlantic relationship in particular. More broadly, we benefited from a widespread feeling that our leadership was benign and that our objectives by and large represented a global good. This was an important source of our legitimacy and made others willing to give us the benefit of the doubt.

Iraq has eroded this moral authority on several levels. First, the invasion itself was seen by many as an act of arbitrary, unchecked power, a unilateral assertion of a US right to act without regard for legitimacy or the views of the rest of the world that was dismaying to our friends, and fodder for our adversaries. Even more damaging have been the revelations about Guantanamo and Abu Ghraib, the accounts and pictures of prisoner abuse, the absence of high-level accountability, the stories of renditions and secret bases in Eastern Europe, and the Administration's wiretappings in the US. These have deeply shocked our friends—many of whom regard them as a betrayal of the ideals and the rule of law that the US was believed to stand for. To others, these

---

[9] Seymour Hersh, "The Iran Plans: Would President Bush go to war to stop Tehran from getting the bomb?" *New Yorker*, April 17, 2006, http://www.newyorker.com/fact/content/articles/060417fa_fact (accessed July 21, 2006); Dafna Linzer Baker and Thomas E. Ricks, "US Is Studying Military Strike Options on Iran: Any Mix of Tact, Threats Alarms Critics," *Washington Post*, April 9, 2006, A01.

[10] Paraphrased from Paul Pillar, "Intelligence, Policy and the War in Iraq," *Foreign Affairs* 85, no. 2 (March/April 2006), http://www.foreignaffairs.org/20060301faessay85202-p0/paul-r-pillar/intelligence-policy-and-the-war-in-iraq.html (accessed July 13, 2006).

revelations have merely confirmed the hypocrisy of our professed commitment to democracy and rule of law.

The negative public opinion polls about America's image and standing in the world post-Iraq are by now a familiar story. Opinions of the US are at an all time low. Particularly striking are the low approval ratings in Britain (56 percent in 2006, down from 75 percent in 2002) and Germany (at 41 percent in 2005, below France where the figure was 43 percent). More significantly, support for the traditional, close partnership between the US and Western Europe on security and diplomatic matters has fallen sharply (26 per cent in France, 39 percent in Germany and 42 percent in Britain). This contrasts with continued high support (66 percent) for such a partnership in the US (which suggests a certain obliviousness to how the rest of the world regards us).[11] In the Middle East of course, the figures are far worse and the virulence of anti-American feeling is unmistakable. Only in Japan and India do majorities have positive feelings about America.[12]

Of course, opinion polls are always to be taken with a grain of salt and several questions are in order. First, how much importance should we attach to these polls? There are familiar arguments. The powerful are always resented and the very powerful are especially resented. The anti-Americanism captured in these polls is about much more than America: fears of globalization, domestic discontents, powerlessness, frustrations, etc. Moreover, as anyone reading the German or French press these days well knows, a kind of caricatured, stereotypical America-bashing has become a particularly trendy national sport. Then too, polls are notoriously ephemeral; American popularity has waxed and waned regularly over the decades. Anti-Americanism has been generally on the rise since the end of the Cold War: perceived American arrogance and triumphalist claims to be the "indispensable superpower" in a unipolar world generated widespread resentment in the Clinton years. Nevertheless, the story these polls tell is not so easily dismissed. It is difficult not to conclude that Iraq has taken anti-American feelings to a new intensity which for the first time extends not just to US government policies but to the American people as well. The strength and virulence of anti-American sentiment in the Middle East and other Islamic countries is particularly disquieting. Iraq of course is not the only reason for the anti-American sentiment in that region; the Israel-Palestine issue

---

[11] Data from Pew Research Center, "Pew Global Attitudes Project: America's Image Slips, But Allies Share US Concerns Over Iran, Hamas," Pew Global Attitudes Project 2006 (June 13, 2006).

[12] Ibid.

has at least as much salience, but Iraq acted as a spark. These views will not be easily reversed.

A second question is how these negative opinions affect the behavior of governments, if at all. The answer is of course that governments act first and foremost in what they perceive to be their own interest. Whatever the outcome in Iraq, the US will remain the single most powerful nation in the world with an immense capacity to influence events, and governments will continue to find it in their interest to work with us across a broad range of issues. The reverse of course is also true. The profoundly negative opinion of America in most European countries in no way changes the need of European governments to enlist our cooperation on a variety of issues. Within a surprisingly short time after the bitter diplomatic quarrel that led up to Iraq, the US and the Europeans managed to patch up our differences—at least on a superficial level— because the alternative was too costly. Common interest trumps emotions. There is virtually no issue of any importance that can be addressed without United States participation—proliferation, the fight against terrorism, the working of multilateral institutions, everything from Iran to Darfur. The interdependence of US and European economies will not be affected by the war. Elsewhere in the world, the experience of Iraq will not change the importance of the US security relationship to Saudi Arabia, the Gulf States or Egypt. Russia and China will not stop talking to us because of Iraq.

If relationships change as a result of Iraq, it will be on the margins, not at the core. That said, it seems also true that Iraq has introduced a new note of wariness and caution into relationships with our friends. Others are more willing to disregard US views. In Europe, we are seeing for the first time a disconnect between the cooperation that governments see as both necessary and desirable and the strong negative emotions of their publics. The tension between the willingness of Arab governments to work with us and the views of the famed "Arab street" has long been a staple of the Middle East. But it is a novelty in Europe and it should give us pause. Leaders who supported the US in Iraq have paid a price at the polls. Sentiment against the war has been a factor in the decision of many governments, particularly in Eastern Europe, to withdraw the small military contingents they sent to Iraq in 2003. The awkwardness of the rendition issue for many of our European friends was compounded by negative public views of America. In the future, we will certainly find it harder to divide the Europeans; in fact it is clear that a determination not to let themselves be again divided by the US was a strong motivation behind the British, French, and German decision to inaugurate joint talks with the Iranians. Even our traditionally reliable British allies have been at pains to distance themselves from us on the possible use of force against Iran. Finally, the experience of Iraq is certain to reinforce European caution about the use of force—among other reasons, because it can have unpredictable and wholly undesirable consequences.

Finally, can we point to specific events or issues where our influence has been in some way diminished as a result of Iraq? This is often difficult to gauge. US power may seem less awesome than before the war. Other large powers may feel more confident in disregarding our views. But it can often be difficult to separate out the impact of Iraq from other factors.

It has, unquestionably, rendered our fight against terrorism more difficult. Whatever gains we have made against the Al-Qaeda network outside Iraq have been more than offset by the upsurge of terrorism in Iraq and the emergence of Iraq as a breeding ground for terrorists, which we have been powerless to stop. It has strengthened Islamic extremism on a global scale.

The US-backed push towards democracy in the Middle East which a year ago seemed to be making modest progress now appears to have faltered. Are we dealing here with diminished US influence—a new willingness to push back—or are we looking at regimes who would, under any circumstances, seek to limit the consequences to their own stability of the chaos in Iraq, the rise of militias in Iraq, and the rise of Islamists throughout the region? Regime survival will always trump a democratization agenda. Is this a result of Iraq or might it have happened anyway?

Similarly, how has Iraq affected on the ongoing saga of Iran's nuclear ambitions? Has the US failure in Iraq emboldened Iran to accelerate its nuclear plans? Or would the advent of Ahmadinejad and the Iranian populist nationalism he seems to speak for have produced the same result in any case? Or did the speed and overwhelming US victory in Iraq— which the Iranians duly noted took only 20 days—strengthen the determination of Iranians to have a nuclear deterrent in order to forestall a similar attack on themselves? Or has our experience in Iraq and the growing pressures to drawdown our forces encouraged the Iranians to think that we will not use force against them, reinforcing their long-standing belief that we lack staying power? The answer may well be yes to all of the above.

Has Iraq affected our own options with respect to Iran? Iraq may have made the use of force against Iran less likely. We lack forces for a large-scale engagement, if not for airstrikes. The areas where Iran could greatly harm our interests now include Iraq. But the reality is that force has always been a bad option for Iran and Iraq does not change this one way or another. The mischief that Iran could create for us in Iraq adds to the negative side of the ledger but it does not in itself alter the option. The experience of Iraq has led others to make clear that we would have no support for military action, not even from the British. It has increased reluctance to include a reference to Chapter VII into the UNSC resolution. But even without Iraq we would have found little support for the use of force in Iran, almost certainly less support than for Iraq.

Russia is increasingly reemerging as a world actor. It is palpably pushing back in the "near abroad," including in those areas where we have established a presence. It clearly has ambitions to be more of a player in the Middle East. But is this because the US is bogged down in Iraq and Putin believes he can be more aggressive in pursuit of Russian interests? Or does it reflect the confidence born of sky-rocketing oil and gas prices, a decade-long accumulation of grievances against the US and the inevitable re-emergence of Russia as a major player? Again, probably all of the above.

Polls in Europe show a new negativity about the United States and point to a growing cultural divide on such issues as the death penalty, the role of religion in public life, genetically modified organisms, etc. Our arrogance is resented. Iraq and the Bush Administration are only part of the story: we have been growing apart since the end of the Cold War and, despite important common interests, will continue to do so.

In sum, it is hard to pinpoint the precise impact of Iraq, but we should not therefore conclude there is none. Iraq will not be a watershed, but there may be significant changes on the margins. We are likely to encounter doubts and apprehension about our leadership that will make it more difficult to persuade others. For many, Iraq has raised serious questions about our judgment and competence. There may be greater reluctance to join forces with us on a given issue. Paradoxically, there may also be worry about our staying power and isolationism (depending on what happens in Iraq). We will no longer be able to count on having the benefit of the doubt. In the Middle East, the legacy of Iraq is likely to be particularly virulent and troubling.

In the final analysis, how the US itself reacts to the experience of Iraq—how Iraq affects attitudes within the United States—may be more important to our future leadership and influence in the world than what the world thinks of us. In the United States, support for the war is dwindling, as we know. It is the first war in 25 years that has produced significant US casualties, reminding Americans that war is a lethal business. Iraq is likely to curb any appetite for large-scale conflict for the foreseeable future. Polls also point to declining support for a US world leadership role. The number of those agreeing that the US should "mind its own business and let other countries get along as best they can" is up to 42 percent from 34 percent in 2004, a level reached only twice in the last forty years: in 1976 after our withdrawal from Vietnam and in 1995, after the end of the Cold War. These figures have rightly been described as reflecting caution rather than isolationism, but they also suggest growing wariness about America's own assertive foreign policy, little support for use of force against Iran and a declining majority (though still a majority) for pre-emptive wars.[13]

The cost of the war will weigh heavily on our future. War expenditures are calculated to reach $94 billion this year, up from $48 billion in 2003, easily surpassing the annual costs of Vietnam, which was $61 billion in today's dollars.[14] The Congressional Research Service estimates put this year's costs at $100 billion.[15] "Shock and awe" are extremely expensive and will become more so as the costs of repairing and replacing equipment rise after three years of war. The impact of these costs–on our budget and external deficits, on our present and future budget choices— will be immense, though they barely to have begun to sink in either on Capitol Hill or in the public consciousness at large.

WHAT IS TO BE DONE?

What policy prescriptions, if any, come out of these observations? In the short-term, it is difficult to see any that will be of much help in restoring our battered reputation or, so long as we are in Iraq, in enhancing our influence. The Bush Administration has made some much needed adjustments—improved consultation and cooperation with allies, engaged in a rejuvenated public diplomacy effort aimed at the Muslim world, etc. A new initiative on Iraq, such as reaching out to Iraq's

---

[13] Andrew Kohut, "A Political Victory That Wasn't," *New York Times*, March 23, 2005, http://www.nytimes.com/2005/03/23/opinion/23Kohut.html?ex=1269234000&en=8309fe1397c4d8b6&ei=5090&partner=rssuserland (accessed July 19, 2006).

[14] Luan Shanglin, "Poor planning to push Iraq war costs to USD1 trillion: report." *Xinhua Online*, April 21, 2006, http://news.xinhuanet.com/english/2006-04/21/content_4459524.htm (accessed July 24, 2006); For updated budget analysis on the cost of Iraq war see the Center for Strategic and Budgetary Assessment reports at http://www.csbaonline.org.

[15] Amy Belasco, *The Cost of Iraq, Afghanistan, and Other Global War on Terror Operations Since 9/11*, Congressional Research Service Report #RL33110 (Washington, DC: CRS, June 16, 2006), http://www.fas.org/sgp/crs/natsec/RL33110.pdf (accessed July 21, 2006).

neighbors and proposing a regional conference, would be welcomed, at least in some quarters, as a fresh start. But changing the world's mind about the US will be very difficult so long as the Bush Administration is in office.

Over the long-term of course, there are many things we can do. Some policy prescriptions on offer are worthy, though of a mind-numbing banality (work with allies, work through the UN, etc). More broadly, we need to come to terms with the fact that America's unipolar moment is over, if indeed it ever existed. We need to rid ourselves of an exaggerated sense of what US military power unsupported by political strategies and diplomacy can accomplish, and of what the US could accomplish alone. We would do well to return to the more limited expectations that were forced upon us during the Cold War: when we accepted, perhaps not willingly, that some of the world's most difficult problems must be managed over the long-term, and were not susceptible to short-term solutions. If diplomacy not backed by force is ineffective, so too is force not informed by diplomacy. Finally, while never abandoning our support for democracy and human rights, we should be more humble about our capacity to engineer social change in complex societies and about our ignorance of other cultures. Regime change is fine as a long-term goal—it was after all our objective for fifty years of the Cold War—but as a short term action goal to be achieved by use of force, it has been a recipe for disaster.

— 8 —
MULTILATERALISM:
LESSONS FROM IRAQ

Daniel Poneman

Multilateralism is a hassle. It takes a lot of time and energy for a government to coordinate its objectives, strategies, and tactics with other governments, each seeking to advance its own— sometimes widely divergent—interests and objectives. Resort to multilateralism can dilute a government's central goals, divert efforts to secondary or tertiary fronts in a military or diplomatic campaign, and create vested interests in third parties who seek to exploit the outcomes from any success and duck those from any failure. Claims of credit and shifting of blame follow similar patterns.

Given all this, one may wonder why the "Wise Men"—the group of US foreign policy leaders who built the post-war world order out of the ashes of World War II, viewed by history as visionaries who conceived and launched the containment policy which ultimately emerged victorious in the Cold War—showed such an affinity for multilateral institutions. Their legacy included the United Nations, the Bretton Woods institutions (the World Bank and International Monetary Fund), the North Atlantic Treaty Organization (NATO), and the Coordinating Committee on Multilateral Export Controls. These early Cold War institutions were later supplemented by other multilateral institutions and treaties of varying impact and effectiveness, including the: Southeast Asia Treaty Organization, Central Treaty Organization, Treaty on the Nonproliferation of Nuclear Weapons (NPT), International Atomic Energy Agency (IAEA), World Trade Organization, Chemical Weapons Convention, Biological Weapons Convention, Organization for Security and Co-operation in Europe (OSCE), and many more.

Why did our leaders turn to multilateral institutions at the very moment when American power relative to the rest of the world had reached a zenith? Our armed forces were second to none, backed by the full weight of American industrial power. Our economy contributed roughly half of total global output. Our allies were exhausted and impoverished, while our enemies lay vanquished and suffering from wholesale destruction of their industrial base. US leaders could have seized the moment and sought to impose a US-dominated *Pax Americana.*

Why, instead, did they take the opposite path, embracing multilateralism and giving it new expression through the creation of a new set of institutions? Because they saw in these institutions the opportunity to forge the kind of alliances that would deter, contain and, if necessary, defeat future Hitlers. They viewed the Bretton Woods system as facilitating the kind of global economy that would promote development, and avoid the kind of trade and monetary instability that had fueled the fires of fascism. In short, the United States viewed these new institutions as extensions of American power, rather than as mere dilutions of that power. American leaders recognized the costs and inefficiencies inherent in multilateralism, but they concluded that these institutions were necessary in a world that was increasingly interdependent, and that they could confer legitimacy on economic, political, and military action unavailable to any nation acting unilaterally.

American leaders did not view their commitment to multilateral institutions as fundamentally impairing their room for unilateral action. To the contrary, they recognized the need to preserve the right and the capability to act unilaterally in defense of American interests, and did so time and again throughout the Cold War and after. Eisenhower sent the Marines into Lebanon (1958); Kennedy launched the Bay of Pigs invasion of Cuba (1961); Johnson sent Marines to the Dominican Republic (1965); Nixon invaded Cambodia (1973); Reagan launched the Grenada operation (1983); George H.W. Bush deployed forces to Panama (1989); Clinton launched air strikes against Sudan (1998) and Iraq (1996).

The United States first faced a fundamental challenge to its global interests after the fall of the Berlin Wall, in Kuwait, when Saddam Hussein invaded and occupied that country on August 2, 1990. In response, President Bush rallied a global coalition, comprised of 660,000 troops from 34 nations, including such key regional players as Saudi Arabia, to confront Saddam Hussein and drive him out of Kuwait. Our cooperation was not confined to the battlefield; US diplomatic efforts garnered $53 billion from foreign donors to underwrite Operations Desert Shield and Desert Storm, sharply curtailing the burden that fell on the American taxpayer.[1] Once the conflict had been won, the US turned

---

[1] "The Unfinished War: A Decade Since Desert Storm," *CNN.com*, In-Depth Special: Gulf War Facts, 2001, http://www.cnn.com/SPECIALS/2001/gulf.war/facts/gulfwar/ (accessed July 20, 2006).

to the United Nations Security Council (UNSC), which passed Resolution 687, establishing the UN Special Commission designed to ferret out Iraq's illicit weapons and verify Iraqi compliance with its obligations not to obtain or possess a wide range of destabilizing weapons.

US reliance on multilateral institutions persisted through the 1990s in a wide variety of fora. The US worked with other governments to combat weapons proliferation through such mechanisms as the: Australia Group, Missile Technology Control Regime, Chemical Weapons Convention, Nuclear Suppliers Group, Korean Peninsula Energy Development Organization (KEDO, formed to implement the Agreed Framework provisions to contain North Korea's plutonium production program), and Nuclear Non-Proliferation Treaty (NPT, extended indefinitely in 1995). The US worked through NATO to respond to Serbia's murderous campaign of ethnic cleansing in Bosnia and to force Serbian withdrawal from Kosovo. The United States also helped shape the transformation of NATO to post-Cold War realities, including its expansion to include member states formerly dominated by the Soviet Union. Additionally, the US also participated in the formation of the Asian-Pacific Economic Cooperation dialogue, hosting its first summit in Seattle in 1993.

The tragic events of September 11, 2001, were followed the next day by the first-ever invocation by NATO of Article 5 of the Washington Treaty, declaring the attacks to be an attack against all NATO members. But that strong expression of collective will was not fully converted into action, as Washington shunned military support from NATO in order to preserve greater autonomy in its military operations in Afghanistan. After the fall of the Taliban, however, the UN was given the leading role in guiding the process to establish a new government and organized a conference in Bonn that provided Afghanistan political forces the opportunity to hammer out arrangements for the transition to self-rule. NATO took command of the International Security Assistance Force (ISAF) in August 2003. ISAF (which is NATO's first mission outside the Euro-Atlantic area) operates in Afghanistan under a UN mandate in support of the government of Afghanistan.

As is well known, the United States relied less on multilateral institutions in both the preparation and execution of the second Iraq war. While the US sought and obtained UN Security Council Resolution 1441 (UNSCR), and persuaded 30 governments to contribute 24,000 of the 156,000 troops deployed to Iraq in support of Operation Iraqi Freedom, the weight of the political argument as well as the burden of the military effort was borne by a US-dominated coalition of the willing. The UN

Secretary-General Kofi Annan did send Sergio Vieira de Mello to Iraq to establish a UN presence in post-war Iraq, but tragically, the Brazilian diplomat was assassinated in a bombing attack on UN Headquarters in Baghdad, effectively ending UN involvement. NATO as an organization "had no role in the decision to undertake the [2003 Iraqi] campaign nor in its conduct."[2] Though NATO members acting individually contributed 17,000 troops to Iraq's stabilization, NATO's formal role has been confined to training Iraqi security personnel and responding to member requests. Under such requests, NATO briefly deployed surveillance aircraft and missile defenses to help protect Turkey against any attack, and provides communications, logistics, and other support to the Polish division serving in Iraq.

> *Suffice it to say that broader multilateral involvement could have added legitimacy as well as economic and military resources to the stabilization and reconstruction of the country.*

Had the UN and NATO been more deeply involved in the Iraq operation, would the reconstruction have been more successful? It is impossible to know for sure. Certainly there would have been costs. More extensive involvement by the UN and NATO would have diluted US autonomy in carrying out the Iraqi stabilization and reconstruction effort and brought the usual bureaucratic baggage and inefficiencies endemic to multilateral efforts. Nor would multilateralization inevitably have altered (or negated the effects of) major decision—such as the disbanding of the Iraqi Army—that shaped unfolding events in post-war Iraq.

On the other hand, UN peacekeeping operations have operated for many years in the Middle East, Europe, Asia, and Africa, the blue helmets often providing a measure of political legitimacy that has helped stabilize areas of conflict. Had well-armed NATO forces been deployed in sufficient numbers to protect Iraq's critical infrastructures in the early days after the fall of Saddam, the early looting and other acts of violence that nourished and then inflamed the insurgency might have been contained. Suffice it to say that broader multilateral involvement could have added legitimacy as well as economic and military resources to the stabilization and reconstruction of the country.

---

[2] NATO Topics, "NATO and the 2003 campaign against Iraq," press release, August 22, 2005, http://www.nato.int/issues/iraq/index.html (accessed July 17, 2006).

Hindsight aside, the struggle to secure, stabilize, and rebuild Iraq continues. At the time of this writing, the four-month deadlock over formation of a new government following the January 2006 elections has ended, opening the possibility that the installation of a Shia prime minister with Sunni and Kurdish support will permit an effective government of national unity. The question remains whether the new government will be able to contain the virulent insurgency that has risen in Iraq and begin to forge a nation-state that can bring its citizens a decent chance to enjoy life, liberty, and the pursuit of happiness, while living at peace among its neighbors.

In order for the the newly-formed government to function effectively, it must at a minimum, guarantee the safety of its citizens, build and sustain effective military and police forces, suppress the insurgency, rebuild public services for power and water, restore sufficient oil production to support these basic government services and lay the groundwork for economic recovery. If it is not able to function effectively, Iraq could continue its descent into chaos and bloodshed, miring its citizens in tragedy and serving as an incubator and training ground for jihadists who will carry death and destruction to the four corners of the world.

Is it too late to multilateralize the Iraq stabilization and reconstruction effort, to help the new government succeed? Given the history of the second Iraq war, the continued reservations of NATO electorates about sending more troops to Iraq, the echoes of the terrorist attack that ended the first UN mission there, and the continuing level of violence, persuading either the UN or NATO to step into the breech would be difficult at best. With Iraqis increasingly responsible for managing their own fate, multilateralization would most likely come at the request of an Iraqi unity government seeking outside support for their nascent efforts to unify and stabilize the country. That request would most likely be honored only if key players—leaders in the Arab world, NATO, and the UN Security Council—concluded that: (1) their own stakes in achieving Iraqi stability warranted the burdens and hazards entailed in entering Iraq; and (2) the effort stood a fair chance of success.

It is not too late to learn the lessons of Iraq, or of the half century of multilateral efforts that preceded Operation Iraqi Freedom. How should we strike the balance between multilateralism and unilateral efforts? To answer this question requires consideration of emerging threats in the coming decades. These certainly include the sadly familiar phenomenon of states failing, and then falling into civil conflicts that boil over into genocide or regional instability. Many of the newer threats that pose the greatest risks to our interests intrinsically transcend boundaries, for example: pathogens; international terrorism; the spread of weapons of mass destruction; and climate change.

None of these problems can be confined by political borders. All are inherently transnational in character. By their nature they operate across international boundaries. That natural feature is amplified by the forces of globalization—increased ease of travel, instantaneous information spread through television and the Internet, the inexorable spread of technology—which can quickly bring the consequences of one failed state or successful weapons proliferator to its neighbors and around the world and turn epidemics into pandemics.

Disturbingly, the economic and military strength of the United States cannot provide absolute protection against the harm that can be inflicted against a society as open and democratic as our own. We present an infinite variety of soft targets to terrorists and we always will. Weapons of mass destruction in the hands of those terrorists present the specter of national catastrophe that could dwarf the tragedy of September 11, 2001.

This suggests that multilateral efforts will be essential to any successful strategy to address these challenges. We will need others to assist in our protection through a variety of mechanisms—multilateral organizations and treaties, bilateral agreements, private sector initiatives involving private businesses and foundations, and non-governmental organizations.

Certainly multilateralism is no panacea. Nor would it be wise to relinquish the right to act unilaterally when our national interests require it. But the fundamental premise of the Wise Men—that we are stronger when we act in concert than alone—is as true today as it was in the 1940s when they designed the multilateral architecture which contained and ultimately defeated Soviet communism. Indeed, for the reasons outlined above, that premise is more valid than ever.

How is that premise translated into an effective toolkit of responses? One approach would be to begin with a survey of those issues that most affect our fundamental interests in the international arena. We should consider, in each of these cases, how US interests converge with or diverge from those of other nations and organizations. For each critical issue, we should seek to emphasize those relationships—with partners, allies, and organizations—where we find the greatest commonality of interest and the greatest ability to affect outcomes. Examples include using the NPT to combat proliferation, the Conference for Security and Co-operation in Europe (CSCE) process to promote democratization behind the Iron Curtain, and NATO to respond to ethnic cleansing in

Bosnia. In many cases, there will be more than one forum that can help contribute to solving—or interfering with—a particular problem. Marshalling the optimal array of forces and fora to bring to bear in each case—and excluding or limiting those which would impede a solution consistent with US interests—constitutes the art of diplomacy.

The underlying premise in this approach is that the United States should act with others when it can and alone only when it must. In some cases, US leadership will be essential to mobilizing the international community to act in concert (as in confronting the dangers of nuclear proliferation). In others, we will be more effective in supporting the efforts of others while remaining more in the background (as in IAEA safeguards, the UN Special Commission implementing United Nations Security Council Resolution 687 to uncover and destroy Iraqi weapons of mass destruction, and UN peacekeeping operations). Our decisions should reflect the constant need to make trade-offs between unfettered discretion and paralyzing consultations, taking into consideration the degree of agreement among the United States and other governments and the priority we place in each case on burden-sharing, maximizing US influence, and other factors.

The choice of forum—be it unilateral, bilateral, or multilateral—can obviously have a profound impact on outcomes. Any student of arms control knows that to refer an issue to the 65-member Conference on Disarmament (CD) in Geneva is tantamount to a diplomatic death sentence; the CD has been unable for years even to approve an agenda, much less negotiate any meaningful agreements. Of course, this fact does not necessarily reflect an intrinsic quality of the forum, or the number of members, but rather the netting out of the degree of political authority that member nations either vest in or withhold

> *We should neither lionize nor vilify multilateralism, but rather use it when and how it most effectively advances US interests in an increasingly complex and interdependent world.*

from that body. Conversely, the 36-member CSCE played a pivotal role in the judgment of many in sowing the seeds for the final disintegration of the Soviet empire.

We cannot run the world, but on vital issues the United States can lead the world and, when we do, multilateral institutions provide the means through which our will is reflected and refracted through other channels.

Thus multilateralism is a means to advance national interests, not an end in itself. It can extend our reach, or dilute our autonomy. It can include the most relevant stakeholders in an issue, or exclude parties indispensable to the resolution of that same issue. It can be used as a mechanism to minimize the political costs for a given action by diffusing responsibility for the decision among more players, or to maximize the risks of least-common-denominator outcomes and policy paralysis. We should neither lionize nor vilify multilateralism, but rather use it when and how it most effectively advances US interests in an increasingly complex and interdependent world.

— 9 —
IMPERATIVES FOR THE INTERNATIONAL COMMUNITY IN IRAQ

Nancy Soderberg

INTRODUCTION

Regardless of how views differ concerning the decision to invade Iraq in 2003, there is a growing consensus that the United States has few good options today, in 2006. Three years into the war, the insurgency continues, the threat of a civil war is real, anti-Americanism is growing, and the US military is stretched beyond its capacity. US interests in the region and beyond are suffering. Over 2,500 soldiers have died, and more than 18,000 have been wounded. The US has already spent $300 billion dollars, roughly what was spent to reconstruct Germany after World War II.[1] Yet most of the population is arguably worse off than before the war—less oil production, less electricity, more corruption, less access to potable water and sewer systems, and 76 percent rating their security situation as "poor."[2]

As the UN Secretary-General has stated, "In Iraq, despite pockets of progress, the situation remains unstable. Recent violence, especially the bombing of the shrine in Samarra, underlines a real and growing sectarian threat."[3] Ashraf Jehangir Qazi, the Secretary-General's Special Representative for Iraq warned during a recent Security Council briefing that the current situation clearly constitutes "a serious obstacle to the effective implementation of infrastructural and income-generating

---

[1] Nina Serafino, Curt Tarnoff, and Dick K. Nanto, *U.S Occupation Assistance: Iraq, Germany and Japan Compared*, Congressional Research Service Report 33331 (Washington DC: CRS, March 23, 2006), 2.

[2] Michael E. O'Hanlon and Andrew Kamons, *Iraq Index: Tracking Variables of Reconstruction & Security in Post-Saddam Iraq* (Washington DC: The Brookings Institution, July 10 2006), http://www.brookings.edu/iraqindex (accessed 14 July 2006).

[3] Kofi Annan, "Message to the Conference of the Parliamentary Union of the Member States of the Organization of the Islamic Conference" (speech, delivered by Mohamed Sahnoun to the Parliamentary Union of the Organization of the Islamic Conference, Istanbul, Turkey, April 12, 2006).

projects designed to address unemployment and the provision of basic services. If not effectively addressed, ongoing violence could prevent donor programmes from having their desired impact."[4]

While the international community recognizes the imperative of a stable Iraq, it is failing to do its part to help the Iraqis achieve that goal. A dramatic shift in approach is needed if the international community is to step in. The election of the Presidency Council, Speaker and Deputy Speakers of the Council of Representatives, as well as the formation of a full-term government led by Prime Minister al-Maliki, offers the opportunity for a new phase of acceptance of the legitimacy of the Iraqi government. An international conference is urgently needed to shift the role of the US away from center stage, forge a new Iraqi political consensus, and pave the way for much stronger international participation. Many think it may already be too late—but we have a responsibility to Iraqis and Americans to try.

WHY THE US NEEDS THE INTERNATIONAL COMMUNITY

Given its broad opposition to the war, driven in no small measure by the way in which the US chose to go to war, the international community has largely chosen to stay out of Iraq, particularly in the realm of security. Of the 48 nations with troops in the coalition in 2003, 26 countries remain. While the US has 130,000 troops, today only the Great Britain, South Korea, and Italy have over 1,000 troops—8,000 British troops, 3,200 South Korean troops, and 2,600 Italian troops. Romano Prodi, Italy's new Prime Minister, has pledged to pull Italy's troops out of the region by December 2006 (in consultation with the US). Poland is considering withdrawing its 550 troops by the year's end. Most of the other 21 countries contribute only a few hundred troops or less. While the US and others have trained an estimated 250,000 Iraqi security forces, it will be years before the Iraqis are capable of taking over the job of maintaining security in the country; especially if it descends into a full-blown civil war.

Therefore, the task of maintaining security in Iraq will remain largely the responsibility of the United States for the near term. However, the very presence of these troops has become a magnet for terrorist recruitment and the insurgency; precipitating the need for a calculated shift in strategy to protect American interests. Absent significant troop

---

[4] United Nations Security Council, 5386th Meeting (AM): Iraq's Political Transition Increasingly Threatened by Inter-Sectarian: Violence, Special Representative Tells Security Council, SC 661, March 15, 2006.

withdrawals, US forces will face difficulties in maintaining current force levels, especially if other regions require troop deployments.[5]

There are several possible courses of action, including an increase in the number of US troops, an immediate cut-off, or a gradual pullout as most prominently recommended by Lawrence Korb and Brian Katulis of the Center for American Progress. Six in ten Americans now favor some form of troop drawdown and as the situation in Iraq continues to deteriorate, the political pressure for such action may force the Administration's hand.[6] Korb and Katulis propose a drawdown of US troops to 60,000 by the end of 2006 and to zero by the end of 2007. They argue that setting a timetable makes it clear that the US is going to leave thus putting pressure on the factions to take responsibility for the future of Iraq. They claim that a "timetable will spur Iraq's battling factions to try harder to reach a compromise before US troops leave."[7]

While a plan for withdrawal is attractive on many levels—most importantly reinforcing the message the US will not keep any permanent military presence in Iraq—it has one major flaw— the US undoubtedly will miss any arbitrary deadline. Why? Because the situation on the ground that will enable US troops to leave at least a somewhat stable Iraq behind cannot be pinned to any specific date. While many are drawing analogies to the Vietnam War,[8] a more appropriate analogy is the US-led effort to create a multi-ethnic state in Bosnia. At the time of US military deployment to Bosnia following the 1995 Dayton Peace Agreement, the Clinton Administration wrongly estimated the troops would be deployed to Bosnia for one year. Although the Administration thought it was an

---

[5] With a slight drop in numbers to a forty-nine brigade equivalent Army and Marine Corps presence, plus some reserve/National Guard units, "we could maintain this rotation for some time, even counting two brigades in Afghanistan." State Department Official, e-mail message to author, May 12, 2006.

[6] Brian Katulis, "Strategic Redeployment Best for All," *Philadelphia Inquirer*, March 27, 2006, http://www.americanprogress.org/site/apps/nl/content3.asp?c=biJRJ8OVF&b=837349&content_id=%7BF8DE4CC3-583A-4C39-914F-5DAD2AFEB873%7D&notoc=1 (accessed July 19, 2006).

[7] Brian Katulis, "US troops won't help calm tensions in Iraq," *Gulf Times*, March 26, 2006; In response to this chapter, Brian Katulis responded: "Our argument is that a timeline is crucial to get the INCREASED cooperation of the international community – the crux of the paper – the US needs to send a clear message that we are not staying there forever. Our argument is that a redeployment timeline is necessary for the Iraqi leadership to have credibility at home – the Iraqi public is restive and most want foreign troops to leave by the end of 2007." Brian Katulis, e-mail message to author, May 25, 2006.

[8] Stephen Biddle, "Seeing Baghdad, Thinking Saigon: The Perils of Refighting Vietnam in Iraq," *Foreign Affairs* 85, no. 2 (March/April 2006), http://www.foreignaffairs.org/20060301faessay85201/stephen-biddle/seeing-baghdad-thinking-saigon.html (accessed July 13, 2006).

accurate estimate, the timetable was set largely to provide clear military goals and to mitigate concerns that Congress would not fund the deployment without having an exit strategy in place. Yet, the political development of a multi-ethnic state lagged and US troops remained for a decade, slowly transitioning the mandate to the North Atlantic Treaty Organization (NATO) and the European Union (EU). Today, 6,300 troops from EU nations remain, with a small NATO headquarters in Sarajevo, and approximately 220 US forces.

Similarly in Iraq, a US withdrawal will depend on both political and military factors. US interests in the region will suffer if the US withdraws precipitously—and any effort to actually meet a meaningful deadline runs the risk of a premature withdrawal. Unlike in Vietnam, the US cannot afford to simply walk away from Iraq. The one possible exception would be if the country descends into total civil war. In such a case the US would have little choice but to pull out. However, having invaded, the US has a responsibility to give the Iraqis a reasonable chance at success. Therefore, the rational course for the US to pursue is to give the Iraqis a clear choice: if Iraq descends into civil war, it will be on its own. But the US will give it adequate assistance for the alternative—a decent political system and a sufficiently capable security force so that following a US withdrawal, Iraqis will have an adequate foundation for success.

Thus, the problem for the establishment of a timetable is that the two key conditions for a responsible US withdrawal—a functioning government and an Iraqi force that can take over the task of securing Iraq—are not tied to any timetable. The United States is faced with essentially two two alternatives:

1. continue to handle Iraq largely on its own; or
2. use its superpower status to secure international involvement in assisting the Iraqis, thus facilitating a faster US withdrawal.

UN, EU, AND ARAB LEAGUE ROLES IN ACHIEVING A STABLE, SECURE IRAQ

Despite the strong opposition of the international community to the US war in Iraq, the United Nations (UN), EU and the Arab League have slowly endorsed the goal of a stable Iraq, and an increasing array of international activities directed at that goal. The UN has called for strong international support. For instance United Nations Security

Council (UNSC) resolution 1546 explicitly put the war behind by welcoming "the beginning of a new phase in Iraq's transition to a democratically elected government...."[9] The resolution also recognized the importance of international support, "particularly that of the countries in the region, Iraq's neighbors, and regional organizations," and that successful implementation of this resolution will contribute to regional stability. [10] The UNSC stated that the "United Nations should play a leading role in assisting the Iraqi people and government in the formation of institutions for representative government."[11] Despite the UNSC endorsement of a robust role for the international community in Iraq, member states have failed to provide the necessary security, funding, and assistance to enable it to do so.

The EU has also recognized it has an interest in a stable Iraq and has endorsed greater engagement with Iraq with three key objectives: the development of a secure, stable, and democratic Iraq; the establishment of an open, stable, sustainable, and diversified market economy; and the political and economic integration of Iraq into its region and the international community.[12] As EU Commissioner for External Relations and European Neighbourhood Policy, Benita Ferrero-Walder said, "The EU and the UN share a vision of a stable, prosperous, unified Iraq with a pluralist democracy—where political differences will be settled by democratic dialogue and not violence. The EU has been the UN's key partner in this essential task."[13] One key step by the Paris Club has been significant debt relief (although Russia has declined to participate).

The League of Arab States, the organization with perhaps the most to lose should Iraq descend into chaos, has taken little action to assist Iraq, including no action on the $40 billion Iraqi debt its members hold. The League has proposed holding a conference on a broader national consensus in Iraq but no such meeting has materialized. Much of the Arab League's focus has been on securing the withdrawal of the US forces. For instance, at the March 28, 2006 Arab Summit in Khartoum, Arab leaders urged Iraqis to quickly form a national unity government to

---

[9] United Nations Security Council, Resolution 1546 (S/RES/1546), 2004.

[10] Ibid.

[11] Ibid.

[12] European Union, *Iraq Assistance Programme 2006*, E/2006/470-C(2006)864 28.03.2006, Chapter 4, March 28, 2006.

[13] European Union, "EU biggest donor for Iraq's elections and referendum," press release, European Commission, October 21, 2005, http://europa-eu-un.org/articles/en/article_5168_en.htm (accessed July 19, 2006).

pave the way for a withdrawal of US-led coalition forces from Iraq. Perhaps the most promising meeting was the 2005 Arab League session in Cairo, in which delegates expressed their commitment to the unity, sovereignty, and independence of Iraq. While the statement issued at the meeting said resistance is a "legitimate right" it stated that "terrorism is not legitimate resistance."[14] According to one senior US official, the Arab League has responded at times to US pressure, such as agreeing to visits to Iraq by senior Egyptian officials and the "generally helpful" communiqués" last November. [15]

Over the past 18 months, the UN Special Representative and his deputies have visited Syria, Turkey, Iran, Jordan and Kuwait, but little progress has been made. One problem is that the League of Arab States does not have some of the organizational capacities that other regional organizations, such as NATO, the Organization of American States (OAS), or the Association of Southeast Asian Nations (ASEAN), have, hampering the region's ability to provide organized support to the Iraqi people, but it could consider channeling and coordinating its assistance and debt relief through the UN or the EU. The US and international community should look to the expected Arab League visit to Baghdad for further progress both in terms of assistance and political support for progress.

Tensions are high between key states of the largely Sunni-dominated Arab League, especially Saudi Arabia, Egypt, and Jordan, and the Iraqi government. It is far from clear whether Arab leaders see a strong, Shia-dominated, democratic Iraq in their interest. Egypt and Saudi Arabia fear a rival to their influence; Iraq's neighbors fear a new Iran-Iraq axis linking Qom and Najaf that might threaten Persian Gulf security.[16] No Arab government has established a permanent diplomatic mission in Iraq, despite specific urging by Iraqi President Jalal al-Talabani to Arab leaders at the Khartoum Arab Summit to increase "their diplomatic representation in the war-ravaged country."[17] Talabani has also criticized the Arab League demands that Iraq's constitution declare itself an

---

[14] Kathleen Ridolfo, "Iraq: Reconciliation Conference Ends With Pledge To Move Forward," *Radio Free Europe*, November 22, 2005, http://www.rferl.org/featuresarticle/2005/11/cafe93f5-6de3-47c0-ad0e-0217ec15294d.html (accessed July 19, 2006).

[15] State Department Official, e-mail message to author, May 12, 2006.

[16] Steven A. Cook, "How Not to Save Iraq," *New Republic*, April 5, 2006, http://www.tnr.com/doc.mhtml?i=w060403&s=cook040506 (accessed July 19, 2006).

[17] "Arab Summit Ends on Note of Apathy," *Aljazeera*, March 29, 2006, http://english.aljazeera.net/NR/exeres/B6DF53F9-0BA4-41C3-942A-F6958576D66D.htm (accessed July 19, 2006).

Islamic and Arab country, claiming it demonstrated a bias as it had not made similar demands on other Arab nations. Iraqi officials are also angered that none of the Arab world's leaders expressed sympathy or offered aid following the stampede of religious pilgrims in Baghdad that left nearly one-thousand dead. The United States has also expressed a desire to see the Arab nations provide additional support. Assistant Secretary of State Welsh stated, "we look to the Arab League and its member states to provide support to the new government and to the people of Iraq… we would like to see a supportive international role, including in the security area."[18]

The leading Islamic multilateral organization, the Organization of the Islamic Conference (OIC), also has failed to play a significant role in Iraq. As Secretary-General Kofi Annan stated in April 2006, the OIC needs to "consider new ways to promote greater regional engagement between Iraq and its neighbors. While countries have legitimate concerns about the current situation in Iraq, they also have an essential responsibility to do everything possible to promote peace and stability there."[19] In mid-May 2006, the OIC discussed bringing all stakeholders in Iraq, "including the occupying powers" to the negotiating table and the possibility of a peacekeeping force under the OIC or the UN.[20] Such statements may indicate a new urgency for much needed Arab leadership.

> *In order for the US to convince a very reluctant international community to support Iraq, a fundamental shift in perceptions and realities of the US role will have to occur.*

"IRAQIFICATION" OF THE POLITICAL PROCESS

In order for the US to convince a very reluctant international community to support Iraq, a fundamental shift in perceptions and realities of the US role will have to occur. Three years into the war, perceptions will be very slow to change—and any such effort is certainly at risk of failure. Success would require the US to relinquish the control it has maintained on the political process to date and undertake a major diplomatic effort to

---

[18] Judy Aita, "United States Urges Arab Nations to Support Iraq," press release, US State Department, March 24, 2006.

[19] United Nations Security Council, *5386th Meeting (AM)*, March 15, 2006.

[20] Datuk Seri Abdullah Ahmad Badawi, "OIC Mulls Plan to End Iraq Violence," *New Straits Times* (Malaysia), May 22, 2006 (accessed July 14, 2006).

secure broader international involvement in Iraq. The US will also need to launch a new diplomatic campaign to convince the international community that a stable and secure Iraq is in its interest.

With the formation of an Iraqi government, albeit after a four-month deadlock, the US can now pursue the "Iraqification" of the political process. Such a process was key in the UN processes in Bosnia, Kosovo, and East Timor. Increasingly, the US must withdraw from its three-year old role as key arbiter in the political process and let Iraqis take control, with the support of non-US actors. Given the dangerous security environment, other nations and non-governmental organizations (NGOs) will understandably be reluctant to increase activities in Iraq. Yet, if the US embarks on a serious diplomatic effort to underscore the world's interest in a stable Iraq, the role of the international community can be greatly expanded, enabling the US to withdraw more quickly and more responsibly. The key to jumpstarting these efforts would be endorsement by the UN, EU, and Arab leaders, and active solicitation by the new Iraqi government.

With this in mind, the Iraqis should call for a Dayton or Bonn-style international conference to secure an internal political agreement to end the insurgency and reach agreement with the international community on its role in assisting Iraq. Of key importance will be a new recognition by nations with influence in Iraq that they have a responsibility to assist the Iraqis—not just the US—in achieving stability. It is time the international community recognizes that Iraq and the United States cannot achieve that goal without substantially increased international engagement, especially on the part of the EU and Arab nations. With strong UN, EU, Arab, and US leadership, such an agreement is possible.

In the aftermath of the 2003 war, UN veteran negotiator Lakhdar Brahimi came in to help forge a consensus on the establishment of an interim government in Iraq. In 1995, Richard Holbrooke brokered the Dayton Peace Accords in which lay the basis for a multi-ethnic state in Bosnia. At the time, both achievements were considered akin to pulling a rabbit out of a hat. A combination of the two processes must now occur. Unfortunately, Brahimi has retired and his 2003 role in forging a consensus left him unpopular with many Kurds and Shias. Yet, someone of close to equal stature can be found.[21] The US should be represented by Secretary of State Condoleeza Rice, or perhaps former Secretary of State James Baker if President Bush is willing to empower him. Key

---

[21] Discussions with UN officials indicate Brahimi would be very reluctant to take on such a role, in part because of the political tensions from his 2003 role.

issues will have to be put on the table, including perhaps the constitutional balance currently in effect. Whether Iran can be convinced to play a supportive role, or even just to remain neutral, will be a key challenge.

A contact group made up of the key players, such as the US, Great Britain, UN, EU, OIC, Saudi Arabia, Turkey, Iran, and Egypt, should be formed to press the Arab world to support a political compromise in Iraq, an end to the insurgency, and a new commitment by the Arab leaders and international community to assist Iraq. The US has made use of such contact groups before with success, both in the Balkans and in Africa. In the 1990s in Afghanistan, a similar arrangement called "six-plus-two" (Afghanistan's neighbors plus the US and Russia) successfully engaged Iran and promoted some stability. An international conference and a contact group for Iraq have a reasonable chance of failure—but the international community owes the Iraqi people a chance at success.

> *A contact group made up of the key players should be formed to press the Arab world to support a political compromise in Iraq, an end to the insurgency, and a new commitment by the Arab leaders and international community to assist Iraq.*

The following discussion does not address the elements of such a political agreement[22] but rather will focus on suggested areas for increased support from the key international actors.

SECURITY/TRAINING

Security remains a concern of the first order. Further international engagement will remain fiction unless the security situation improves. The instability in Iraq threatens the reconstruction effort as well as the overall success of the transition. Despite increasing calls for the withdrawal of US troops, the US will most likely continue its lead role, since at the current rate, the Iraqis are years away from being able to provide adequate security throughout the country. Therefore, additional

---

[22] Senator Joseph Biden and Leslie Gelb of the Council on Foreign Relations have suggested an effort to maintain a united Iraq by decentralizing it, giving each ethno-religious group — Kurd, Sunni Arab and Shia Arab — room to run its own affairs, while leaving the central government in charge of common interests. They also recommend a regional non-aggression pact; Joesph R. Biden Jr. and Leslie H. Gelb, "Unity Through Autonomy in Iraq," *New York Times*, May 1, 2006, A19.

assistance in operations and training for the new Iraqi police and army is essential to ease the US burden and expedite a US withdrawal.

One cause of concern for the region is the belief that the US plans to establish permanent military bases in the region and to control Iraq's oil. It is important that the Administration make clear its intention to respect fully Iraq's sovereignty on both points. Any continued military presence, including bases in the region, would only be at the request of the countries involved. The US must continue to make clear that it has no designs on controlling Iraq's oil, but rather stands prepared to assist the Iraqis in re-building Iraq's oil production capacity.[23] It must emphasize that it will support Iraq's territorial integrity and that it will oppose any invasion of Iraq (in particular by Iran and Turkey). In all likelihood, even after a withdrawal from Iraq, the US is likely to maintain an over-the-horizon force for years. For instance last August, the head of the Air Force said that after the withdrawal of US ground troops, the US will continue a rotational presence "more or less indefinitely."[24]

An immediate task is to engage the international community in providing security and enhanced training for the Iraqi police and armed forces. NATO and the Arab states should assist with training and the Arabs should provide stronger border security. The private sector should also be considered for protection of civilian workers, including NGOs.

NATO

At NATO's summit meeting in Istanbul on June 28, 2004, its Heads of State and Government agreed to assist Iraq with the technical assistance and the training and equipping of its security forces. In July, NATO established a Training Implementation Mission and Joint Staff College for this purpose and is now running a training center for senior security and defense officials on the outskirts of Baghdad. Any combat role is ruled out.

While NATO claims all its member countries are contributing assistance, either in Iraq, or outside of Iraq, through financial contributions or donations of equipment, more clearly can and should be done. NATO should expand its training and mentoring of middle and senior level

---

[23] While the US recognizes it must clarify the long term security relationship, to date, it has been reluctant to make such an unequivocal statement.

[24] Eric Schmitt, "US General Says Iraqis Will Need Longtime Support From Air Force," *New York Times,* August 30, 2005, http://select.nytimes.com/gst/abstract.html?res=F00B14FD3D550C738FDDA10894DD404482 (accessed July 13, 2006).

personnel from the Iraqi security forces in Iraq and outside of Iraq, at NATO schools and training centers. It should also train police and soldiers at the infantry level. The Alliance should also play a larger role in coordinating offers of equipment and training from individual NATO and partner countries by actively identifying needs and soliciting sources for them.

ARAB LEAGUE/OIC

Given the difficult neighborhood in which Iraq lies, border security is essential to a stable Iraq. Turkey, Syria, Jordan, Kuwait, Iran, and Saudi Arabia all have a responsibility to ensure insurgents and other terrorists do not use their territory as a transit route into Iraq. Iraq is rightly sensitive to any neighboring troops entering its territory. Thus the international community will need to monitor the border, perhaps even establish a UN mission as it did along the Iraq-Kuwait border throughout the 1990s. Should any of these nations need assistance in securing their borders, Muslim nations should agree to provide assistance, including troops. The country in question could request international assistance, including from NATO, other organizations, or bilateral assistance.

In addition, capable Arab states can do more to assist the US and NATO in training and equipping Iraqi police and military forces. Certainly, Jordanian, Egyptian, Moroccan and even Indonesian soldiers could join the effort. The less western the program is, the faster the perception that the US intends to occupy Iraq indefinitely will fade.

PRIVATE MILITARY COMPANIES

While controversial, private military companies are already playing a significant role in Iraq in protecting civilian contractors. In addition to the US, private military companies from Great Britain, Nepal, Chile, Ukraine, Israel, South Africa, and Fiji are all working in Iraq. They tend to be very effective, using their elite training as Rangers, Green Berets, Delta Force, SEALS, and the British Special Air Services. They are expensive, some paying employees as much as $1,200 a day. Such high pay also runs the risk of luring lesser-paid active duty military into the private sector.[25] But given the drain on the US military services and the need for protection for any increased international presence, such an

---

[25] David Isenberg, "A Fistful of Contractors: The Case for a Pragmatic Assessment of Private Military Companies in Iraq," *British American Security Information Council Executive Summary and Key Conclusions* 2 (September 2004), http://www.basicint.org/pubs/Research/2004PMC.htm (accessed July 21, 2006).

option must be considered. Funding for the NGOs could come from Iraq's oil sector, if necessary.

NON-SECURITY ASSISTANCE

UNITED NATIONS

UNSC Resolution 1546 established the mandate of the UN Assistance Mission for Iraq (UNAMI) as requested by the government of Iraq. Those tasks include:

- assisting in the establishment of the government and holding elections;
- the promotion of a national dialogue and consensus-building on the national constitution;
- advising the government of Iraq in effective government;
- coordination of the delivery of reconstruction, development and humanitarian assistance;
- the promotion of human rights, justice, and national reconciliation; and
- holding of a consensus.[26]

While making it clear it is not the job of the UN, the resolution also welcomes the efforts by the government of Iraq to develop Iraqi security forces such as effective police, border enforcement, and other institutions for the maintenance of law and order and recognizes that the multinational force will assist in the building of the these capabilities and institutions. Importantly, the resolution also requests that member states, international and regional organizations, contribute assistance to the multinational force to help meet the needs of the Iraqi people for security and stability, for humanitarian and reconstruction assistance, and to support the efforts of UNAMI. This resolution provides the necessary political support for the international community to step in and help the Iraqis—regardless of its strong opposition to the war.

UNAMI intends to increase its assistance activities in seven key areas, focusing on strengthening the management capacity in the ministries, coordinating the provision of basic services and supporting the restoration of public infrastructure. On March 15th 2006, Ashraf Jehangir Qazi, Special Representative of the Secretary-General for Iraq, again asked for an increase in the number of UNAMI staff operating

---

[26] United Nations Security Council, Resolution 1546 (S/RES/1546), 2004.

throughout Iraq. He asked for active UNAMI participation as the political process continued to unfold in the constitutional phase, as amendments were considered and laws enforcing constitutional provisions were drafted by the first parliament. He noted that the work of reconstructing the country's political institutions was only now beginning, and the UN has much to offer in that respect.[27]

In order for the UN to fulfill additional tasks, as well as the six key tasks outlined in UNSC 1546, it will need significant international assistance and enhancement of the necessary capacities within UNAMI. The UN has repeatedly requested—with little response—dedicated air assets to assure greater operational mobility and flexibility.[28] In order for the UN to fulfill its mandate, it must secure these, most likely from NATO.

EUROPEAN UNION

Greatly divided over the war in Iraq, the EU has now recognized it has an interest in Iraq's success and is taking steps to assist the Iraqis. By the end of 2005, the EU had expended approximately 518.5 million € for Iraq's reconstruction efforts. Having endorsed the goals of a secure, stable, and democratic Iraq with a market economy, and integration of Iraq into its region and the international community, it should greatly increase its assistance and use its influence in the Arab and Muslim world to garner further support for Iraq. It should also consider further assistance in each of the six UN areas identified above. The EU should take the lead in ensuring the UN Development Group Trust Fund is fully funded. While the Paris Club has acted to reduce Iraq's debt, more can be done, including stronger leadership to encourage Russia and the Arab states to follow suit.

ARAB LEAGUE/OIC

The most important step the Arab League can take is to give strong legitimacy to the new government of Iraq, gain Arab and Muslim agreement to strangle the insurgency, secure their own borders, and oppose any interference in the affairs of Iraq.[29] It can also lend support

---

[27] United Nations Security Council, *5386th Meeting (AM)*, March 15, 2006.

[28] To date, UNAMI has received an aircraft order and the US is considering providing another; State Department Official, e-mail message to author, May 12, 2006.

[29] Joseph McMillan, *Saudi Arabia and Iraq: Oil, Religion, and an Enduring Rivalry*, Special Report No. 157, Iraq and Its Neighbors series (Washington DC, United States Institute of Peace, January 2006); Geoffrey Kemp, *Iran and Iraq: The Shia Connection, Soft Power, and the Nuclear Factor*, Special Report No. 156, Iraq and Its Neighbors series (Washington DC, United States Institute of Peace, November 2005; Henri J. Barkey, *Turkey and Iraq: The Perils (and Prospects) of Proximity*,

to the efforts of the UN and EU for the development of Iraq, including channeling its significant potential for assistance through these bodies. The Arab states and OIC should work with the EU to ensure the UN Development Group Trust Fund is fully funded. Arabs must also do their share in providing Iraq debt relief, especially Saudi Arabia with the largest debt at $32 billion.[30]

NGO SECTOR

The role of NGOs in Iraq can be crucial in developing civil society and assisting in the humanitarian relief effort. Funding over the next few years will remain important for key organizations aimed at assisting Iraqis in establishing and supporting political parties, academic organizations, human rights groups, trade unions, and independent media. Yet, in 2006, the administration sought to end a USAID grant to two US organizations dedicated to promoting democracy, the National Democratic Institute and the International Republican Institute. After Congressional protests, the Administration changed course and provided $54 million to these organizations, as well as the National Endowment for Democracy. A realignment of the Administration's budget priorities is key. For instance, the Administration has budgeted $254 million for enhancing the rule of law but only $10 million toward promoting democracy in Iraq.[31] The international community should focus on quick impact efforts that can demonstrate progress to an already disaffected population.

SUMMARY OF RECOMMENDATIONS

The US should give the Iraqis every opportunity to develop a stable political system and a sufficiently capable security force so that following a US withdrawal Iraq will have an adequate foundation for success. The US should use its superpower status to secure international involvement in assisting the Iraqis, thus facilitating a broader basis of support for the new Iraq. Such support could speed reconstruction and security, paving the way for a faster US withdrawal.

Special Report No. 141, Iraq and Its Neighbors series (Washington DC, United States Institute of Peace, July 2005); all available at http://www.usip.org/iraq/neighbors.html (accessed 14 July 2006).

[30] Megan K. Stack. "Hands-Off or Not? Saudis Wring Theirs Over Iraq," *LA Times*, May 24, 2006, http://www.latimes.com/news/nationworld/world/la-fg-saudi24may24,1,5495022.story (accessed July 14, 2006).

[31] Peter Baker, "Democracy in Iraq Not a Priority in US Budget," *Washington Post*, April 5, 2006, A01.

The US must relinquish control of the political process and undertake a major diplomatic effort to secure broader international involvement in Iraq. It must now pursue the "Iraqification" of the political process. The US must also launch a diplomatic effort to convince the international community it now has a responsibility to help the Iraqis succeed. To jump start increased international engagement, the Iraqis should call for a Dayton or Bonn-style international conference to secure an internal political agreement to end the insurgency and reach agreement with the international community on its role in assisting Iraq. Key issues will have to be put on the table, including perhaps the constitutional balance currently in effect. A contact group made up of the key players, such as the US, Great Britain, UN, EU, OIC, Saudi Arabia, Turkey, Iran, and Egypt, should be formed to press the Arab world to support a political compromise in Iraq, an end to the insurgency, and a new commitment by the Arab leaders and international community to assist Iraq, including through debt relief. It is additionally important for the US to make clear it has no intention of establishing permanent bases or securing access to Iraq's oil. It must emphasize that it will support Iraq's territorial integrity and that it will oppose any invasion of Iraqi territory (in particular Iran and Turkey).

SECURITY AND TRAINING

NATO and the Arab states should provide additional assistance in increasing overall security and conducting training for the new Iraqi police and army. Iraq's neighbors, with outside assistance where needed, should provide stronger border security. The private sector should also be considered for protection of civilian workers, including NGOs. Capable Arab states should assist the US and NATO in training and equipping Iraqi police and military forces. While controversial, the use of private military companies must be considered, with possible funding from Iraq's oil sector if necessary.

NON-SECURITY ASSISTANCE

The international community, particularly the UN, EU, the Arab League and the OIC, should provide all necessary assistance to UNAMI as it increases its assistance activities in seven key areas, focusing on strengthening the management capacity in the ministries, coordinating the provision of basic services, and supporting the restoration of public infrastructure. It should also generously meet the funding requests at the upcoming fifth meeting of the Donor Committee of the International Reconstruction Fund Facility for Iraq in June, and ensure the UN

Development Group Trust Fund is fully funded. Debt relief must be a higher priority.

NATO should also immediately grant the UN's request for more dedicated air assets to assure greater operational mobility and flexibility. The US Administration, and the international community, should generously fund support to civil society in Iraq and ensure democracy programs are fully funded. The international community should focus on quick impact efforts that can demonstrate progress to an already disaffected population.

— 10 —
PUTTING IRAQ IN A
REGIONAL AND GLOBAL CONTEXT

Michael Kraig

INTRODUCTION:
THE INTELLECTUAL CHALLENGE OF IRAQ

Psychologically within the policy community of the United States, Iraq has taken on the status of an intellectual burden that hardly anyone wants to shoulder, but which literally no analyst can afford to ignore. The Iraqi situation seems impervious to the usual American penchant for "rational choice," step-by-step logical approaches to problem-solving. This is in part because it defies any analyst's attempt to evaluate the true situation on the ground, which makes it extremely hard to outline US policy options that can apply equally tomorrow and one month from now. In a situation so fluid, in which cultural, linguistic, ethnic, and religious realities resist western modes of analysis and problem-solving, how can one identify the main players; their stakes, interests, incentives and disincentives; the levers of influence on those groups; and the US economic, military, and political options that maximize the probabilities of success?

In short, our difficulty with Iraq represents more than a failure to understand Islam, or the Arab world, or the Middle East in general; it represents a central challenge to the post-Cold War legacies of security thought and practice that still define Washington (and US academic) analysis and decision-making. Iraq embodies nearly every characteristic of the "new" type of security threat in the twenty-first century global system. As a weak and failing state in the middle of the world's most oil-rich region, it poses an indirect economic threat to the stability of the globalized world. As a territory being used and abused by stateless, radical, anti-globalist terror groups, it directly strengthens these actors and therefore indirectly exposes the rest of the world to future transnational terror threats. As a multi-ethnic, divided religious polity with increasing amounts of inter-group distrust, it poses a humanitarian and human protection threat because of the ever-present potential for massive ethnic cleansing. As a state losing its grip on sovereignty, it poses a regional threat to neighboring states who are fractured by ethno-religious divisions and who are still engaged in an arduous, long-term state-building exercises. Iraq's growing black market economy—which mixes equal doses of corruption and mafia-like criminality—threatens neighbors who themselves suffer from corruption and black-market forces. Finally, as a divided Shia and Sunni Islamic state in which religious radicalism of various shades is undermining religious tolerance, Iraq's precarious security situation indirectly threatens regional stability as a whole, given that the Middle East itself is divided between different versions of these same two Islamic schools of thought, as well as between those who would separate religion and government, and those who would ardently join them together.

Thus, what started out as a threat defined by the United States in traditional, state-to-state, strategic terms has become a multifaceted threat that has nothing to do with high-tech weaponry or the usual balance-of-power. The familiar and comfortable terminology of containment and deterrence is essentially useless in dealing with the Iraqi problem. An escalation of choice by America that was originally defined in terms of interstate competition, coercive diplomacy, and victory through war has become a conflict that is immune to Cold War-era threats based on the US ability to escalate conflicts through the use of precision weaponry or placement of aircraft carriers. The magic promised in the "revolution in military affairs" (now dubbed "transformation") is largely powerless to affect either realities on the ground or Iraqi elite decision-making in Baghdad. It is, in short, exactly the type of civil, social conflict that has been evident in other regions ever since the demise of Yugoslavia, with characteristics reminiscent of Kosovo, Chechnya, Indonesia, Somalia, and other vacuums of state identity and state power in the post-Cold War world. And as with these other hard cases, both the United States and the international community at large seem too befuddled and incoherent to take effective action.

The primary thesis of this chapter is simple: until the domestic stability of both Iraq itself and the regional environment becomes the central factor in US decision-making, the problems will persist and stability will be elusive. Until now, the United States has insisted on defining the conflict in ways amenable to application of traditional military capabilities (a unified insurgency that opposes stability and democracy and can be defeated through campaigns). Moreover, beyond Iraq itself, the question of Persian Gulf and Middle East security as a whole have been defined in traditional strategic terms, with weapons of mass destruction (WMD) counterproliferation constituting the primary focus for US policymakers.

Thus, a so-called "rogue state" such as Iran has been viewed through the prism of counterproliferation as an ideological competitor or "emerging power" who challenges US regional hegemony—rather than being viewed more correctly through the prism of twenty-first century globalization, i.e., as an example of an isolated, stagnating state whose own delicate internal balances are potentially threatened by the breakdown of rules and order in Iraq. Similarly, Turkey has been viewed as a North Atlantic Treaty Organizations (NATO) ally whose bases might be used for military operations against a nuclearizing Iran, rather than as a state undergoing its own internal socio-political transformation, one that is potentially threatened by the export of ethno-religious divisions from Iraq. What is clearly needed is a push of the intellectual "reset" button to put Iraq in its proper regional context, and to put regional security overall within the global context of maintaining order and stability in an interdependent, inter-connected, globalized system consisting equally of sovereign states and transnational actors—as opposed to the present course of stressing US strategic dominance and military primacy through counterproliferation, containment, and deterrence of regional rogues such as Iran and Syria.

The chapter will proceed as follows. First, the present US strategic focus will be outlined, both in terms of regional strategy and in terms of larger global goals, and this strategic vision will be critiqued and challenged. Second, an alternative set of strategic US and international goals will be outlined for Iraq, the Persian Gulf, and the Middle East, based not only on the need to stabilize Iraq and Gulf security but also on the requirement of setting positive precedents for similar hard cases within the larger post-Cold War global system. Third, it will assess the difficulties of engaging Iraq's neighbors in a concerted effort to contain civil violence in Iraq, given various competing and contradictory interests within and between Middle East states. Finally, the conclusion will stress the need for both Iran and the United States to "hit the strategic reset button" to reorder their priorities toward each other, toward Iraq, and toward the region as a whole.

THE PRESENT US STRATEGIC WORLDVIEW AND ITS DISCONNECT FROM GLOBAL AND REGIONAL REALITIES

Many regional experts and analysts are confused with the lack of strategy in the current US approach to the Persian Gulf, an approach which is characterized by a failing occupation in Iraq alongside bilateral military arrangements with Gulf Arab monarchies and the complete isolation of Iran. In fact, the United States does have a strategy, one that intertwines counterproliferation and the Bush Administration's Global War on Terrorism, based upon a flexible mix of deterrence, compellance, coercive diplomacy, global military superiority, and the preventive or preemptive use of military force.

Since the terrorist attacks on the World Trade Center on September 11, 2001, the Bush Administration has sought to link the counterproliferation approach (which stresses the threat of "rogue states" like Iraq or North Korea) with a counterterrorist approach that stresses the future threat of transnational terrorist cells to the US homeland.

A broad counterproliferation/counterterrorist strategy involves several aspects:

- Dissuasion of competing military buildups by potential state adversaries like China, Iran, Russia, or others through the solidification of indefinite US global military superiority. This will presumably convince rising middle powers in key regions to embrace US-style liberal democracy and forego military expansion in their own spheres of influence;

- deterrence of those rogue states or future "near peer competitors" who manage to acquire weapons of mass destruction or significant conventional forces that challenge US hegemony at the regional level in the Middle East, Persian Gulf, South Asia, Southeast Asia, and Northeast Asia;

- deterrence of transnational terrorists by threats to strike their networks within the boundaries of failed states; and

- preventive/preemptive military strikes, or the threat of such strikes through coercive diplomacy in the event that dissuasion and deterrence are not feasible or desirable. This includes covert aid to those Third World states perceived to be too weak to effectively police their own territory and rid themselves of threatening terrorist cells without US intervention.[1]

---

[1] This approach has also been labeled "The Preventive War Strategy, and is reprinted here from previous publications by this author. See Lawrence Korb and Michael Kraig, *Strategies for US*

In turn, each of the above elements could be seen as an overall strategy of compellence, in that the presumed superiority of US values, culture, political institutions, economy, and global military power will act together as a combined package to compel (or convince) others to embrace secular, liberal, capitalist democracy for their own future development and forego threats to US leadership in key regions of the world.

As defined operationally by the US government since the early 1990s, counterproliferation consists of technology denial methods directed at the developing world (export controls) as well as new methods of deterrence, defense, and preemption (precision-guided and more lethal conventional munitions alongside the existing nuclear arsenal). The perfection of defense, deterrence, and preemptive policy options has become the major goal of the national security planning community.

Under this vision of global politics, globalization of the free market is selective, insofar as dual-use commercial advances with military applications are to be uniformly denied to developing countries that may use them to gain political strength or military power. Security is therefore seen in cooperative, multilateral, or mutual terms only with regard to friends and allies, those who band together in their economic and military relations to defend against intractable and potentially irrational enemies. Both ideological and resource competition are seen as endemic to international relations and as an unavoidable reality that necessitates improved methods of control to minimize unpredictability and uncertainty in relations with potentially hostile actors.

The counterproliferation approach views US diplomatic relations largely in terms of discrete bilateral and multilateral relationships, i.e., in terms of formal alliances or informal security understandings among friends. Examples of such friends include NATO, South Korea, Japan, Israel, Australia, non-allied Southeast Asian countries such as Thailand and Singapore, and the Gulf Cooperation Council (GCC) states in the Middle East, all of whom receive preferential US aid, trade relationships, military technology-sharing arrangements, and, in the case of the GCC states, large sales of off-the-shelf, high-technology military items. From this perspective, technological diffusion and development are positive only insofar as they occur within this circle of friends and allies.

National Security: Winning the Peace in the 21st Century, Report of the Stanley Foundation Independent Task Force on Strategies for US National Security, Muscatine, Iowa, December 2003, http://sns.stanleyfoundation.org; Michael Kraig, "Forging a New Security Order for the Persian Gulf," Middle East Policy Council, XIII, no. 1 (Spring 2006), http://www.mepc.org/journal_vol13/0603_Kraig_ft.asp (accessed July 21, 2006).

Security is a fungible good that can (and should) be divided among opposing camps. Moreover, according to this approach, the sovereign nation-state is still the primary actor, insofar as transnational terror networks are thought to be produced, guided, funded, encouraged, equipped, or otherwise supported by rogue states like Iran or Syria.

It is within this context that we must examine the US problems in Iraq. Simply stated: although Iraq is host to tens of thousands of US soldiers who are exposed to death and destruction every day, and although Iraq is clearly battered by transnational terrorism, the unfortunate reality is that the US still acts as if the most important regional security problem is not a failed Iraq, but rather, a strong Iran. The main motivator of US policy toward the Middle East is not a vacuum of power and the decline of public order in Iraq, but rather, the potential rise of a coherent, relatively strong sovereign actor who might be on the path to latent nuclear weapons capabilities. While Iraq is in the headlines every day with the death of US servicemen and women, as well as Iraqis, it is not the loss of sovereign order that is concerning US decision-makers the most. More troubling, it seems, is the presence of a potential counter-vailing sovereign actor with a different ideology than the United States. Overall, it is the US global strategic position that constitutes the de facto and primary factor motivating US regional security practices in the Persian Gulf.

As strange as it may seem, the United States is not intent, at the moment, on creating an inclusive regional order based on the sovereign preferences of all Persian Gulf states so as to get their willing aid to stabilize a war-torn Iraq. Despite the impending disaster of Iraqi civil war, the United States is not overly interested in either a rough balance of power or a rough balance of interests (based on reassurance measures) with all of Iraq's neighbors as a way of garnering their consistent support for an Iraqi stabilization agenda. Instead, the United States is intent on a larger counterproliferation mission that is simultaneously regional and global, military and ideological, economic and social. Its goal is to prevent the emergence of a nuclear-capable competitor with an ideological mission or identity that is antithetical to the presumed objective global goal of spreading liberal capitalist democracy as the path to prosperity, peace, and stability within all regions of the globe.

LOGICAL FAULTS OF THE PRESENT US STRATEGIC WORLDVIEW

Inherent in the current US strategic worldview is the assumption that regional security cannot exist in the presence of competitive WMD programs, especially nuclear weapons programs. This unstated, but very real, driving assumption of US policy is rather strange from a historical point of view. History has shown that Chinese and US arsenals, based on mutual assured destruction calculations and on second-strike forces, can very comfortably co-exist alongside quite positive economic, social, and diplomatic relations. One might wonder why no one in Washington is therefore comparing, as a serious academic exercise, the US-Iranian case with the US-Chinese case.

Instead of making such comparisons, the overriding US assumption (never clearly stated) is that the Persian Gulf will not, cannot, and should not be secure, prosperous, and stable in the presence of nuclear proliferation. In short, the unstated assumption is that a nuclear Iran will upset Persian Gulf stability and security, will be aggressive, will try to resort to its old goals of spreading the Islamic vision of statehood within the region, and will give its WMD to questionable politico-terrorist groups such as Hezbollah or Hamas. Or, more to the point, a nuclear Iran will undermine the overall strategic position of the United States, both globally and regionally, in a way that clearly has not been the case with a nuclear China.

It is hard to see how these unstated assumptions are automatically true, however ingrained they may be in all of our various government policies toward the region. Iran is, in fact, more democratic than China is or ever was, despite the corruption of the recent parliamentary elections in Tehran. At the very least, Iran has a much freer press than China (despite periodic attempts by conservatives to shut major news outlets down), and its citizens are generally more pro-western and pro-US .

To be fair, however, to the persistent GCC concerns of Iranian hubris and hegemony, Iran does believe that it should have influence roughly commensurate with its geo-strategic position, its rich cultural and religious heritage, and its important economic resources (particularly oil and gas).[2] Obviously, Iran does not have this influence and has not had it since the Shah was deposed. Whether the Iranian wish for increased influence is based on arrogant desires for hegemony, as many Arab Gulf analysts argue,[3] or whether it can be interpreted as just another example of the historical desire of states to be given their due, is largely beside the

---

[2] Statements by Iranian participants from a not-for-attribution, informal roundtable discussion sponsored by the Stanley Foundation and the Institute for Near East and Gulf Military Analyses in Dubai, January 2004, as summarized by Michael Kraig, "Conference Report," *Middle East Policy Journal* 11, no. 3 (September 2004): 1-39.

[3] Ibid.

point. Iran is a major regional state, and it will always wish for influence commensurate to its geopolitical weight, whatever the domestic or regional political context.

It is under this fervent Iranian desire that nuclear weapons are relevant. Simply stated, US neoconservative visions of a radically Islamic, theocratic, and transnational terrorist-supporting Iran wielding nuclear weapons to cow neighbors and commit indirect terrorist attacks abroad (including on US soil) are wild beyond imagination. President Ahmadinejad's role and power have been radically over-emphasized within the western press. The same people who said Khatami was a figurehead with little real power (largely true) are now doing an about-face and saying Ahmadinejad has displaced the real centers of power and is now influencing everything from Israeli policy to nuclear policy without any real checks on his actions.

The reality is that those who were skeptical of the power of the Iranian Presidency were, and are, correct in their views. When you take into account the preferences of the Supreme Leader and elites such as Rafsanjani, Iran begins to look a lot more like China circa the 1960s-70s. Repeated Stanley Foundation dialogues over the past six years have created a picture of a hidebound elite who are steadily giving up on earlier idealistic goals of spreading the Shia Islamic Revolution, and are instead taking a realpolitik turn toward increasing Persian influence and hegemony within Iran's immediate locale, as with other emerging or rising powers in the past. Even as President Ahmadinejad is successfully consolidating his institutional authority through wide-ranging purges of existing officials at all levels of government, he ultimately is beholden to the Council of Guardians—and most of all, to the personal preferences of Ayatollah Khamenei. Given that Iran, under Khamenei, seriously attempted to initiate a new process of détente or rapprochement with the United States in 2002-2003—including a stated willingness to put all issues, including aid for anti-Israeli groups, on the table—it is unrealistic to assume the Ahmadinejad will be given free reign on nuclear decisions or a deciding finger on the nuclear button. What matters most are the long-range preferences of the overall clerical elite in Tehran, and the indications of the past several years have shown a decided turn away from spreading Shia fundamentalism to all corners of the Middle East, and a turn toward traditional state security for the Islamic Republic of Iran, defined in a very recognizable, nationalist sense.

As with China over the past 30 years, this ultimately means more integration with the global economy. The top elites now know that if they want the Islamic/democratic experiment to succeed, it requires much more economic growth and prosperity to do so, at least if they want to appease their restive, increasingly cynical youth population.[4] Iran wants global and regional recognition as a contributor to religious philosophy and civilizational evolution within the Middle East. It also desperately wants to be free from existential threats to its current Islamic identity, whether from Israel, the United States, or from a future potential Taliban-ized Afghanistan and Pakistan.

Given the realities outlined above, it appears that Iran wants a "light switch" latent nuclear capability, not an arsenal of bombs ready to explode on the territory of infidels. What Iran wants is what Japan already has: a set of credible security assurances that allows it to develop without having to weaponize.[5] Obviously, Iran will never get security assurances in the form that Japan has them: US nuclear threats against Japan's potential enemies and coverage by the US nuclear umbrella. Iran can, however, credibly demand that its Islamic regime finally be recognized by the west, by the United States in particular, and that any high-tech weapons deployments by the GCC states (or by the United States within GCC states) be purely defensive in nature (just as the GCC and the United States have a right to demand that Iranian military deployments be defensive, not offensive, in nature). Iran's pursuit of a full fuel cycle, especially a low-enriched uranium (LEU) fuel cycle, is essentially an insurance policy, very similar to the insurance policy that Japan currently has with its overflowing plutonium stockpiles. It is also similar to India's various nuclear programs in the 1950s and 1960s, before India decided it was indeed isolated in the world with a hostile and arrogant China on its Himalayan doorstep and needed to weaponize its latent capability.[6]

Finally, Iran's pursuit of an LEU capability is directly related to hyperbolic domestic political trends in Tehran. The Iranian nuclear program has become a political football, and both sides want to score the

---

[4] Ray Takeyh, "Security Architectures in the post-Saddam Middle East" (presentation, Center for Contemporary Conflict Conflict of the Naval Postgraduate School and the Center for Naval Analysis, Alexandria, VA, February 9, 2004); and Mark Gasiorowski "Security Architectures in the post-Saddam Middle East" (presentation, Center for Contemporary Conflict of the Naval Postgraduate School and the Center for Naval Analysis, Alexandria, VA, February 9, 2004).

[5] Ray Takeyh , "WMD Proliferation in the Middle East: Directions and Policy Options in the New Century" (lecture, Naval Post Graduate School Center for Contemporary Conflict Conference, Monterey, CA, June 28-30, 2004), http://www.ccc.nps.navy.mil/events/recent/jun04mideast.pdf (accessed July 14, 2006).

[6] Dr. Nassar Hadian, "Iran's Nuclear Program: Contexts and Debates," in *Iran's Bomb: American and Iranian Perspectives*, ed. Geoffrey Kemp (Washington, DC: The Nixon Center, April 2004), 51-67.

same touchdown. The International Crisis Group commissioned polls that, when analyzed by an Iranian expert alongside other domestic polls in Iran, showed decisively that most of the Iranian public (and many officials) do not want a nuclear bomb.[7] However, they do want a full nuclear fuel cycle for prestige as well as for scientific, economic, and identity-based concerns. Nuclear technology, in the Iranian collective psyche, means symbolic sovereign equality and international respect.[8] Unlike in Europe and the United States, this pro-nuclear majority in Iran does not see an automatic connection between a fully-monitored, internationally-safeguarded energy program and a nuclear weapons capability. A majority of Iranians would point out that Japan and others also have this latent capability and are legally monitored and verified by the International Atomic Energy Agency (IAEA), just as Iran would be.

Further, Iran's relationships with Hezbollah and other groups indicate that it will never share WMD with non-state actors. Surrendering control over its strategic assets could bring worldwide condemnation upon Iran and effectively nullify any conceivable chances of economic integration with its neighbors or with the world. Iran recognizes that it is safe from US military strikes only if it sticks to truly local, politically-motivated terrorism based on Shia irredentist goals vis-à-vis Israel and avoids aiding transnational, apocalyptic zealots whose goal is to bring down the entire global economic system. Hezbollah does not equal Al-Qaeda; Hezbollah is not a "scream against globalization," to use the words of one prominent Washington security analyst.[9] Al-Qaeda, in contrast, is indeed very publicly against the prevailing global order. Iran does not provide significant aid to the latter type of terrorists (beyond harboring some under tight domestic conditions for a bargaining chip with the United States), and Iran certainly would not countenance handing them a nuclear weapon.[10]

---

[7] Karim Sadjadpour, "Iranians Don't Want to Go Nuclear," *Washington Post*, February 3, 2004, A19.

[8] Hadi Semati, (lecture, Carnegie Nonproliferation Conference, June 22, 2004), www.ceip.org/files/projects/npp/resources/2004conference/home.htm, (accessed July 14, 2006).

[9] Robert Litwak, "WMD Proliferation in the Middle East: Directions and Policy Options in the New Century" (Naval Post-Graduate School Center for Contemporary Conflict Conference, Monterey, CA, June 28-30, 2004), http://www.ccc.nps.navy.mil/events/recent/jun04mideast.pdf (accessed July 14, 2006).

[10] There is, of course, a hot debate in Washington policy circles over the issue of some 9/11 terrorists crossing Iranian territory earlier in 2001. However, despite all the hyperbole, it is still unclear whether Iranian authorities knew about the exact locations of these transnational terrorists in their travels from Afghanistan and Pakistan to points further West; or whether the Iranians knew, but passively accepted, that such groups occasionally traversed their territory from Afghanistan to other Gulf states and Turkey; or whether the authorities in Tehran actively aided and abetted such

In sum: a strong Iran can be deterred and balanced, cajoled and threatened, rewarded and punished, according to the issue and event at hand. Non-state factions engaged in civil strife cannot be similarly targeted. Thus, whereas any sovereign actor (even Iran) is open to some level of control and influence via the normal levers of statecraft, non-sovereign actors fighting for their very identifies and livelihoods in an atmosphere devoid of trust and order are largely beyond the control of external actors, the world's lone superpower included.

Iranian leaders of all ideological stripes have something that could be called "Persian pride," which can be both useful as well as detrimental to regional security. Pride can be massaged diplomatically; it can be pandered to; it can be assuaged. Persian pride is unsurprising in its effects and character because it is a national attribute shared by all factions in Tehran: Shia theocrats and ardent secular nationalists, leftist socialists and radical populists, authoritarian technocrats and democratic idealists. The Persian pride that runs Iran afoul of its neighbors and the international community, via issues such as nuclear reactors and islands, is the same nationalist pride that could lead Iran to be part of a regional coalition for supporting the reinstitution of effective sovereignty in Iraq.

SETTING NEW STRATEGIC PRIORITIES

The United States largely has to reverse its strategic priorities. State failure in the Gulf (and throughout the globe) should be viewed as the primary threat to the United States and its long-term goals of global economic growth, political liberalization, and military security. Traditional interstate competition between Middle Powers, Great Powers, and the lone superpower—including strategic competition with Iran—should take a definite backseat to a concern about sovereign collapse in Iraq.

---

individuals. From a larger geopolitical standpoint, as argued in this paper, the claim of active Iranian aid makes little sense, and in any case pales in comparison to the top-down creation and support of al Qaeda-linked groups by the Pakistani Inter-Service Intelligence apparatus in the decades leading up to 9/11. Furthermore, it is doubtful that Iranian authorities would have known of these individual's concrete plans. Just because there are some individuals of very dubious reputation crossing borders from one state to another, this does not mean that the authorities of all the states in question (including Germany in 2001) actually knew about these men's exact plans for catastrophic terrorism against the Twin Towers in New York. Prior to 9/11, it was the standard practice of governments of many countries, both western and eastern, to more passively track, analyze, and monitor the travels of such individuals without actually arresting and detaining them on a regular basis.

PREVENTING THE CONTAGION OF CIVIL CONFLICT IN A REGION COMPOSED OF STRUGGLING SOVEREIGN STATES

What the US implicitly believes about Iran should be explicitly assumed about Iraq: a collapsed Iraqi state will upset Persian Gulf stability and security, result in the spread of noxious forms of radical, anti-western terrorism, lead to worse relations between Muslims and the west (and between different Islamic sects), and thus endanger political, social, economic, and military order throughout the region. Sovereign collapse in Iraq will cause friends and allies within the region to feel more insecure as a direct result of US actions—from Turkey to Saudi Arabia, from the Levant to the Gulf. Ultimately, a failed Iraqi state and a period of indefinite internecine warfare will undermine the security of the average US citizen far more than a strong Iran with a potential, latent nuclear weapons infrastructure. Thus, for the United States to succeed in Iraq and the region, the problem of regional stability should be redefined as the construction of a multilateral coalition to prevent the spread of the "contagion" of civil violence in a Middle East composed of relatively new sovereign states.

> **What the US implicitly believes about Iran should be explicitly assumed about Iraq: a collapsed Iraqi state will upset Persian Gulf stability and security, result in the spread of noxious forms of anti-radical, anti-Western terrorism and lead to worse relations between Muslims and the West.**

The reason that Iraq is a regional security problem is not only its own weakness, but the historical weakness of its neighbors. No state in the region can claim success in the task of sovereign state development. Whether one is speaking of small, rich, and globalized, tribally-based oil monarchies (Oman, Kuwait, Qatar, Bahrain, and the United Arab Emirates), large and rich but illiberal and un-globalized Islamic-theocratic states (Saudi Arabia, Iran), large and secular but very poor and authoritarian, Arab-nationalist states (Syria, Egypt), or states that embody a fluid mix of democracy, authoritarianism, capitalism, secularism, and Islamism (Jordan, Turkey, Lebanon), the simple fact is that none of the current Middle East states is completely immune from some mix of ethnic, religious, and economic conflict that could jeopardize the entire state-building exercise.

All of them still have high rates of poverty and unemployment when compared to fully developed countries in the West (including Israel, if the Arab-Palestinian population is considered as part of the Israeli polity). All of them rely on a heavy dose of military or police control to shore up the ship of state. All of them are simultaneously trying to figure out their niche in a global economy that has largely left them behind (the unsustainable oil rents of Gulf states notwithstanding). Except for the oil-rich states, all of them depend a great deal on external economic aid, and even the oil-rich states have a high "security dependence" in the form of externally-provided military training, weapons, and technological inputs. All of them have overloaded defense and domestic security budgets (Israel included). All of them have relatively high levels of corruption and black-market economic behavior.

Some of them have identities that put them at odds with the global economic system: Iran and Saudi Arabia have brands of theocracy that blend religion and economy in a way that results in political control of markets, which in turn means an antipathy to liberalization. Syria and Egypt have similar antipathies based on a blend of Arab pan-nationalism, socialism, and domestic politics. The result is that for these four states—and perhaps others—economic liberalization and strengthened ties to the international trading system mean a loss of political control, a weakening of bureaucracies or tribal networks and an undermining of the very Arab or Islamic nationalism upon which the states were originally built.

In such a regional environment, the primary threat is not likely to be the use of nuclear weapons by a rogue government against its neighbors. Rather, it is the spread of uncontrolled sectarian violence across and within relatively fragile, rigid, and calcified state structures, whose national identities are still under challenge from cross-cutting tribal, religious, ethnic, and other ideological identities. Identity conflict, social violence, and under-performing governments—not traditional interstate conflict—are the primary threats not just to the Iraqi state but to all Middle East states over the next several decades (Israel included). In this context, reestablishing sovereign authority and stability in Iraq is a minimum requirement for the productive socio-economic development of all Middle East societies. This is a goal enunciated by nearly every US analyst, and certainly championed by both Democrats and Republicans in their ongoing statements about grand US foreign policy goals in the twenty-first century.

Simply put: positive civil society developments such as independent judiciaries, liberalized economies, open media, strong political parties, and dynamic institutions are currently held hostage to the basic lack of international and transnational security in the region. As the failed states of Yugoslavia, Somalia, and others have shown in spades, without security, there is no development and there is no justice. Security—defined as basic political and social order—is a prerequisite for meeting the pro-democracy goals of the new Bush *National Security Strategy of the United States* (NSS).[11]   Paradoxically, even as the Bush Administration has made clear (at least implicitly) that it values a destabilized Syria and Iran over a strong, sovereign Syria and Iran, the overarching goals of the NSS can only be met if there is a re-commitment to the value of sovereign order in a divided region.

GETTING OTHERS ON BOARD

One obvious conclusion of this analysis is that the United States should do all it can to engage a domestically-divided Iran as part of a strategic reorientation of the bilateral US-Iranian relationship. However, it is not just the populist and radical President Ahmadinejad of Tehran who presents difficulties in reorienting US foreign policy toward the containment of civil violence in Iraq. The fact is that all Iraqi neighbors are divided internally about how they should feel in regard to Iraq's fate, and thus, building a stable coalition for action will be extremely difficult. Nonetheless, it must be tried.

THE "STRATEGIC TIGHTROPE PROBLEM": NO ONE WANTS A STRONG IRAQ OR A DISUNITED IRAQ

One of the most basic problems is that beyond Jordan, no neighboring state wants either a strong Iraq or a failed Iraq. Hence, excepting Jordan's unique historical position (in which the economic concerns and strong bilateral trade relations have trumped nearly everything else) every state in the region wants a weak but functional Iraq. This is because a strong Iraq – depending on the nature of its strength—could challenge its neighbors militarily, symbolically (through leadership on pan-Arabism or pan-Islamism), or ethnically.

Moreover, every neighbor seems to want a weak Iraq that is dominated by its favored coalition of forces. Turkey would prefer a secular, non-Islamist Iraq whose secularism is not dominated by the Kurds, but is shared between the Kurds and others who can check Kurdish designs for autonomy. Iran wants a broadly Islamist Iraq where the Shia are

---

[11] George W. Bush, *The National Security Strategy of the United States of America* (Washington DC: White House, September 17, 2002), http://www.whitehouse.gov/nsc/nss.html (accessed July 14, 2006).

dominant, but not so dominant they challenge the symbolic leadership of Qom and the actual leadership of transnational groups like Hezbollah. Syria wants an Iraq that does not strengthen any other Middle East player against Syria. It is not really clear that Syria cares whether Iraq is tribal, Islamist, or secular, as long as no faction challenges Syria's internal situation, and no Baghdad government allies with either external powers or Middle East states against Damascus. This is because, in general, Syria's internal and external situation is the most uncertain out of all Middle East states, even Lebanon. The Ba'athist leadership has failed to achieve any of its long-term developmental goals, and it is casting about for a new identity—but what kind of identity is not exactly clear or predictable.

Saudi Arabia would like a secular Iraq, given that an Islamic-defined Iraq would probably be a Shia Islamism (as is currently evolving), rather than the Saudi Wahhabi cultural-ideological version of Sunni Islamism. Overall, however, the main thing Saudi Arabia desires is normality, predictability, and stability. As long as the final resolution is stable, predictable, and does not permanently disenfranchise Sunni groups vis-à-vis others—and, does not empower a hegemonic Iran through a purely Shia definition of Iraqi identity—the leaders in Riyadh will be relatively content and relieved.

Meanwhile, Israel does not want an Iraq that, as in the case of Saddam, can build long-range munitions under the banner of anti-Zionist pan-Arabism (or the potential of a pan-Islamic ideology that is equally noxious to Israeli security). And the small Gulf Arab monarchies want an Iraq that does balance Iranian hegemonic designs, but does not pose an equally hegemonic threat of its own.

Jordan just wants a stable Iraq that does not create a dominant Shia arc (which puts Jordan at the intersection of such an arc, from the Gulf in the East to the Levant in the West), and which does not create either war or an economic vacuum, so that the traditionally lucrative flow of goods, oil, and black market items can be re-instituted. Jordan likes to think of itself as the puzzle piece in the Middle East that links East and West, North and South—but it wants this linkage to be economic, largely secular in character, and to some extent controllable by the leadership in Amman. It does not want such a linkage to be what is currently the case: transnational terrorist zealots, arms smuggling, and drug trafficking. It also does not want the final government in Iraq to view itself as a challenger to neighbors of both countries, because Jordan wants equally good relations with those states as well. So, a strong Iraq is fine, but not the kind of strength that presents an ideological or military challenge to

Israel or the Gulf states, which would put Jordan in the difficult position of choosing between friends (which was the case with Saddam in 1990).

Finally, none of Iraq's neighbors want Iraq to be a stomping ground for extremist, unpredictable, and uncontrollable fundamentalists whose main goal is simply the destabilization of every regional government. This probably constitutes the only truly shared interest among both Iraq's neighbors and across all external parties as well.

CONCLUSION: AVOIDING INTERNAL IRAQI HEGEMONY

Given the sheer diversity of geopolitical views outlined in short form above, there are really only two Iraqi domestic futures possible: a united Iraq that avoids internal hegemony by any one socio-political group, or a disunited Iraq in which all groups strive for domestic hegemony, based on aid from competing neighbors. The latter reality is what is currently forming, to the detriment of everyone, and to the benefit of Bin Ladenists who thrive on chaos.

In this regard, the worst malefactors are the two most hegemonic powers overall: the United States and Iran. It may seem strange to put them in the same boat, but think about the contributions thus far by all the other actors above. Syria is manipulating tribesmen and possibly even Islamists in areas immediately neighboring Syria's border with Iraq. Destructive nightmares like Fallujah are the result of indigenous resistance to Sunni disempowerment at the hands of Kurds, US occupiers, and Shia alike. Syria is neither "pro-Sunni" nor "pro-Shia," nor, for that matter, pro-Islamist or pro-secularist. None of the worst atrocities of the past three years can realistically be blamed on Syria, despite its itinerant meddling; because its meddling has lacked any predictable, strategic character, other than making sure no Iraqi force threatens Syrian unity. Syria has no overall vision for the future of Iraq that can truly act as a destabilizer and regional threat overall. This is because Syria has no strategic vision for itself and its own future. Syria's own internal confusion has kept it from being a major player for either good or ill in Iraq.

Meanwhile, Turkey has a minimalist, defensive goal: no Kurdish state, no permanent Kurdish autonomy from Baghdad. This is a goal shared by both Syria and Iran, so Turkish actions to keep the Kurds from threatening its own unity will inevitably be of strategic benefit to Syria and Iran. If the Kurds are not threatening the sovereign experiment in Ankara, they are also probably not threatening the sovereignty of either Syria or Iran. Turkey's main goal is also endorsed by all external powers, who do not want a Yugoslavia-type mess after the exhausting years of repeated Balkan crises in the 1990s. The Turkish threat to Iraqi stability is really latent and deterrent in character: if the Kurds were to get too big for their britches, then Turkey might be forced to intervene through ugly paramilitary and/or military actions across the border.

Similarly in the south, Saudi Arabia's goals will not be a threat, as long as it does not feel impelled to start acting on its fears of Sunni disempowerment and Shia dominance. Saudi Arabia, though viewed by many as radical in its internal Wahhabi vision and its transnational support of madrassas in Pakistan and Central Asia, is a conservative power in the Middle East itself. Stability has always been its main goal within its own region, as witnessed by Al-Arabiya's biased trumpeting of the secular Iraqi parties in the December elections, at Saudi behest. If, however, things become too lopsided in Iraq on an ethnic and religious (Sunni) basis, in a way that threatens Sunni Islam as a whole and Saudi Arabian identity in particular, Saudi Arabia has the means, and could have the will, to support some very virulent and nasty players in Iraq. This is a latent threat that has not yet materialized, and the entire region and all external actors have an interest in keeping Saudi involvement small, cautious and conservative in nature.

So, we are left with an embarrassing reality: two countries with great power designs on the Middle East region overall that also have been destabilizing things via hegemonic pursuits within Iraq itself. The United States is equally at fault as the Iranians in this regard. While Iran has made sure the Shia bloc is dominant, the United States also has indirectly supported this exact same goal through its overweening focus in the first year of occupation on total dismantlement of a pan-Arabist government structure.

Many were confused by de-Ba'athification, but it makes perfect sense if one assumes that the US did not just want a democratic Iraq, but also a certain type of democratic outcome that forswore strong Arab nationalism that would challenge Israel or the US vision for the entire region. The United States has never been happy with socialist-leaning, pan-Arabist visions, as witnessed by its strengthening of Saudi Arabia throughout the Cold War. In Iraq, it had the chance to dismantle one of the last pan-Arabist states, from top to bottom, and the US took it. The hope was to create a globalized, liberalized state of the kind that Robert Zoellick and other free-trade, democratic idealists have trumpeted, as reflected in our bilateral Free Trade Agreements (FTAs) with neighboring Gulf Arab states. Pan-Arab nationalism has not traditionally been kind to this distinctly libertarian, Wilsonian vision, and has been a proud, nationalist thorn in the side of western designs for decades now (hence the US leveling of all Ba'athist institutions in Baghdad). The US insistence on a right to keep military bases is clearly meant to provide a landed intelligence and Special Forces capability for potential future pressuring (and even use) against rogue states such as Syria and Iran, who challenge US regional dominance.

Meanwhile, paradoxically, this US goal has served Iran's goal of becoming the dominant Gulf hegemon (and potential Middle East hegemon), via the strengthening of a Shia bloc and the production of a thoroughly biased Iraqi Constitution that does not guarantee equality of oil profits or social or political power among contending ethnicities and religious groupings. But, Iran is ultimately failing in its machinations, as well: the Shia groups are becoming discordant and downright distrustful of each other, each of them trying to trump the leadership of the other, and the Supreme Council for the Islamic Revolution in Iraq (SCIRI) and Muqtada Al-Sadr harbor their own strong, independent militias toward this political end. The result has been an angry and disillusioned Kurdish bloc as well as an alienated and largely powerless Sunni bloc, and the complete undermining of secularists of all stripes. In other words: Iranian and US meddling have together created an Iraq on the edge of sovereign collapse.

The only way out of this Iraqi-cum-regional disaster is to work multilaterally for a balance of interests both throughout the region and within Iraq domestically. If neither Iran nor the US give up on the goal of dominating the region ideologically, economically, and militarily, their macro-level hegemonic goals will continue to be reflected in their internal Iraqi actions, creating a failed Iraq and hence, an insecure region with an unsure oil supply to the global economy, which will hurt Iran and the US.

It is not clear, unfortunately, if it is still possible to turn the ship of Iraqi state toward a more balanced outcome. Despite the recent formation of a government, which has a relatively moderate Shia elite calling for the disbanding of paramilitary groups and militias that have been guilty of atrocities against each other and against Sunnis, stability could still be tenuous because the original constitution on which the new government is based is extremely flawed. The Shia groups with strong militias and domestic supporters are not likely to agree to a renegotiation of the Iraqi Constitution—something that objectively must happen, if the secularists and the Sunnis are going to feel secure and confident in their future. And it is not clear if the Kurds are willing to give up their own designs on areas such as Kirkuk.

The US has finally started pressuring various groups in Baghdad to go back to the negotiating table for a fair and balanced outcome, but this pressure may be coming too late. With troops clearly on the edge of a drawdown due to lack of support on Capitol Hill, what exactly is the leverage of the United States over either Kurds with de facto autonomy in the North, or Shia with de facto political control in the South? Meanwhile, it is also not clear if Iran still has real influence over the separate components of the United Iraqi Alliance (Hizb Al-Dawah, SCIRI, and Muqtada Al-Sadr), or if various groups have become powerful enough on their own to do what they want, dragging Iran into their own designs rather than reflecting Tehran's and Qom's external preferences.

In any case, a balanced outcome in Iraq—a non-hegemonic domestic outcome expressed through a new constitution that accepts (and in fact trumpets) a diversified and heterogeneous Iraqi national identity—will be impossible to produce if the United States and Iran both continue their larger regional strategies, as currently defined. The current definition of security for both is to beat back or weaken other sovereign competitors. In the view of both, other states national strength is a potential threat, not a potential asset. But for Iraq to come out of this tragedy as a unified actor, the US and Iranian pursuit of strategic hegemony against other states—which holds out the goal of weakening others—must take a backseat to sovereign equality between states, as expressed in a balance of interests among all regional players. The main threat to the US is not Iranian strength, and the main threat to Iran is not US strength; rather, the threat to both (and to all others in the region) is Iraq's eternal weakness and even dissolution. The goal must not be to win a strategic competition, but rather, to ensure sovereign order.

— 11 —
IRAQ AND AMERICA...AND IRAN:
A POLICY CONUNDRUM

Ellen Laipson

In Spring 2006, the central Middle East policy preoccupation for the Bush Administration shifted from Iraq to Iran. Iraq policy, for better or worse, is on the wane, with efforts increasingly focused on limiting political fallout, reducing casualties, and transferring the burden for governance, security and reconstruction to the Iraqis. Iran policy is on the rise, to measure by frequency of pronouncements and high level meetings on the subject. But the two policies are intertwined, in no small measure because the countries are neighbors, and what the United States does in one can directly affect the other. How they relate to each other also has consequences for US interests, and their relations are in flux as US policy attention shifts. This triangular dynamic is complicated and requires careful calibration. A strategic policy process that envisions long-term goals for the United States in both countries would establish a useful framework; the consequences will be significant for US global leadership and credibility.

CHANGING LINKAGES IN US POLICIES
TOWARDS IRAN AND IRAQ

The United States has long struggled to manage and relate its policies regarding the two large regional states and would-be hegemons, Iran and Iraq. Over the last quarter century, we have attempted different approaches to the region. In the twin pillars policy in the 1970s, we embraced Iran as our strategic partner (along with Saudi Arabia) against radical Arab nationalism. During the Iran-Iraq war, we rooted for both to lose, but, once Iran had the upper hand and was on Iraqi soil, discreetly provided some assistance to Iraq, judging that a victorious Iran was the greater danger to US interests.

In the 1990s, dual containment was premised on the need to isolate both Iran and Iraq, in the hopes of encouraging more moderate policies and more buy-in to international norms and values. The end of the Cold War eliminated the need to justify building up one regional actor as a proxy in the superpower struggle.

At the turn of the new century, both countries continued to defy the new international order, and were again conceptually linked in the new Administration's foreign policy formulations. Both were seen as outliers, as rogue states. There was a symmetry of sins: both were objectionable for their weapons of mass destruction policies, their support for terrorism, their opposition to the Arab-Israeli peace process, and their poor human rights records at home.

But after September 11, the policies diverged. Although the two countries were linked in the famous "Axis of Evil" speech of January 2002, the Administration decided to move first on Iraq. Asserting that the danger of Iraq was imminent, Iraq became the second front in the Global War on Terrorism. Preparations for the war that was launched in 2003 were visible throughout 2002, while a sometimes half-hearted diplomatic process continued. The Administration used weapons of mass destruction (WMD) as the primary thrust of its rationale for war, and made another critical judgment that distinguished the policy from that towards Iran. In the case of Iraq, the Administration judged that regime change could not occur from within; the system of repression was too strong, and the Iraqi people could not win back their own freedom.

By contrast, Iran policy lagged, with virtually no policy decisions or actions. On the issue of regime change, Iran was seen as more open politically and its people more capable of taking matters into their own hands. Therefore, strategies of regime change need not include military action. In addition, Iran's WMD ambitions were initially understood to be on a slower trajectory. Compared to North Korea, the Administration seemed to think there was time to take a measured approach, albeit with strongly critical rhetoric. The policy was defined by continued sanctions, harsh rhetoric and open skepticism about the value or purpose of engagement.

This recent history of US policies towards Iran and Iraq is defined by *negative* interests: we knew what we didn't like, and we acted to prevent and deter action by and interaction with these two states. Our policy tools were containment and sanctions, and we saw the isolation of both states, not engagement, as the most effective means to achieve our stated goals there. As a result, economic and cultural connections withered, and human contact between the two societies was severely curtailed. There are few American interest groups who promote positive relations with either state, other than émigrés with complicated political agendas. This is not a trivial handicap when formulating new policies under different circumstances.

At present, US policies are driven by immediate requirements, from actions to persuade Iran to suspend its nuclear program to a host of political and military decisions aimed at bringing more domestic calm to Iraq. There is little evidence of strategic planning for a different or more desirable future: is our goal normal, stable relations with both states? To create an environment for them to live peacefully as neighbors? Do we expect Iraq to be a key partner of the United States and potential leader in the Arab world, as Egypt and Saudi Arabia have been? Can we engage the regional states in meaningful consultations about their strategies for regional security, and the role US forces would play in a different security arrangement? These kinds of questions are difficult for policymakers to ponder when the current situation requires countless tactical decisions, and when the situation is too fluid to allow for focus on a distant horizon. But this focus on the near-term demands can create unintended tensions or contradictions that need to be addressed.

DECONFLICTING CURRENT US POLICIES

At present, the divergence of policy energy and momentum has begun to take its toll. The Bush Presidency will be defined by its engagement in Iraq, and until recently, it looked at Iran through the Iraq prism. Was Iran's behavior undermining US policy objectives? How could Iran's special access to rising Shia power centers be contained so that Iraq did not become a new Iran, from the vantage point of Islamic political institutions? More immediately, was Iran a key source of support to radical groups attacking US troops and the fledgling Iraqi security forces? Was Iran developing ties to Sunni insurgents as well as their natural allies in the Shia community? Our policy of seeking more engagement by Iraq's neighbors was premised on not letting Iran monopolize Iraq, but Arab reluctance to invest political capital there presented the enduring challenge of trying to manage or set limits on the extent of Iranian influence in Iraq.

The rise of Iran on the US foreign policy priority list could be accelerated by the ongoing situation in Iraq. In a best case, success in Iraq would have a salutary effect on Iran, persuading Iran to cooperate with the international community over its nuclear program and other acute issues. Assuming no such easy outcome, however, the Administration may hope to engage Iraq as a supporting player in Iran policy; this presupposes that Iraq's leaders agree with their fellow Arabs that a nuclear-armed Iran will be a disaster for the Arab world. But it is more likely that Iraq will avoid such a hard choice and see its own vital interest lying more in developing a normal relationship with Tehran rather than associating itself with US goals.

They are uncertain about our real intentions regarding democracy: in Iraq, we want citizens to give the state a chance to succeed, while in Iran we want to further stimulate public disaffection and even disobedience towards the state.

The US government probably has little insight into how current decision makers in Baghdad and Tehran relate to each other and how they talk about the American role in the region. US policies towards both Iraq and Iran are surely on the agenda when Iraqi and Iranian ministers hold their increasingly frequent meetings. Iraq and Iran may harbor some separate but parallel concerns about America's strategic agenda; at one level, they may welcome US moves to weaken or contain the difficult neighbor, but they may fear US over-confidence about inducing change, which could result in greater instability for both. When the US threatens the use of military force if diplomatic efforts fail in stopping Iran's nuclear program, Iraqis must worry how such a development would affect them, whether it leads to an unwelcome quick drawdown of US forces, or engages their territory in an attack on such an important neighbor. Iran, according to some experts, could respond to such pressure by stirring the pot in Iraq, mobilizing clandestine forces to create more violence to dissuade the US military from action in Iran.[1] In the event of open hostilities between Washington and Tehran, Iraqi Shia might feel solidarity with Iran, but many Iraqis would find no solace in such an outcome, and would fear both Iranian defiance, and US ambition to see change in Iran; both would bring only more chaos.

In both countries, popular attitudes towards the United States are complex and subject to mood swings. One legacy of the long periods of non-engagement has been our severely limited ability to anticipate or understand how the people in the two countries will react to various US policies. We are prone to very simplistic and self-serving formulas: they will like us because we have liberated them from a dictator, or from the

---

[1] Geoff Kemp, *Iran and Iraq: The Shia Connection, Soft Power and the Nuclear Factor*, Special Report 156 Iraq and its Neighbors Series (Washington DC: US Institute of Peace, November 2005), 15.

failures of the revolution. In reality, both societies harbor deep resentments about the lack of support from the international community, and from the toll of many years of US or UN-imposed economic sanctions. They are also uncertain about our real intentions regarding democracy: in Iraq, we want citizens to give the state a chance to succeed, while in Iran we want to further stimulate public disaffection and even disobedience towards the state. This divergence of tactics and approach can lead to some surprising responses to new US policies; such unpredictability in public opinion warrants care and humility in structuring our policies and public pronouncements.

EVOLVING IRAQ-IRAN RELATIONS

By now, the cartoon image of cunning Iranian operatives pulling the strings of their Iraqi puppets and bankrolling their every act of violence has been replaced with a more nuanced and multi-dimensional appreciation of Iraq-Iran relations. Iran and Iraq are attempting to build a more normal relationship, to regulate some of the informal networks of trade and religious travel, and to impede insurgent or paramilitary activity across the border. In 2004, the two countries restored formal diplomatic ties, which had been severed for over 20 years. The level of representation was restored to full ambassadorial level in May 2006. There has been one presidential level visit (President Talabani visited Iran in November 2005), and countless ministerial exchanges have taken place.

Trade is growing; in 2006 Iran had plans for over $1 billion in investment in revitalizing Iraq's industrial sector.[2] Iran provides electricity to Basra. The two energy sectors also have a trade relationship, and rely on each other for refining capacity, swaps and transit arrangements. There are policies to regulate the flow of pilgrims; an estimated seven-thousand Iranian pilgrims visit shrines in Iraq per week, often with security forces guarding them, and a comparable level of Iraqis are permitted to enter Iran for religious purposes as well.[3] These are just some examples of the multiple ways the two societies interact.

---

[2] Muthana Aidan, "Iran to invest $1 billion in Iraq," *Azzaman*, March 2, 2006, http://www.azzaman.com/english/index.asp?fname=news%5C2006-03-02%5C206.htm (accessed July 14, 2006).

[3] "Iranian Pilgrims to Iraq have Doubled to 7,000 a Week," *IranMania*, June 28, 2002, http://www.iranmania.com/news/ArticleView/Default.asp?NewsCode=10894&NewsKin (accessed July 14, 2006).

There are, of course, more complex interactions in the security arena. Iran has trained and supported several of the key militia (the Badr Brigade, Dawa, and the newer Mahdi Army loyal to Moqtada Sadr) that are now supposed to be integrated into the national forces, or disbanded. Iran will almost certainly look for ways to maintain assets and capabilities in the Iraqi security forces, even if its direct allies are merged into the national structure. The two governments cooperate on illegal migration; some scores of Iranians who entered Iraq illegally are in Iraqi prisons, but it is hard to gauge what percent of the total traffic that represents. Iran will continue to have multiple security agendas in Iraq: it wants the central government to develop the competence to defend its borders and maintain internal security, but it will almost certainly take measures that subtly undermine the ability of the Iraqi state to fully control the means of violence in the country, and will hold in reserve agents who can serve Tehran's agenda should subversion or sabotage be deemed necessary.

The new Iraqi government has begun to take charge of its relations with Iran, and to distance itself from US policy towards Iran. Foreign Minister Hoshayr Zebari must have pleased his Iranian counterpart when he told the press in late May 2006 that "Iran doesn't claim that they want to obtain a nuclear weapon or a nuclear bomb, so there is no need that we ask them for any guarantee now."[4] Other statements by Iraqi officials regarding immunity for US soldiers, etc., must assure Iran that Iraq is not allowing Washington to dictate its foreign policy. US Ambassador to Iraq, Zalmay Khalilzad, however, sees Iraq's political class as gaining confidence and therefore, more likely to perceive that they have many options in the region, and should avoid over-reliance on Iran.[5] The argument that Iraq can hold its own in relations with Iran depends, however, on the Arab world giving Iraq more attention and support, so that Iraq can establish a balanced regional posture. This is an issue on which Iraq and the United States strongly agree.

GETTING TO WIN-WIN-WIN?

After three years of bruising engagement with Iraq, it is time to revisit how Iraq policy and Iran policy relate to each other. Consistency is not the objective, but effectiveness is. The two policies need not mirror each other, but they need to take into account what is happening next door,

---

[4] "Iraqi Minister Defends Iranian Nuclear Program," *CNN.com*, May 26, 2006, http://www.cnn.com/2006/WORLD/meast/05/26/iraq.iran (accessed July 14, 2006).

[5] Zalmay Khalilzad, "Iraq: A Status Report" (speech, Center for Strategic and International Studies, Washington, DC, July 11, 2006).

and, ideally, might be contained in a single strategy for the region that would maximize prospects for peace and stability for all regional actors, including the United States.

It should not be viewed as political criticism to assert that neither US policy toward Iran nor policy toward Iraq have been successful; it is empirically true that we have not achieved our stated goals in Iraq, and our Iran policy has been a default policy for decades. Is it possible to use the current high-level attention to both countries as an opportunity to find a more promising and positive trajectory? We need to look for ways to have the two policies reinforce each other, and work towards common strategic objectives. While deeply immersed in the hard work of today, there should be more evidence of planning for tomorrow. We need to catch up for many years of estrangement from both Iraq and Iran. This is work that must be done by the national security community, but it can also involve diverse actors in our respective societies, building bridges for a more promising time.

> *For now, we seem to believe that American military power and presence constitutes the regional system, for better or worse. There must be more than could be done to think strategically with the regional players about alternative systems that rely more on local capabilities.*

There is no guarantee that new American initiatives would be received positively by either Iraq or Iran. There is deep suspicion across the Muslim world about American intentions, and publics in these two relatively literate and modern societies are still prone to seeing an American hand when anything goes wrong in the region. But the toll of decades of estrangement, the new challenges of Islamic extremism and insurgency in Iraq, and the realities of globalization all provide incentives for some fresh thinking and new vocabulary in dealing with the regional powers.

First, we should develop a more positive vision for Iran, for a more promising time in US-Iranian relations. Such a public discourse would be useful in communicating to the Iranian people over the heads of their leaders, and removing some of the uncertainty in the Iranian public's mind about our long-term goals. It would be helpful to express our hope for a "normal" relationship, and for resumed cultural, economic and societal contact.

Second, we need to begin to consider a range of roles Iraq might play in the region. A confident, stable Iraq will be a positive outcome for US policy, but it does not necessarily mean that Iraq will be a reliable partner for all US plans and intentions in the region. We may want to encourage Iraq to step forth when it is ready as a regional leader, as it was in the past, but that will have consequences for the region and for US relations with other key players.

We also need to be clearer and more open about the US role in regional security. For now, we seem to believe that American military power and presence constitutes the regional system, for better or worse. There must be more that could be done to think strategically with the regional players about alternative systems that rely more on local capabilities. This will require more transparency on our part and theirs about energy security as well as more traditional concepts of security.

For the short-to medium term, the US project in Iraq is likely to produce more uncertainty and instability, even if over a decade, the Iraqis themselves manage to create a more stable and representative state and society. It is hard to imagine a breakthrough in US-Iran relations for the remainder of the Bush presidency, and until Iran's president is ready to act in a less defiant way towards the international community. But given the record of US policies towards these large, ambitious, and independent states over several decades, it is worth pondering if a larger frame that articulates a positive vision for US engagement with both would be a useful first step in building a more effective regional policy.

— 12 —
POST-COMBAT STABILIZATION AND RECONSTRUCTION: THE LESSONS FOR US GOVERNMENT ORGANIZATION AND NATIONAL SECURITY RESOURCE PLANNING

Gordon Adams[1]

INTRODUCTION

Once the initial phase of full combat ended in Iraq, the United States government found itself in the unanticipated role of a long-term occupying power, with major responsibilities for post-conflict stabilization and reconstruction (S&R).[2] The successes and failures of the past three years of occupation have raised troubling questions about the way in which the US government is organized and carries out budgetary planning for this kind of responsibility.

---

[1] This paper is based, in part, on research on national security resource planning and budgeting that the author is conducting jointly with Dr. Cindy Williams of the Security Studies Program at the Massachusetts Institute of Technology. The author's work is being supported by the John D. and Catherine T. MacArthur, Smith Richardson, and Compton Foundations and the Ploughshares Fund. The author wishes to thank Brian Harding, Cindy Williams and the members of the working group on national security budget processes supporting the research project, as well as Ellen Laipson and Maureen Steinbruner, for their help and advice.

[2] A number of terms have been used to describe US military and civilian operations that follow or are not full-scale military combat. In the 1990s, the Defense Department commonly used the term "Military Operations Other Than War" (MOOTW), or "peacekeeping," to describe these operations. The term "contingency operations" was generally used to describe the Somalia, Rwanda, and especially Haiti and the Balkans deployments, security and reconstruction activities. In the early twenty-first century, "nation-building," though often disparaged, was frequently used to describe operations that required both military and civilian activity in countries where government had failed, forces had been deployed, and rebuilding of some kind was needed after a more combat-driven phase of operations. By 2004, the term "stabilization and reconstruction" came to be used, with specific reference to Afghanistan and Iraq. This article will use this latter phrase (S&R) to describe government actions of any magnitude that follow active combat use of US military force or involve both the military and the civilian capabilities of the federal government to seek to bring order and stability to a country, combined with programs that target socio-economic recovery and the strengthening of governance in that country.

US government structures, programs and resource planning for S&R in Iraq fell manifestly short, including failure of the interagency process for policy-making, inadequate planning, serious underestimation of costs and requirements (both military and civilian), an overestimation of the absorptive capacity of the Iraqi economy and major problems with program implementation and reporting.

These weaknesses and failures in governmental planning and budgeting have had important consequences for broader national security processes, which no longer function as they should in laying out clear choices and options, setting priorities and providing the detailed analysis required for sound policy-making. As a consequence of the Iraq experience, moreover, the executive branch is struggling to restructure itself and reform its processes for dealing more effectively with the challenges of future S&R operations. The Iraq experience also has exposed significant weaknesses in Congressional structures and processes for policy oversight and resource planning that will need to be addressed to cope with the cross-cutting realities of twenty-first century national security challenges. It is important to codify these lessons for the future, since, as in the recent past, the US is highly likely to be involved in future S&R operations, albeit possibly on a less dramatic scale than those in Iraq.[3]

Iraq is not the first S&R challenge the US government has faced. On a major scale in Germany and Japan, and a smaller, but not insignificant scale in Somalia, Haiti, Rwanda, Kosovo, East Timor, Afghanistan, and a large number of humanitarian interventions, post-conflict S&R operations have been a significant part of the US use of military force overseas for more than 50 years.[4] While the lessons of earlier S&R operations could have been harvested and applied, virtually every US post-combat S&R operation since the end of the Second World War has been created and managed as a one-off, with little learning applied to subsequent cases.

The Clinton administration made an effort to generalize from the intervention experiences of the 1990s, proposing a process for more

---

[3] A 2004 Defense Science Board summer study, led by Craig Fields and Philip Odeen, concluded that since 1990, the end of the Cold War, the US has started stabilization and reconstruction operations every 18-24 months, with operations lasting typically 5-8 years. Defense Science Board, *Transition to and from Hostilities*, 2004 Summer Study (Washington, DC: Office of the Under Secretary of Defense for Acquisition, Technology and Logistics, December 2004).

[4] James Dobbins, et al., *America's Role in Nation-Building: From Germany to Iraq*, (Santa Monica, CA: RAND Corporation, 2003).

systematic planning for post-conflict S&R.[5] But the proposed process was not implemented in the subsequent intervention in Kosovo. The Bush administration entered office highly critical of what it called the "nation-building" and peacekeeping uses of US military forces, but rapidly found itself facing this kind of challenge following the use of combat forces in Afghanistan and Iraq. As a result of these experiences, the Administration has increasingly focused on how to structure the government to deal more effectively with similar future cases.[6]

This discussion begins with a brief review of the planning and implementation of post-conflict operations in Iraq. It then evaluates some of the lessons learned to date from that experience: information/intelligence/planning assumptions; institutional and planning issues; implementation of S&R operations; flexible spending authorities; budgetary issues; and Congressional budgeting and oversight.

THE CASE OF IRAQ

Given the size of the deployment, the duration, the financial costs, and the enormous consequences for the US military of the Iraq occupation, it constitutes perhaps the limiting case for examining such S&R operations and provides a number of potential lessons learned. According to the Congressional Research Service, through fiscal year (FY) 2006, Congress will have appropriated roughly $350 billion for Iraq operations, including both military and foreign assistance activities.[7] Moreover, annual appropriations for Iraq have risen regularly over the past four years from $51 billion in FY 2003, to $77 billion FY 2004, to $87 billion

---

[5] Presidential Decision Directive, *Managing Complex Contingency Operations, PDD/NSC 56*, (May 1997), http://clinton2.nara.gov/WH/EOP/NSC/html/documents/NSCDoc2.html (accessed July 14, 2006).

[6] US Department of Defense, Military *Support for Stability, Security, Transition and Reconstruction Operations*, Directive Number 3000.05 (November 28, 2005), http://www.dtic.mil/whs/directives/corres/pdf/d300005_112805/d300005p.pdf (accessed July 16, 2006); National Security Presidential Directive, *Management of Interagency Efforts Concerning Reconstruction and Stabilization*, NSPD-44 (December 7, 2005), http://www.fas.org/irp/offdocs/nspd/nspd-44.html. NSPD-44 superseded PDD-56.

[7] Amy Belasco, *The Cost of Iraq, Afghanistan, and Other Global War on Terror Operations Since 9/11*, Congressional Research Service Report #RL33110, (Washington, DC: CRS, June 16, 2006), 4; This number includes a pro-rated estimate (by this author) of the $50 b. "bridge fund" likely to be voted by the Congress as transition funding to a future FY 2007 supplemental budget request. The Congressional Budget Office estimates that all US military operations in Iraq, Afghanistan and the global effort to combat terrorism could cost an additional $371 b. between FY 2007 and FY 2016; Congressional Budget Office, *An Alternative Path Assuming a Reduction in Spending for Military Operations in Iraq and Afghanistan and in Support of the Global War on Terrorism* (Washington DC: CBO, February 24, 2006), http://www.cbo.gov/ftpdocs/70xx/doc7048/02-24-AlternativePath.pdf.

in FY 2005, to \$100 billion in FY 2006.[8] US military forces in Iraq, generally said to be around 138,000, are actually closer to 200,000 if one counts forces in the entire theater, including those at sea, that are relevant to Iraq military operations.[9]

From the early planning stages for the post-combat period to budget planning, implementation of the policy, and oversight and evaluation, post-conflict S&R in Iraq may be the poster-child for negative lessons, despite the considerable funding and serious effort made by government officials and private contractors. Lessons from past S&R operations were not taken into account, initial planning was short-sighted and based on erroneous assumptions, budgets were not prepared for the post-conflict period, ad hoc structures were created to implement the policy and then changed on the ground in rapid succession, execution has been slow and relatively ineffective both with respect to stabilization and reconstruction, and Congressional oversight of this operation has been virtually non-existent.

The failures of pre-conflict planning for Iraq S&R have been widely reported.[10] The Department of Defense (DoD) lacked the planning, budgeting, statutory authorities, staff and training to plan or implement the kind of stabilization and reconstruction operation that proved to be needed.[11] Moreover, DoD planners systematically sought to exclude foreign policy and assistance agencies from the planning effort. The State Department had coordinated a "Future of Iraq" study for more than a year, involving both interagency representatives and substantial participation by Iraqi exiles.[12] The DoD, however, had prevailed in the

---

[8] Belasco, *The Cost of Iraq*, 4. On a monthly basis, CRS estimates that the Department of Defense will be spending around \$8 b. a month. Ibid., 13, 15.

[9] The total relevant force is difficult to calculate for a variety of technical and reporting reasons. Ibid., 25-28, 29.

[10] George Packer, *The Assassins' Gate: America in Iraq* (NY: Ferrar, Straus and Giroux, 2005) 3-148; Larry Diamond, *Squandered Victory: The American Occupation and the Bungled Effort to Bring Democracy to Iraq* (New York: Times Henry Holt & Company, 2005) 67-102; Michael R. Gordon and General Bernard E. Trainor, *Cobra II: The Inside Story of the Invasion and Occupation of Iraq* (New York: Pantheon Books, 2006); David L Phillips, *Losing Iraq: Inside the Postwar Reconstruction Fiasco*, (NY: Westview, 2005); Interviews with members of the working group on national security budget processes.

[11] James Dobbins, who was involved in post-war relief operations in Somalia, Haiti, Bosnia and Kosovo, felt the decision to create ORHA was a mistake. Katherine McIntire Peters, "Blind Ambition," *Government Executive*, July 1, 2004, http://www.govexec.com/features/0704-01/0704-01s3.htm (accessed July 14, 2006).

[12] The complete overview and 12 reports from the 17 working groups in the Future of Iraq Project can be found at "Reports From the Future of Iraq Project," Reports from State Department, (Future

interagency discussion over "unity of command," and had been put in charge through National Security Presidential Directive (NSPD) 24. Gen. Jay Garner, the head of the Office of Reconstruction and Humanitarian Assistance (ORHA), the first institution given responsibility for post-war Iraq, focused on humanitarian issues. Military planners made it clear that the US would rely on the Iraqi army, police forces, provincial government, and ministries, funded by oil revenues, to establish order and carry out reconstruction.[13] Such funding as was needed for post-combat S&R was provided as part of the operating costs for DoD forces in the region.[14]

In addition to the relatively ad hoc way in which post-conflict S&R institutions were created, funded and staffed, the specific management organizations for administering the operations also evolved over time. Planning, priority-setting, and oversight over reconstruction programs passed through the Development Fund for Iraq (DFI, non-US funds), as well as the Iraq Reconstruction and Relief Fund (IRRF). DFI-funded projects were selected, and contracts decided by an ad hoc Program Review Board in the Coalition Provisional Authority (CPA) headquarters in Baghdad. Contracting services were provided largely by the Army Corps of Engineers and the US Agency for International Development (USAID). Projects were implemented and supervised by an ad hoc Program Management Office (PMO), the Army Corps, AID, State, and a number of other agencies. Once the US embassy took responsibility for post-conflict S&R operations in June 2004, a new oversight and contract authority was created – the Iraq Reconstruction and Management Office (IRMO), with a supporting Project Contracting Office (PCO) run largely by the Army Corps of Engineers.

This evolving architecture has been responsible for the management of more than $25 billion in US appropriated funds and, until June 2004, for more than $20 billion in Iraqi resources.[15] In addition, the DoD has

---

of Iraq Project, October 2001) http://www.thememoryhole.org/state/future_of_iraq/ (accessed July 21, 2006); Phillips, *Losing Iraq*.

[13] Gordon and Trainor, *Cobra II*, 144.

[14] ORHA and CPA officials have noted in private interviews that ORHA had difficulty finding funding from the Army, which was understandably focused on prosecuting the military campaign. Given the pressure from policy officials at DoD to execute the military campaign with a constrained force, military planners were reluctant to give priority to Garner's desires for forces assigned to post-war S&R operations. Steven W. Peterson, "Central but Inadequate: The Application of Theory in Operation Iraqi Freedom," (seminar paper, National Defense University, National War College, Washington, D.C. 2004,) 11.

[15] Curt Tarnoff, *Iraq: Recent Developments in Reconstruction Assistance* Congressional Research Service Report RL31833 (Washington, DC: CRS, October 24, 2003) 2, 6.

operated its own programs for reconstruction and stabilization operations, the largest single part of which has been the Commander's Emergency Response Program (CERP).[16] The CERP program grew out of the realization, as combat was ending, that US forces would need resources to deal with budding emergencies well before CPA or any contracting authority could act.

The initial resources for CERP came from the discovery of caches of dollars in the homes of former Iraqi regime officials. With quick action from Washington, these resources were made available at once for such tasks as cleaning streets, collecting garbage, providing rations, repairing roofs, wells, sewers, doors and the like, rehabilitating jails and police stations and meeting urgent medical needs. In June 2003, this ad hoc program became CERP, which would allow commanders "to respond to urgent humanitarian relief and reconstruction requirements within their areas of responsibility, by carrying out programs that will immediately assist the Iraqi people and support the reconstruction of Iraq." Over time, the CERP program grew from $300 million to $500 million, to $850 million in May 2005.[17]

The ad hoc nature of post-conflict S&R operations in Iraq has been mirrored in the way the administration and the Congress have dealt with resourcing Iraq policy in Washington. The first, most serious policy mistake was to underestimate the difficulty and therefore the resources that would be needed to meet the challenge. The administration provided no hard estimate for the military and S&R costs of Iraq operations, but public statements tended to suggest the total cost might be less than $50 billion.

Once the resource implications of Iraq became clear, the normal budgeting process was not used as a channel for managing Iraq-related resource planning. Instead, since 2003, the administration and the Congress have considered resource requirements through a series of out-of-cycle emergency supplemental requests. Virtually all of the $350 billion allocated for Iraq has been funded in this way. Emergency supplemental requests from DoD have been prepared outside the normal agency budget planning processes.[18] In the case of foreign assistance

---

[16] For details on the CERP program, see Special Inspector General for Iraq Reconstruction, *Management of the Commander's Emergency Response Program for Fiscal Year 2005*, SIGIR-05-025 (January 23, 2006); Mark Martins, "No Small Change of the Soldiering the Commander's Emergency Response Program in Iraq and Afghanistan," *Army Lawyer*, February 2004, 1-20.

[17] Special Inspector General for Iraq Reconstruction, *Management*, 1.

and diplomatic operations, the initial $21 billion request from State/USAID was actually drawn up at the CPA in Baghdad, working against a severe deadline and with little budget-quality information.[19]

Normally, the documentation that supports national security budget requests is voluminous, with detailed program descriptions, discussion of program priorities, and details on the ultimate objectives for the program or project. For Iraq, emergency supplemental budget requests rarely provided detailed backup of this kind. Congress, in turn, has held virtually no budget or oversight hearings on post-conflict S&R spending in Iraq. The consequences for the national security budget process are discussed below.

Congress did act to require some detailed reporting on Iraq resource planning. As part of the initial post-conflict S&R approval, Congress required a quarterly report from the State Department describing in detail the categories of spending for which the funds would be used, and reporting on the execution of those amounts. These Section 2207 reports provide the most detail that exists on S&R spending in Iraq, broken down into ten categories. Congress also enacted another important provision, creating the organization which has become the Special Inspector General for Iraq Reconstruction (SIGIR), which has been in operation since 2004, and provides some tracking of program execution and problems in the S&R operation.

This brief summary of planning, implementation, and budgeting for Iraq post-conflict S&R indicates why the program has been subject to criticism. Inadequate pre-conflict planning, ad hoc structures for implementation, personnel difficulties and thin budget planning and scrutiny in Washington, all have created serious concern and a sense that some, perhaps a substantial part of the more than $50 billion invested in security and reconstruction activities may have been wasted, or is at least hard to track.

The consequences of poor planning, shifting needs on the ground, a lack of clear priorities and inadequate administration, have been intense criticism of the program, a failure to create the impact desired in Iraq, and growing realization that some, perhaps even a substantial part of the

---

[18] DoD supplemental budget requests have focused on overall requirements for counter-terror operations and Afghanistan, as well as Iraq; Iraq funding has consumed roughly three quarters of such requests.

[19] Interviews with members of the working group on national security budget processes.

more than $40 billion in overall funds from all sources devoted to reconstruction alone have been wasted. Given the inadequacies of reporting, tracking performance and waste is difficult.[20] As the executive branch and the Congress cope with the Iraq experience, a number of lessons can be drawn that may provide guidance for future S&R operations.

PRELIMINARY LESSONS

Though the entire story of post-conflict stabilization and reconstruction operations in Iraq has yet to be told, a number of preliminary lessons can be drawn for future S&R planning, budgeting and program implementation. A first important set of lessons involves information, intelligence and planning assumptions, which will drive planning and implementation decisions. A second concerns how the executive branch should be organized to plan and execute S&R operations. A third related set has to do with how the funding for such operations should be integrated into the overall federal budget process. A fourth concerns how Congress can provide effective oversight over S&R funding and programs.

INFORMATION, INTELLIGENCE AND PLANNING ASSUMPTIONS

Perhaps the most important lesson of Iraq for future post-conflict stabilization and reconstruction operations involves the information, intelligence and planning assumptions that were the starting basis for thinking about what the post-conflict situation might require. Such information and administration assumptions will have a direct influence on how planning and budgeting is done in anticipation of post-conflict operations. The information available to date on the administration's pre-war thinking about post-war Iraq suggests that the failures and problems in implementation were driven, in part, by the assumptions made at the start.

Briefly, there were several key assumptions and judgments about Iraq that drove pre-war planning and budgeting:

---

[20] The most detailed available reporting on Iraq budgets has been provided by the Congressional Research Service, an agency of the Congress. The greatest detail on actual implementation has been provided by the reports and audits of the Special Inspector General for Iraq Reconstruction, which are available at www.sigir.mil.

- The Iraq operation should be carried out with a minimal number of US forces, relying on technological superiority and the use of "shock and awe" on the Iraqi military.

- The US experience of "nation building" in the 1990s— primarily in the Balkans— had incentivized depending on the US for presence and assistance. This was unacceptable and should not be reproduced in Iraq.

- The United States would carry out the invasion and post-conflict operations with only a small coalition of international support, of which the largest part would be British forces. Reconstruction operations would be small, short-term, Iraqi-led and largely self-funded through oil revenues.

The consequence of making these assumptions and relying on these judgments with respect to Iraq was that planning for post-war Iraq S&R operations was simply not done in the length of time and detail required for effective stabilization and reconstruction to take place.[21]

Although, as Field Marshall von Moltke is said to have observed, no battle plan ever survives contact with the enemy, the absence of a US government plan, driven by these assumptions and judgments, played a key role in leading to the ad hoc, inadequately funded efforts of ORHA and the CPA. The disorganization of the US executive branch and the "on the job" learning curve for organizations responsible for implementation in Iraq might have been avoided, had the assumptions and judgments been different or had differing views been taken into account in the policy process.

INSTITUTIONAL AND PLANNING ISSUES

Sound policy implementation, budgeting and oversight over post-conflict S&R programs depend, to some degree, on the clarity and transparency with which the executive branch is organized to plan and execute such programs. As noted, there was relatively little clear structure for planning and implementation of post-conflict S&R operations in Iraq.

Post-conflict experience clearly suggests that some kind of architecture was needed, to shape clear policy goals, plan for budget requirements, oversee execution, and correct the course, as needed. Such an

---

[21] Gordon and Trainor, *Cobra II*, 503.

organization needed to coordinate a broad number of agencies, communicate clearly and hold implementers accountable.

Despite the history of S&R operations by the United States, the National Security Council and agency infrastructure has never been well prepared for post-conflict realities.[22] This continued to be true in the case of Iraq. The agency tasked by NSPD-24 to lead the effort—the Defense Department— did not develop a specific architecture for Iraq planning and implementation inside the Pentagon, though it did play a central role in the creation of ORHA and the CPA, both of which reported to the Secretary of Defense. The National Security Council (NSC) did task a Senior Director and an executive group to oversee Iraq policy implementation, but that organization left the planning and implementation tasks to the agencies, especially DoD.

The Iraq experience, combined with Afghanistan and smaller interventions in Haiti, the Sudan, and Liberia, has led to efforts to organize the executive branch more systematically for post-conflict stabilization and reconstruction. Both the DoD and the State Department have been affected, as has the interagency process dealing with post-conflict S&R issues.

The Defense Department has come to accept the reality that the US military is likely to be called on to carry out post-conflict operations involving security, reconstruction and governance. Defense Directive (DD) 3000.05, issued November 28, 2005, recognizes this likelihood and treats such operations as equal in mission status with combat operations.[23] DD 3000.05 describes S&R missions as "a core US military mission," which, in the long-term, should "help develop indigenous capacity for securing essential services, a viable market economy, rule of law, democratic institutions, and a robust civil society." This Directive explicitly recognizes that civilian officials may be best able to perform the tasks of developing local governance, promoting economic activity, rebuilding infrastructure, and developing local capacities, but that the military may have to begin such tasks early in an intervention.

---

[22] Neither Defense nor State considered S&R to be core missions, leading to ad hoc structures and policies in every successive intervention. Dobbins, et al., *America's*, xxviii.

[23] Department of Defense Directive 3000.05, *Military Support for Stability, Security, Transition, and Reconstruction (SSTR) Operations* (Washington, DC: Department of Defense, November 28, 2005), http://www.dtic.mil/whs/directives/corres/pdf/d300005_112805/d300005p.pdf (accessed July 19, 2006).

The Directive lays out a path to implement these intentions fully through the DoD policy, acquisition, and budgeting stovepipes. In particular, it instructs the services to make these missions an integral part of training and exercising the forces, and tasks the DoD Comptroller to ensure that the Department's planning, programming and budgeting process has "addressed the resource requirements for stability operations." It also instructs DoD to "work closely" with other relevant US government agencies in such operations.

The administration also has recognized that putting stabilization and reconstruction operations under the responsibility of DoD, which was done in Iraq through June 2004, was not effective. As a result, the DoD directive is paired with a National Security Presidential Directive (NSPD-44), of December 2005, giving the State Department responsibility for managing interagency efforts for Reconstruction and Stabilization.[24] NSPD-44 notes the need for a focal point for a more coordinated stability and reconstruction effort by the US government and the related need to coordinate such efforts more closely with military planning and operations in such cases as complex emergencies, failing and failed states, and transitions from peacekeeping and military interventions.

NSPD-44 calls for the State Department to lead an integrated US government process preparing, planning for, and conducting post-conflict S&R efforts. This responsibility includes creating a process to identify states at risk of instability or collapse, developing strategies and plans for the US response and ensuring program and policy coordination among agencies. While NSPD does provide for a National Security Council level Policy Coordinating Committee in this area, State is given primary responsibility for coordination with DoD, foreign governments, international organizations and non-governmental organizations for these operations. In particular, the NSPD charges State with the responsibility to "resolve relevant policy, program, and funding disputes" among government departments with respect to S&R operations. Other agencies are to coordinate with State in preparing budgets covering these programs and activities.

The DoD Directive and NSPD-44 clearly represent progress, based on the Iraq experience, though Iraq operations have not been included in the NSPD process. These documents and the process they have created may

---

[24] White House, "Management of Interagency Efforts Concerning Reconstruction and Stabilization," *National Security Presidential Directive NSPD-44* (December 7, 2005), http://www.fas.org/irp/offdocs/nspd/nspd-44.html (accessed July 19, 2006); This NSPD superseded PDD-56.

not, however, be adequate to resolve the issues raised by the Iraq experience.

One set of issues involves the Department of Defense. DoD and the military are being asked to walk a difficult path in the Directive and take on major responsibility for reconstruction and governance, at least at the start of an operation, while ensuring that effective coordination takes place with other government agencies, principally State and USAID. One of the major reasons for making DoD responsible for Iraq post-conflict S&R was a sense that the State Department (and USAID) had not been effective in the Balkans and Afghanistan, reflecting mistrust in DoD that State was capable of coordinating and managing such operations. It is still unclear whether Defense officials believe State is capable of leading, coordinating, and implementing such operations. At the same time as issuing the Directive, DoD has recognized that State may have difficulty raising funds to support its coordinating activity. To cope with this problem, DoD has urged, and Congress approved, making $200 million in DoD funds available for S&R operations at State.[25] At the same time, DoD has sought, and is slowly being granted, additional authority to carry out S&R activities of its own, including humanitarian assistance, training and equipping foreign military forces, and engaging more widely in the kind of reconstruction programs funded by the CERP program in Iraq.[26]

There are also continuing issues with respect to the role of State in executing the responsibilities given it in NSPD-44. The State Department created an office of the Coordinator for Stabilization and Reconstruction (S/CRS) in 2004, which was tasked in NSPD-44 as responsible for interagency coordination on post-conflict S&R.[27] The office has been active for the past two years, establishing a process for identifying collapse-prone states, creating a staff of roughly 60 drawn from a number of agencies, developing a planning framework for S&R

---

[25] Section 1206 of the National Defense Authorization Act of FY 2006 makes $100 million in DoD funds available for each of two years, for transfer to State for "immediate reconstruction, security, or stabilization assistance to a foreign country." This authority would need to be renewed for subsequent years. Congress, House, National Defense Authorization Act for Fiscal Year 2006, 109th Cong., H.R.1815, Sec. 1206. Authority to Build the Capacity of Foreign Military Forces, H12739-13175.

[26] Some of this authority (T&E) was legislated in the FY 2006 authorization act; the remainder is in the legislative process deliberating on the FY 2007 National Defense Authorization Act. These additional authorities were agreed on in the executive branch between State and Defense and provide, generally, for the concurrence of the Secretary of State as decisions are made on specific programs and projects.

[27] S/CRS explicitly has no responsibilities with respect to Iraq, Afghanistan or counter-terror operations.

operations, developing plans for a civilian reserve corps, and planning "pilot project" missions in Haiti, sub-Saharan Africa, Congo, and the Sudan.[28]

There remains concern, however, that S/CRS will not be adequate to all of the tasks it has been given.[29] Internally, the organization ranks relatively low in the overall structure of State, making it unclear how effectively it can coordinate other parts of the department or USAID, or have an influence on internal budget decisions. The role of regional bureaus and country desks, which are major players in State decision-making, has not been specified, nor is it clear how S/CRS responsibilities might relate to such important offices as the newly created Office of the Director for Foreign Assistance, or the office responsible for International Narcotics and Law Enforcement. Other organizations in the foreign policy community continue to jockey for turf, concerned that S/CRS may seek to be a program management and implementation office, in addition to coordinating the interagency effort.[30]

It has also been difficult for S/CRS and State to raise the funding for its operations. Budgets for its personnel have been low, limiting the staff size.[31] A two-year effort to acquire a contingency fund of $75-100 million for initial operations has failed in Congress. And the office continues to struggle with defining and creating a civilian reserve corps that could be available for rapid deployment to another country at the early post-conflict phase of operations.[32]

NSPD-44 represents a minimalist model for interagency coordination, defining tasks and responsibilities without changing the existing structure. In Iraq the Army Corps of Engineers, CERP, USAID (through

---

[28] A rather complete description of S/CRS activities and programs is available at http://www.state.gov/s/crs/; See also "An Interview with Carlos Pascual," *Joint Forces Quarterly*, 42, no. 3, (2006): 80-85.

[29] Interviews with government officials.

[30] Interviews with executive branch officials.

[31] Former coordinator Ambassador Carlos Pascual estimates that S/CRS should be funded at $60 million for personnel and operations, another $50 million for a civilian reserve corps, and $200 million for a contingency response fund. Actual funding is $21 million for personnel and operations, with no contingency fund. "An Interview," *Joint Forces*: 85.

[32] S/CRS has personnel and administrative budget of roughly $17 million and no contingency funding to start planning operations or conducting early missions. State has requested $75 million for a Conflict Response Fund that would enable S/CRS to initiate planning in specific contingencies; a similar request for $100 million in the FY 2006 budget was denied by the Congress.

several offices—the Office of Transition Initiatives, the Office for Foreign Disaster Assistance's Disaster Assistance Response Teams, and Development Assistance offices), State Department Economic Support Funds, Treasury Department technical assistance programs, and Justice and FBI training programs all pursued separate agendas that were only "loosely coordinated." To properly integrate the planning, budgeting and implementation machinery, an office like S/CRS would need to have higher status and be significantly better endowed with resources. While S/CRS may make some progress in identifying future states at risk, and in encouraging some pre-planning, as currently envisioned, it will likely lack the strength and resources to change the current way of doing business, which tends to stand up new operations as they appear on the horizon, create ad hoc coordinating mechanisms, and hope the implementation works. The coordination model, especially one run out of one Department, is likely to leave such missions poorly planned and under-resourced.

It is not clear that the civilian coordination and integration responsibility has been put at the right level for effective post-conflict S&R operations. It is difficult to empower one federal department to coordinate the actions of other departments. Asking one department to resolve disputes and budgetary issues with another is often a recipe for stalemate; it is even more difficult if the responsible office is relatively low within the hierarchy of the responsible department. This is particularly true, as the Iraq case suggests, when one is dealing with State and Defense, two of the most powerful agencies in the national security arena. Should the leadership of these agencies be at loggerheads, a situation which clearly obtained during the buildup to the Iraq invasion, there is little hope that one of them can prevail without White House intervention.[33]

History suggests that only the NSC can bring the President's authority to bear over disputing departments, when it comes to national security policy. The importance of the task and the difficulties integrating two or more key agencies' activities (along with the work of dozens of less powerful agencies) may demand a more integrated approach, based at the NSC. Future operations are likely to be considerably more effective if the planning and oversight processes are directly coordinated and institutionalized at the NSC level, which has the experience and authority to resolve interagency disputes. This process could and should be closely linked to the Office of Management and Budget (OMB), which

---

[33] Gabriel Marcel, "National Security and the Interagency Process," in *US Army War College Guide to National Security Policy and Strategy*, ed. J. Boone Bartholomees (Carlisle Barracks, PA: Army War College, July 2004), 253.

has greater capability than any one department to affect the budget allocation decisions of the agencies.

A model of this kind has been proposed by the Center for Strategic and International Studies, among others.[34] It would create a new Senior Director at NSC and an office responsible for developing Presidential guidance for complex contingency operations, integrating interagency planning, and enhancing civilian agency capacity for planning such operations. Operations would be implemented by the agencies, but the NSC would retain a policy integration and oversight role, while Interagency Crisis Planning teams would be created to develop campaign plans.[35]

The foundation for planning, coordination of interagency activity, and policy, legal, and budgetary dispute resolution needs to be established at a more authoritative level than a single department. Should such a structure and process be created, its first task should be to undertake an institutional review of structures, budgets and authorities relating to S&R operations. This process should lead to a proposal for NSC and OMB restructuring to allow timely focus, careful interagency planning, investment in appropriate agency capabilities for such operations, and the redeployment of offices and capabilities to eliminate redundancy and clarify responsibilities. Appropriate distribution of agency responsibilities for S&R should follow from such a review.[36]

---

[34] Clark Murdock and Michele Flournoy, *Beyond Goldwater-Nichols: US Government & Defense Reform for a New Strategic Era; Phase 2 Report* (Washington, DC: Center for Strategic and International Studies, July 2005). The Lugar-Biden bill passed by the Senate, like the CSIS proposal, would create a directorate at NSC to oversee interagency contingency planning. "Reconstruction and Stabilization Civilian Management Act of 2006," S.3322, 109th Cong., Congressional Record S5394-5397 (May, 26, 2006); Marcell, "National Security," 253.

[35] The Clinton administration also made an effort to build on its experience of complex contingency operations through Presidential Decision Directive 56. PDD 56 called for integrated planning of such operations, requiring the development of a political-military plan defining issue that needed to be resolved in advance of an operation and assigning agency responsibilities. The process was to be overseen by the NSC Deputies committee. An Executive Committee would be created for each new operation to supervise day-to-day management of the US role, gather together the appropriate agencies, and ensure legal and fiscal issues were resolved. An "after action" review would be done of each operation. PDD-56 was never fully implemented and was superseded by NSPD-44.

[36] For a summary of various reform proposals for the interagency process, see Nayla Arnas, Charles Barry, and Robert B. Oakley, *Harnessing the Interagency for Complex Operations* (Washington, DC: Center for Technology and National Security Policy, National Defense University, Washington, DC, August 2005), http://www.ndu.edu/ctnsp/Def_Tech/DTP%2016%20Harnessing%20the%20Interagency.pdf (accessed July 19, 2006).

IMPLEMENTATION ISSUES

The Iraq experience exposed a number of implementation issues involving human and fiscal resource decisions that need to be dealt with in any subsequent post-conflict S&R operation. Many lessons were learned the hard way on the ground in Iraq, but are slowly being codified into an agenda for the agencies responsible for planning, interagency coordination and oversight.

The first issue is who or which agencies should have responsibility for implementation on the ground. In Iraq, a bewildering array of organizations had implementation responsibility, working for a series of ad hoc agencies responsible for coordination. What is needed is one clear, institutionalized office, supported by an interagency presence, based either in an embassy or presidential representative, with authority over post-conflict operations and a clear division of responsibility and working relationship vis-à-vis the military commander in the field. This office should be linked to an authoritative dispute resolution organization in Washington.

This office needs to be empowered to make decisions about program priorities, spending and contracting, with tasking being done to the many agencies involved locally. The program officers delivering reconstruction projects for such agencies as USAID, State, Justice, Health and Human Services, and Defense should be accountable to this office. Full use needs to be made of the capabilities already at hand in the US government to implement such programs – particularly the USAID capabilities housed in the Office of Transition Initiatives and the Disaster Assistance Response Teams (DART) experienced in humanitarian and disaster relief.[37]

Human resource issues are a second important problem exposed by the Iraq experience. It was extraordinarily difficult to recruit civilian personnel to serve in Iraq, the time in service in-country was highly variable, private personnel contracting was difficult, security for civilian personnel was a major problem, the right skill sets were not always available, and inexperience was common on the CPA staff. All these problems spilled over into lack of efficiency in operations and effectiveness of performance for the CPA.

---

[37] Ibid., 20; and Diamond, *Squandered Victory*, 104.

Virtually every study and directive concerned with future S&R operations has focused on the human resource problem, calling for better and different staff training and education at civilian agencies, the creation of a "surge capability" such as a reserve corps of civilian specialists that could be rapidly deployed to post-conflict areas, flexibility in hiring and contracting rules for personnel, greater inter-agency coordination on personnel policies and human resource regulations (including some form of joint service for personnel likely to be involved in post-conflict operations), and planning for security for civilian personnel.[38] Defense has now focused on training and exercising personnel for S&R operations (Directive 3000.05) and S/CRS is developing a concept for a civilian reserve corps, which is supported by the Lugar-Biden bill pending in Congress. These actions, while important, will not provide near-term solutions to the personnel problem. A third issue is flexibility of funding and contracting mechanisms. As noted, the provision of appropriated funds for post-conflict Iraq S&R was slow, due in large part to the failure to anticipate the requirements. While DFI funds filled the gap and could be used flexibly, questions were raised about the accountability with which these funds were contracted and spent. In addition, cumbersome federal spending and contracting practices seriously slowed the delivery of appropriated funds, creating a substantial lag between the time the funds were made available and their actual obligation to a project.

As a consequence, considerable attention has been devoted to both flexibility and accountability in funding.[39] The Special Inspector General for Iraq Reconstruction recommends greater flexibility in the uses of contracting rules, a more clear definition of program requirements, the use of flexible funding instruments, and greater attention to long-term costs of projects and their sustainability by the receiving government. Flexibility is a key consideration. The CERP program appears to have combined flexibility and accountability successfully, allowing rapid delivery of local projects.[40] Similar initiatives such as the Accelerated Iraq Reconstruction Program (AIRP-

---

[38] Murdock and Flournoy, *Beyond Goldwater-Nichols*; Defense Science Board, *Transition to and from Hostilities*; Department of Defense Directive 3000.05, *Military Support for Stability*; White House, *National Security Presidential Directive NSPD-44* (This NSPD superseded PDD-56 NSPD-44), all pay attention to this issue; In particular, the Special Inspector General for Iraq focused his first lessons learned report on human resources; Special Inspector General for Iraqi Reconstruction, *Iraq Reconstruction: Lessons in Human Capital Management* (January 2006), 30; This report described CPA as a "pickup team" with high turnover.

[39] Celeste J. Ward, *The Coalition Provisional Authority's Experience with Governance in Iraq*, Special Report 139 (Washington, DC: US Institute of Peace, May 2005) 11.

[40] Martins, "No Small Change," 15.

developed by the CPA) and the Rapid Contracting Initiative for the electricity sector also seem to have dealt with the need for flexibility, and deserve further study and possible institutionalization.

Along with flexibility comes accountability. A number of questions have been raised, based on the Iraq experience, about the accountability for spending and contracting. In part to deal with this problem, the assistance appropriated in the fall of 2003 was left in the hands of OMB to "apportion" to the appropriate agencies. Congress also required regular reporting on the functional allocations of this funding by the CPA, through the 2207 reports, and created the Special Inspector General for Iraq Reconstruction to audit the spending. There remains concern, however, that data systems have not been created to track expenditures and that contracts and fiscal reporting mechanisms are slow or non-existent.

The precedent of the SIGIR is a good one that could be institutionalized more generally. In addition, it will be important to ensure that trained contracting personnel deploy with any local office responsible for post-conflict S&R operations, to ensure proper contracting practices. In addition, it will be critical to create clear and timely reporting requirements from the local S&R office to the executive branch and the Congress, permitting appropriate oversight over S&R programs and projects.

FLEXIBLE SPENDING AUTHORITIES

One issue which connects implementation and broader federal budget considerations is the flexibility with which the Defense Department can conduct programs that would normally fall under the authority of the State Department. Operations in Iraq, as well as in Afghanistan and against terrorist organizations, have brought the military more centrally into the arena of foreign assistance than ever before. As a result, the Department of Defense has been seeking a broad expansion of its authority to carry out foreign assistance-like programs directly.

DoD has moved in this direction in part to acquire the capacity to act directly in support of post-conflict S&R and counter-terror operations without seeking State Department approval, as is required under the Foreign Assistance Act for such programs as Foreign Military Financing. The result has been a growing effort to redefine and, to some extent, reallocate the authority to carry out S&R and security assistance activities between State and Defense. In virtually every emergency supplemental budget request, DoD has sought to expand its authority to support friendly and allied governments for contributions to counter-terror operations and for training and equipping non-American forces for such operations, in Iraq and elsewhere—without invoking State Department authorities. The result has been a persistent tug-of-war between State and Defense over what State has seen as an erosion of its prerogatives under the Foreign Assistance Act.

In the FY 2006 National Defense Authorization Act, DoD did receive new authority, allowing the President to direct the Secretary of Defense to support (through training, equipment and supplies) building the capacity of other country's militaries to conduct counter-terrorist operations or to "participate in or support military and stability operations" in which US forces also participate. The Secretary of Defense was to jointly formulate such programs with the Secretary of State, and coordinate with State in the implementation of the program. Defense could draw on up to $200 million of its defense-wide operating and maintenance budgets to fund such programs.[41]

In its legislative proposals for FY 2007, Defense has sought to expand on this authority and add others. These proposed changes were made with the agreement of the Secretary of State, who is generally required to "concur" in DoD actions under the authorities. The Section 1206 authority provided in the FY 2006 bill would be expanded to allow training and equipping programs to build capacity in a broad cross-section of allied or coalition forces—military, gendarmes, internal defense, civil defense counter-terror and border protection. DoD would be authorized to carry out such programs directly, or it could transfer up to $750 million from any DoD operating funds to State or any other agency for this purpose.

In addition, DoD is seeking authority to allow using up to $100 million from DoD operating funds, with the concurrence of the Secretary of State, to provide logistic support, supplies and services to allied forces in a wide range of contingencies, including peacekeeping, S&R, and humanitarian relief. Another proposal would allow DoD to transfer military equipment and communications to allied forces. Still another would allow DoD to use operating funds to allow commanders to respond to urgent humanitarian relief or reconstruction requirements to

---

[41] National Defense Authorization Act for Fiscal Year of 2006, HR.1815, 109th Cong., Section 1206 (April 26, 2005): H12739-13175.This Act also asked the President to report to Congress in a year on changes that might be needed to the Foreign Assistance Act of 1961 to facilitate building the capacity of foreign governments and militaries to support such operations, including the resources and funding mechanisms that might be needed to ensure adequate funding for such programs. This report has not been submitted as of May 2006.

benefit the local populace, up to $550,000 per case, with the concurrence of the Secretary of State, which would effectively institutionalize and broaden the application of the CERP program. [42]

These issues of authorities and funding flexibility could help solve some of the rigidities and inflexibilities of the current, stove-piped budgetary system, which hamper counterterrorism and S&R operations. The Defense proposals recognize an important reality: Congress is reluctant to provide significant funding and flexible contingency authority to the State Department for S&R operations. The compromise would be for Defense to be provided the funding and the authorities, as long as decisions require the concurrence of the State Department.

Some in the State Department see this compromise as a gradual erosion of State authorities over foreign assistance, with long term implications for the Secretary of State's ability to direct US foreign relations overseas. Others worry about orienting significant foreign assistance funds more toward military purposes and operations, at the cost of investment in government capacity-building more broadly.

It seems clear that the current capabilities and structures of the State Department are not yet ready to take on the full civilian planning function that S&R operations demand. As long as such missions are being carried out, funding and capabilities are more abundant at DoD, even though the Iraq campaign has highlighted severe limitations in what Defense is capable of doing in the areas of reconstruction and governance. A fully capable State/USAID, that can plan, fund and carry out S&R operations may be years away and will require substantial cultural changes in the State Department (greater training and capabilities for program operation) and USAID (greater focus on ability and government capacity-building). [43]

BUDGETARY ISSUES

The Iraq experience, combined with Afghanistan and broader counter-terrorist operations, has raised significant issues for federal budgeting for national security. These issues include the adequacy of national security budget resources, their location in appropriate agencies, the discipline

---

[42] Grants could go above $500,000, but would then require the approval of the Secretary of Defense.

[43] Secretary Rice's focus on "transformational diplomacy," announced in January 2006 includes greater attention to training foreign service officers for program management and delivery, consistent with this goal of cultural change. "Transformational Diplomacy," fact sheet, US Department of State, January 18, 2006, http://www.state.gov/r/pa/prs/ps/2006/59339.htm (accessed July 19, 2006).

and transparency of internal and cross-agency resource planning processes, and problems of oversight and reporting.

The first fundamental budget question is whether the US government budgets adequately, and in the right places, for post-conflict contingency operations. It is clear that, in the Iraq case, the government did not. Actual funding for Iraq operations, following open combat, has fallen far short of the requirement. On the military side, operations over the past three years have substantially surpassed expectations, due to a longer and larger presence, the insurgency and instability in Iraq and wear and tear on equipment. There continue to be problems to the present day, including the expectation by the Army and the Marine Corps that resetting the force with overhauled and new equipment will cost substantially more than currently projected budgets.

On the civilian side, reconstruction funding has fallen far short of the need and little in the way of additional funds is expected from the Congress.[44] As the Defense Science Board put it, only eighteen months after the end of Iraq combat, "We have learned to provide adequate resources for 'as long as it takes' for combat, but we often don't provide adequate resources for a sufficient period for stabilization and reconstruction."[45]

No conflict plan can accurately anticipate the exact funding requirement for a war and its aftermath. Adequate budgeting for post-conflict S&R, however, could be estimated. The first requirement would be to provide adequate funds for the civilian capability needed to plan and put in place the capability to respond to a post-conflict S&R need. As already noted, these funds, largely for staff, civilian reserves, and planning office operations, have been hard to obtain from the Congress. Equally important is providing adequate funds to permit early-entry operations in a failing state or invaded state. These are contingency funds, by their very nature, since no system can accurately predict where the next post-conflict operation is likely to take place. As noted, contingency funding for State or any other civilian response capability has been hard to raise in the Congress. The US clearly does not budget adequately to allow appropriate advance preparation and initial response.

The consequence of erroneous projection of the requirement and need for a reactive response has led to the second major budgetary issue growing

---

[44] Joel Brinkley, "Give Rebuilding Lower Priority in Future Wars," *New York Times*, April 8, 2006.

[45] Defense Science Board, *Transition to and from Hostilities*, 8.

out of Iraq operations: the continuing use of emergency supplemental budget requests, at very high dollar levels. The consequence of repeated reliance on emergency supplementals has been a serious breakdown in the federal budget process, both in the executive branch and the Congress. Budget discipline in national security—meaning the provision of detailed justifications for budget requests, pushed through a normal agency budget process, and given adequate oversight by the White House and the Congress—has been seriously eroded by Iraq, Afghanistan, and counter-terror operations.

For Defense, the need to respond to the attacks of 9/11, the Afghanistan campaign and the Iraq war seriously compressed the timing for defense budget decisions, leading to an internal DoD budget planning process that ran parallel to and bypassed the normal DoD resource planning process. The first national security emergency supplemental, for $40 billion requested a month after the 9/11 attacks, had no program justification and, because of the pressure of events, was appropriated by the Congress in record time. As operations continued in Afghanistan and then in Iraq, budgeting through emergency supplementals became the norm for DoD. The normal budget continues to be submitted to the Congress, but parallel requests amounting to nearly 25 percent of all DoD funding between FY 2003 and 2006 have been submitted off schedule.

> *The consequence of repeated reliance on emergency supplementals has been a serious breakdown in the federal budget process, both in the executive branch and the Congress.*

The DoD has argued that it cannot accurately predict future Iraq costs and will continue to need funding on an emergency supplemental basis to cover requirements in a timely way. The Department points to past experience, when wartime costs have been unpredictable and required rapid, supplemental funding. However, in past conflicts, supplemental or unbudgeted funding has generally only been supplied at the start of a conflict, with budget requests reverting to normal budgetary planning channels by the second or third year.[46]

---

[46] Stephen Daggett, *Military Operations: Precedents for Funding Contingency Operations in Regular or in Supplemental Appropriations Bills*, Short Report RS22455 (Washington DC: Congressional Research Service, June 13, 2005).

The distinction between the regular DoD budget request and these emergency supplemental requests has become increasingly blurred. As the Iraq operation continues, equipment that has been heavily used requires repair and replacement. The result is a growing emergency supplemental request for procurement dollars to repair and replace the equipment. It is increasingly unclear how much of that replacement is Iraq war-driven and how much may simply be an acceleration of procurement plans the services already had in place, which would have normally appeared in the regular defense budget request.

The relationship between Iraq and broader plans to restructure the Army are also unclear. Until FY 2007, the Army was seeking "modularity" funding through the emergency supplemental route, justified by the need for autonomously operating brigades in Iraq. On the other hand, this modularity was a predictable, long-term planning and budgetary process for the Army and not an emergency, so it might have been included in the normal budget. Over time, the grey area between the regular, systematic DoD budget planning process and the emergency supplemental process has been growing.

The danger for national security budget discipline is that budget planning in DoD for emergency supplementals does not go through the same process as the regular budget. Supplementals tend to be planned at a high level, in the Office of the Secretary of Defense, rather than through the services programming processes. They move quickly through the DoD process, are reviewed quickly and not in detail at OMB, and are transmitted to the Congress. Congress, as noted below, gives these requests considerably less scrutiny than they do the normal budget. In DoD, this process can create a strong temptation to game the budgetary system, putting in the less scrutinized supplemental service requests that might have been trimmed in the normal resource planning process.[47]

The same problem exists, on a smaller scale, for the State Department, USAID and the foreign policy agencies. Including the FY 2006 emergency supplemental, between Iraq and Afghanistan, over $36 billion in foreign assistance, embassy construction and operations have been provided, over 75 percent of it for Iraq.[48] Normally, annual foreign assistance requests would range from $18-20 billion a year. Here, too, emergency supplemental budget requests are not subject to the same detailed program scrutiny regular budget requests receive, leading to

---

[47] Interviews within Congress and the executive branch.

[48] Amy Belasco, *The Cost of Iraq*, 12; Since then $4 billion in International Affairs spending has been added.

thinly articulated justifications and unclear definitions of budget priorities. The practice is even more risky for the international affairs agencies, as the Defense Science Board notes, since members of Congress have less appetite for continuing to fund these programs over time than they have for supporting forces deployed in the field.

This breakdown in budget discipline will take time to repair. For DoD, it will require returning most budget decisions to the normal process. This can now include substantial parts of Iraq spending, as troop levels and pay are relatively predictable, as is the rate at which equipment is being used, repaired and replaced. Should deployments shrink, the net result is a savings, which can be reflected in future budget requests. For foreign affairs, the correction will involve putting Iraq, Afghanistan and other counter-terror spending into the normal budgetary mix and setting priorities for overall spending before budgets are transmitted to OMB.

Congress has begun to focus on the issue, as members note the use of supplementals for DoD and seek a more fully justified and disciplined process. The Senate version of the National Defense Authorization Act includes a requirement that, starting in FY 2008, the President's budget "shall include a request for funding for such fiscal year for ongoing military operations in Afghanistan and Iraq," an estimate of all funds needed for that year, and a detailed justification.[49]

Discipline on the planning end of the budget also needs to be matched by oversight on the execution end. As noted, however, reporting on budget execution for Iraq is intermittent and incomplete. The allocation of foreign assistance programs is reported regularly, but not their execution. The Defense Department has failed to respond to the requirement to report on Iraq, Afghanistan and counter-terror costs and to estimate future costs legislated in three different statutes. In addition, such data as exist on DoD obligations for the war are inconsistently defined and exclude some costs, making them hard to track.[50]

---

[49] This amendment was introduced by Sen. McCain, supported by the Chair and Ranking Member of the Armed Services Committee (Sens. Warner and Levin), and the Chair of the Budget Committee (Sen. Gregg) among others. Senate Amendment, "Levin Amendment," amendment 4320 to S. 2766, National Defense Authorization Act for Fiscal Year 2007, 109th Congress, 2nd sess., June 22, 2006.

[50] Amy Belasco, *The Cost of Iraq*, 1, 31-32.

A broader budgetary implication of the war in Iraq, as well as Afghanistan and counter-terror, is the constraint these operations necessarily put on other national security spending and federal spending in general. Despite the use of emergency supplementals, these operations have potential consequences for future resources available to the Defense Department, the foreign affairs agencies and to the federal budget. At DoD, continual growth in spending for Iraq is already constraining resources that may be needed to execute programs focused on defense transformation—the technologies that will magnify combat capabilities in the future. Manpower and operating costs in Iraq (and elsewhere) are digesting resources at a rate approaching $10 billion per month. If there are overall constraints on future defense budgets and this spending rate continues, future resource planning could be severely compromised.

> *Despite the use of emergency supplementals, these operations have potential consequences for future resources available to the Defense Department, the foreign affairs agencies and to the federal budget.*

The same stress could be felt in the foreign affairs agencies. Resources for crises such as Darfur, the tsunami, or the Pakistan earthquake are difficult to obtain. There is little stretch or internal flexibility inside existing foreign affairs budgets, so these emergencies tend to require emergency supplemental funding. Iraq costs, both in personnel and in assistance resources, are consuming a growing proportion of overall foreign affairs spending and are not always well integrated into ongoing foreign assistance operations. As Congress presses for a more integrated approach to foreign affairs budgets, the State Department may well find itself pushed to reduce other spending in order to accommodate demands for Iraq and related funding.

This budgetary pressure is amplified in the federal budget as a whole. Iraq spending continues to be high, as do intelligence and homeland security budgets. There also has been significant growth in Medicare, education and transportation costs. The result has been rapid growth in the federal deficit and national debt. While deficits are projected by OMB to decline in future years, these projections are based on current legislation, not taking into account the costs of reform in the Alternate Minimum Tax and the extension of current tax cuts. Nor do they include long-term projections for Iraq and related spending, which are budgeted year-by-year. As deficit pressures grow, the politics of deficit reduction have begun slowly to reappear, with potential consequences for other federal spending. For example, under the spending ceilings proposed by the administration for FY 2007, which protect projected growth for national defense, domestic spending over the next five years would be forced to decline by $152 billion from the Congressional Budget Office (CBO) current services baseline.[51]

CONGRESSIONAL BUDGETING AND OVERSIGHT

Through its oversight, legislative, and budgetary responsibilities, Congress is an important part of the post-conflict S&R equation. Problems in Executive branch planning, organization, budgeting and implementation could be addressed, in part, through congressional scrutiny of policies and budgets. Over the past four years, however, Congress has held few committee hearings on Iraq, influenced perhaps by unitary government and a reluctance to appear to be undermining troops deployed in the field. In addition, while Congress has been willing to support budgets for the military, there is a widespread reluctance among members to commit additional funding to foreign affairs in general, or to post-conflict S&R operations in the State Department in particular.

The result has been minimal attention to proposals that address post-conflict S&R requirements through changes in the executive branch. One exception is the Lugar-Biden bill, which would create a slightly different version of NSPD-44 (a State S/CRS lead), authorize $100 million a year for operating funds for State S/CRS, and authorize a readiness response corps and reserve to support civilian deployments for S&R operations.[52] With the support of the Chair of the Senate Armed Services Committee, this bill passed the Senate in May 2005. Rep. David Drier has introduced a different bill in the House that would create an Undersecretary of State for Overseas Contingencies and Stabilization, a civilian overseas contingency force, a joint task force at NSC for stabilization, reconstruction and contingency operations, and a support fund for these activities at State (to be offset by reductions in foreign assistance programs). There has been no action on the Drier bill.[53]

---

[51] Center on Budget and Policy Priorities, *Five-Year Discretionary Caps Would be Unwise at this Time* (Washington, DC: Center on Budget and Policy Priorities, March 27, 2006), http://www.cbpp.org/3-27-06bud2.htm (accessed July 19, 2006).

[52] Stabilization and Reconstruction Civilian Management Act of 2004, S. 2127, 108th Cong., (March 18, 2004): S108-247.

Congressional oversight of Iraq operations also has been rare, neither the Foreign Relations nor Armed Services Committees have devoted significant attention to the conduct of the war itself. Only the appropriating committees have been engaged in a sustained way on these issues, but both regular and emergency supplemental budget requests move through the process with little scrutiny of Iraq spending. Congressional appropriations staffers have noted, privately, that they see the emergency supplemental budget process as weakening overall defense budget discipline.[54] The foreign assistance and State operations budget requests for Iraq receive attention from committee staff, but rarely from members. In general, both authorizers and appropriators are uneasy about the wisdom of expanding DoD authority to conduct foreign assistance activities. They are, however, equally leery of providing the State Department with increased funding, particularly contingency funding for post-conflict S&R.

Relative inattention, minimal oversight, budgetary reluctance, and institutional skepticism in the Congress pose major problems for dealing with post-conflict stabilization and reconstruction operations long-term. One underlying issue is that the committees in Congress that legislate and oversee defense and foreign affairs rarely communicate as committees and almost never hold joint hearings. Yet the issues of authorities and accountability, which cut across agencies in the executive branch, also cut across the structure of Congress.

This is especially apparent in the case of Iraq and post-conflict S&R. Congress simply cannot legislate or conduct oversight on S&R programs without stumbling across the relationship between Title 10 of the US Code (which governs the Defense Department) and Title 22 and the Foreign Assistance and Arms Export Control Acts (which govern State and the foreign affairs agencies). At the very least, joint oversight and legislative hearings are needed to deal with this relationship as it appears in new legislative proposals. If nothing else, such hearings would inform committee members and staff about the relationship between the two departments and the importance of strengthening foreign affairs capabilities as one tool to lessen the S&R burden on the military.

The same lack of communications exists, even more rigidly, with the appropriating committees. Once the Appropriations Committee Chair

---

[53] International Security Enhancement Act of 2005, H. R. 1361, 109th Cong., 1st sess., (Mar 17, 2005).

[54] Bipartisan source on the Hill have described the defense budgeting and appropriations processes as "bankrupt," as a result of the supplemental process. Confidential interviews.

has allocated funds to the appropriations sub-committees, the subcommittees do not regularly interact. Three subcommittees deal with defense funds—Defense, Military Quality of Life and Veterans Affairs (House) or Military Construction and Veterans Affairs (Senate), and Energy and Water. For foreign affairs funding, there is one major subcommittee in the Senate (State, Foreign Operations), but two in the House (Foreign Operations and Foreign Operations, Export Financing). The appropriations subcommittees will need to be in communication on the fiscal and budgetary issues that cut across agencies over which they have jurisdiction, or it will be difficult for executive branch reform to be effective.

Ultimately, the challenge will be to sustain Congress's attention on post-conflict S&R operations. The Congressional attention span is limited. An issue like post-conflict S&R can come and go, but is unlikely to be sustained, which raises serious questions about Congressional support for long-term post-conflict programs. Policy failures, such as those seen in the first two years in Iraq, will further erode Congressional interest in providing additional support or contingency funding to agencies with what is seen as an uneven track record.

THE PATH AHEAD

Regardless of the wisdom of the decision to invade Iraq, planning and implementation for post-conflict stabilization and reconstruction have been severely flawed, with major consequences for policy success. It is important to cull the lessons from the Iraq experience and to apply them to future operations, lest each be treated as a one-off, reproducing the same flaws and discovering new ones.

A lessons-learned exercise, focusing on planning, resource allocation, implementation and evaluation is critically needed, in an atmosphere free of partisan or political judgment, lest the only lessons learned be that one party or the other is at fault. Effective future planning and resource allocation for such exercises will depend on the fairness and truthfulness of that evaluation.

Second, reporting needs to be an early reform in approaching such exercises in the future. In the rush to implement, DoD has been left virtually free of reporting requirements, while State/USAID reporting is incomplete. Evaluation, none of which is provided today, needs to be included in that requirement. Without accurate reporting and evaluation, agencies will remain forever critical and mistrustful of each others' capabilities and unwilling to coordinate or integrate operations. Without accurate and transparent reporting, congressional mistrust of the executive branch will guide responses to the request for greater flexibility and agility in planning and funding mechanisms.

Third, a way needs to be found to create and empower planning mechanisms that truly integrate executive branch capabilities and allow the government to anticipate future contingencies. These planning mechanisms need to be institutionalized and provided with adequate authority to make programmatic and budgetary trade-offs in advance of a post-conflict stabilization and reconstruction operation. The executive branch needs to have flexible and agile mechanisms that allow resources, human and fiscal, to move swiftly into an S&R operation. These need to be created in dialogue with the Congress, to reassure the latter that information and accountability will be adequate for their oversight and legislative tasks.

America cannot avoid being engaged in the twenty-first century world. The key to success in that engagement will be the way in which it takes place. It is important to remember that the best planning in the world will not survive in a country whose population does not want US forces and civilian agencies to enter or stay. Therefore, the most critical decisions will involve the use of force and the speed, effectiveness and responsiveness with which post-conflict programs are resourced and implemented—to stabilize, provide assistance, bring order, and ensure security. Having tools in the national security toolkit that are flexible, agile, effective and realistically focused will be an important part of that engagement. Iraq demonstrates at least that such tools—for planning, resource allocation, and execution – are not in place and are badly needed.

— 13 —
SHORT TERM FOCUS ON LONG TERM CHALLENGES: THE ADMINISTRATION, CONGRESS AND IRAQ

Denis McDonough

Military operations in Iraq are well into their fourth year, American casualties have topped 2,500 and early in the next fiscal year American expenditures in Iraq and Afghanistan will surpass half a trillion dollars.[1] These numbers foreshadow Iraq fatigue in Congress and among the American public. Policymakers in the Executive and Legislative branches must head off this sentiment if the United States is to maintain a sufficiently robust military and non-military presence to ensure a unified and stable Iraq.

As America's political leaders consider policy changes for Iraq, and their consequences, they must prepare to fight institutional roadblocks in Congress to sustain high-level attention on post- conflict reconstruction efforts. This chapter examines those roadblocks and lays out a strategy to avoid them while making sure that Congress is a responsible partner for policymaking in Iraq.

In 1996, I witnessed a memorable discussion between a senior, experienced member of the House of Representatives and a Haitian leader. Like many other American leaders at the time, the Congressman was trying to cajole the Haitian leadership into some kind of cooperation and compromise to resolve a political impasse that was all too familiar in the winner-takes-all Haitian democracy. "I want to warn you," he said, "Haiti will not be able to count on the kind of attention and support it currently enjoys for very long. Another problem will force itself on to the front page in the US and Haiti will fade from the agenda in Washington."

---

[1] Peter Cohn, "War-related costs will exceed $500 billion next year," *Congress Daily*, June 27, 2006, http://www.govexec.com/dailyfed/0606/062706cdam1.htm (accessed July 19, 2006).

The look on the Haitian leader's face changed from joy, from having Congress off his back, to concern as he calculated Haiti's share of foreign assistance approved each year by Congress.

Another senior US Senator, years later and discussing another topic, told a visiting scholar interested in national security policy, "you have to understand that Congress is essentially a reactive body—reactive to public opinion; at the same time, it suffers from attention deficit disorder, meaning it is difficult to sustain attention on any given challenge for an extended period." This will be doubly so in the coming years as Congress is forced to consider a range of pressing foreign policy choices relating to Iraq, Iran and North Korea, as well as fiscal policy decisions on issues such as the long term viability of Medicare and Social Security, in the context of a daunting federal debt.

The challenge of sustaining high-level Congressional attention, even from experienced and senior Members of Congress, is important to keep in mind as policymakers struggle to fashion a workable long-term policy for Iraq. In addition to the expert views expressed in this collection of essays, among national security experts more generally it is widely assumed that Iraq will demand sustained American investment, regardless of the levels of American troops deployed there, over the course of many years.

For example, in his recent assessment of the Department of Defense's quarterly report on *Measuring Stability and Security in Iraq*, Anthony Cordesman identifies its misleading picture of facts on the ground in Iraq as its chief failing. He does so, he writes, because "it does not prepare the Congress or the American people for the years of efforts that will be needed even under the 'best case' conditions and the risk of far more serious forms of civil conflict."[2]

The rationale for a long-term American effort in Iraq is understandable, particularly when one considers the potential negative impact a failing Iraq would have on a strategically important region. Yet the public

---

[2] US Department of Defense, *Measuring Stability and Security in Iraq*, Report to Congress, May 2006, http://www.defenselink.mil/news/Oct2005/d20051013iraq.pdf (accessed July 19, 2006); The findings of that report will lead many members of Congress to argue the opposite of the general view espoused in this collection of papers and by Cordesman, among others; Anthony H Cordesman, *The Quarterly Report on 'Measuring Stability and Security in Iraq:' Fact, Fallacy, and an Overall Grade of 'F'* (Washington DC: Center for Strategic and International Studies, June 5, 2006), http:www.csis.org/media/csis/pubs/0605_iraqquarterlyreport.pdf (accessed July 17, 2006); Curt Tarnoff, *Iraq: Recent Developments in Reconstruction Assistance*, Congressional Research Service Report RL31833 (Washington, DC: CRS, October 24, 2003) 2,6; CRS identifies increased Iraqi oil revenues, rampant corruption, and unfulfilled commitments from other international donors as potential sources of additional, non-US reconstruction assistance.

debate in the United States, and in Congress in particular, has focused very little, if at all, on what a long-term American effort in Iraq will entail or demand.

This has been true throughout the debate. In the run-up to the war, in public and closed testimony, Administration officials cited the lowest estimates for the costs of the Iraq operation in general and reconstruction in particular. Mindful of the American public's general disregard for foreign assistance programs, reconstruction assistance was rhetorically and procedurally linked to funding for ongoing military operations—a tactic that was very apparent in the earliest and largest request for reconstruction assistance. For instance, the $18 billion second supplemental was identified publicly as being equally important to the security of American troops in Iraq as the $66 billion for military operations in the same request, by the President, Ambassador Bremer and Secretary Rumsfeld.

Meanwhile, the recent debate in Congress on Iraq policy makes clear that Congress's focus will continue to be dominated by our troop presence in Iraq with scant reference to the longer term challenges of rebuilding Iraq. The debate centered almost exclusively on the issue of the length of the deployment of American troops, with little consideration of other, non-military American efforts or responsibilities in the region while we maintain a presence there, or while we drawdown that presence.

The one exception to this general posture among the legislative proposals debated and voted on in the House and the Senate over a two-week debate was Senate Amendment 4320, offered by Senator Carl Levin (D-MI). This amendment referenced the long term challenges that will surely confront the United States and the sovereign Iraqi government as the American military presence changes. It stated the Sense of the Congress that, "during and after the phased redeployment of United States forces from Iraq, the United States will need to sustain a nonmilitary effort to actively support reconstruction, governance, and a durable political situation in Iraq."[3]

While not necessarily a clear statement of long-term support for investments in the reconstruction of Iraq, it is the most robust statement of long-term commitment uttered in the two weeks of debate. In fact, it is as robust a statement of sustained commitment to Iraq as Congress has

---

[3] Senate Amendment, "Levin Amendment," amendment 4320 to S. 2766, *National Defense Authorization Act for Fiscal Year 2007*, 109th Congress, 2nd sess., June 22, 2006.

sought to make since the initial hearings on Iraq and US policy there in the summer of 2002.[4]

A review of the hearings conducted by Congress on Iraq during the current Congress (the 109th, which convened in January 2005) shows that Congress's oversight, like its legislation, is focused almost exclusively on immediate funding and operational military challenges in Iraq and minimally, if at all, on the long-term sustainability of reconstruction.[5]

An exception to this general rule is a hearing that was held in the House Government Reform Committee on October 18, 2005 entitled, "Iraq: Perceptions, Realities, and Cost to Complete." Testimony during that hearing identified concerns from the Special Inspector General for Iraq Reconstruction (SIGIR) and from the General Accounting Office about sustainability of existing reconstruction projects, so much so that the SIGIR recommended the establishment of an "Office of Sustainability" within the Iraq Reconstruction Management Office (IRMO).[6] SIGIR estimated that operating and maintaining US-funded reconstruction projects will require $650 million to $750 million in annual expenditures by an Iraqi government that is already operating a budget deficit.[7]

---

[4] Senator Biden convened hearings in July and August 2002, and the hearings were dominated by discussion of post-Saddam Iraq and the difficulty of that challenge. Senator Biden has been one of the few voices in the Congress regularly urging a clear message to the American people that success in Iraq will demand long and sustained engagement by the United States. Hearings included: US Foreign Relations Committee, *Advancing Iraqi Political Development*, 109th Cong., 1st sess., July 18, 2005; US Foreign Relations Committee, *Advancing Iraqi Political Development*, 109th Cong., 1st sess., July 18, 2005; US Foreign Relations Committee, *Improving Security in Iraq*, 109th Cong., 1st sess., July 18, 2005.

[5] A review of the Iraq hearings in the 109th Congress suggests that Congress's attention on Iraq is dominated by recent developments. The following titles of hearings give a sense of Congressional concerns: House Armed Service Committee, *Current Operations and the Political Transition in Iraq*, 109th Cong., March 17, 2005; House Armed Service Committee, *Status of Tactical Wheeled Vehicle Armoring Initiatives and Improvised Explosive Device Jammer Initiatives in Operation Iraqi Freedom*, 109th Cong., May 5, 2005; Senate Armed Services Committee, *Readiness and Management Support for Operation Iraqi Freedom and Operation Enduring Freedom*, 109th Cong., February 7, 2006; House International Relations Committee, *Iraq: Update on US Policy*, 109th Cong., April 26, 2006; House International Relations Committee, *Review of Iraq Reconstruction*, 109th Cong., June 8, 2006; Senate Foreign Relations Committee, *Accelerating Economic Progress in Iraq*, 109th Cong., July 20, 2005.

[6] House Committee on Government Reform, Iraq: *Perceptions, Realities and Cost to Complete,* 109th Cong., Oct 18, 2005, http://reform.house.gov/NSETIR/Hearings/EventSingle.aspx?EventID=35714 (accessed July 21, 2006).

[7] SIGIR also testified in the House GROC hearing and found in a series of audits mentioned in this CRS study a growing "Reconstruction Gap," which CRS defines as "a project originally promised to the Iraqis and for which funds were appropriated by Congress and cannot be completed with the sums allotted," Curt Tarnoff, "Iraq: Recent Developments in Reconstruction Assistance," Congressional Research Service Report RL31833 (Washington, DC: CRS, October 24, 2003) 2, 6.

Nevertheless, statements and questions from the members of Congress present at the hearing focused less on the long-term sustainability of reconstruction efforts and more on successes, or lack thereof, of reconstruction to date. And at the end of the day, notwithstanding the title of the hearing and its reference of costs to complete Iraq's reconstruction, there was no estimate or approximation of the time or resources needed for this task.

Congress's focus on the short term in Iraq has been exacerbated by the way the Administration has chosen to budget and pay for the war in Iraq. Public Law # 109-234, the latest supplemental appropriations bill to pay for the wars in Iraq and Afghanistan, was signed by President Bush on June 15, 2006.[8] It is the ninth supplemental appropriations bill enacted since September 11, 2001, bringing emergency supplemental appropriations for the wars in Iraq and Afghanistan to $420 billion in total.

Emergency supplemental bills are, as the name would suggest, debated for less time and given less scrutiny than regular appropriations bills. Moreover, the spending included in such bills need not be considered within the confines of the budget constraints Congress puts on itself, meaning that Congress and the Administration are not forced to make trade-offs to fund supplementals, as they would be forced to do if they considered war budgets in the context of the regular annual appropriations bills. Lastly, since the supplementals fund ongoing war activities, they are "must-pass" bills, meaning that if they are not enacted the Pentagon will be forced to suspend ongoing missions. Such must-pass measures become large targets for riders proposed by senior members of either chamber, be they legislative riders or special projects.

Senator John McCain (R-AZ) explained his concerns with reliance on supplemental appropriations this way:

> First, unless we take action, "emergency" funds will continue to be employed as a way to add spending above that contained under the budget caps... Second, supplemental appropriations have diminished responsible budget decisions and proper oversight by Congress... Third, budgeting annually through

---

[8] Armed Services Committee, National Defense Authorization Act for Fiscal Year 2007, S. 2766, 109th Cong., 2nd sess., (April 6, 2006): 109-452.

emergency supplemental appropriations bills encourages pork-barrel spending.[9]

In addition to the problems identified by Senator McCain, Gordon Adams has laid out in convincing detail in the previous chapter the negative repercussions for internal Pentagon, as well as inter-agency, planning and budgeting of over-reliance on supplemental appropriations law.[10]

The reliance on supplemental funding for Iraq also exacerbates the Congressional tendency to focus on immediate challenges in Iraq with insufficient consideration of whether sustainability of America's presence there may require some trade-offs in the short run. By making appropriations in this extraordinary manner, members of Congress and the Administration continue to operate under the false assumption that the most robust portion of America's engagement in Iraq will be only for the near term. As a result, Congress has not prepared itself—or the public—for a sustained, substantial and necessary American investment in Iraq.

THE FOCUS ON THE SHORT TERM IN IRAQ IS CONSISTENT WITH CONGRESSIONAL PRACTICE

While the circumstances in Iraq are certainly unique,[11] the general tendency of Congress to focus on the immediate aspects of any particular

---

[9] Congress, Senate, Senator John McCain of Arizona speaking in the context of the McCain-Byrd amendment, *Senate Amendment 4242*, 109th Cong., 1st, Congressional Record S5860 (June 14, 2006); McCain's remarks were made in the context of a Senate debate on the McCain-Byrd amendment (Senate Amendment 4242), an amendment that requires the regular FY07 budget submission from the President to Congress include funding for ongoing operations in Iraq and Afghanistan be included in the regular appropriations bills. Senator Byrd had offered and the Senate accepted five similar amendments in Senate debates on supplementals over the last three years. The McCain-Byrd amendment, unlike the previous Byrd amendments, is binding on the Administration. It passed 98-0.

[10] Gordon Adams, "Post-Conflict Stabilization and Reconstruction: The Lessons for US Government Organization and National Security Resource Planning," in *Iraq and America: Choices and Consequences*, ed. Ellen Laipson and Maureen S. Steinbruner (Washington, DC: Henry L. Stimson Center, 2006).

[11] Among the many unique aspects of the Iraq operation one must consideration the Administration's reliance on supplementals for funding. A recent Congressional Research Service (CRS) analysis of precedents for the use of supplementals for war operations found that "supplementals have been the most frequent means of financing the initial stages of military operations [but] in general past Administrations have requested, and Congress has provided, funding for ongoing military operations in regular appropriations bills as soon as even a limited and partial projection of costs could be made;" Stephen Daggett, *Military Operations: Precedents for Funding Contingency Operations in Regular or in Supplemental Appropriations Bills*, Congressional Research Service Report RS22455 (Washington, DC: CRS, June 13, 2006).

challenge has been true for some time. A brief review of US policy in post-conflict operations during the last decade makes clear that Congress's attention, and the taxpayer's dollars, generally follow the troops. That is, as American troops are deployed to a particular region, Congress's attention to—and investment in —that region peaks, and as troops redeploy Congressional attention and investment lag.

Success in Iraq will demand robust American investment over the long term.[12] Therefore, a survey of choices and consequences for US policy in Iraq must include recognition that continued Congressional support for robust investment in, not to mention troop deployment to, Iraq is not guaranteed.

This is a fact that the Administration already recognizes. As it finalized its FY 2006 budget for rollout earlier this year, the Administration leaked that it did not intend to seek additional reconstruction assistance,[13] while its latest supplemental request did not include funding for democracy programs in Iraq—though Congress did insist on including democracy funding in the final supplemental appropriations law signed by the President.

> *Congress has not prepared itself—or the public—for a sustained, substantial and necessary American investment in Iraq.*

To Follow the Money, Follow the Troops

A review of Congressional reaction to US commitments overseas over the last decade shows the nature of the challenge facing this and subsequent Administrations that want to maintain investments in and attention to post-conflict Iraq. Appropriated assistance, accumulated

---

[12] Robin Raphel, "US Economic and Reconstruction Assistance to Iraq: Principles for the Next Phase," in *Iraq and America: Choices and Consequences*, ed. Ellen Laipson and Maureen S. Steinbruner (Washington, DC: Henry L. Stimson Center, 2006); Barbara Bodine, "Setting Priorities: Security and Legitimacy." in *Iraq and America: Choices and Consequences*, ed. Ellen Laipson and Maureen S. Steinbruner (Washington, DC: Henry L. Stimson Center, 2006).

[13] Ellen Knickmeyer, "US. Has End in Sight on Iraq Rebuilding: Documents Show Much of the Funding Diverted to Security, Justice System and Hussein Inquiry," *Washington Post*, January 2, 2006, A01, http://www.washingtonpost.com/wp-dyn/content/article/2006/01/02/AR2006010200370.html (accessed July 17, 2006); Ellen Knickmeyer, "US Plan to Build Iraq Clinics Falters: Contractor Will Try to Finish 20 of 142 Sites," *Washington Post*, April 3, 2006, A01, http://www.washingtonpost.com/wp-dyn/content/article/2006/04/02/AR2006040201209.html (accessed July 17, 2006).

from the US Agency for International Development (USAID) Greenbook, and the number of hearings on our policy towards that country are convened in Congress shows that concerted Congressional interest in and support for a certain policy is strongest when American troops are preparing to be deployed and weakest when they leave.[14]

Somalia

Year	Troops	Appropriated Assistance	Hearings Convened
1992		$69,700,000	5
1993	6345	$127,200,000	7
1994	933	$32,100,000	4
1995	419	$17,400,000	1
1996	-	$10,900,000	-
1997	-	$6,800,000	-
1998	-	$14,400,000	-
1999	-	$12,700,000	-
2000	-	$12,800,000	-
2001	-	$20,400,000	1
2002	-	$34,400,000	-
2003	-	$30,900,000	-
2004	-	$30,700,000	-

Haiti

Year	Troops	Appropriated Assistance	Hearings Convened
1994	17496	$124,700,000	9
1995	1616	$185,600,000	8
1996	277	$111,700,000	9
1997	239	$116,700,000	1
1998	356	$121,600,000	-
1999	59	$106,900,000	1
2000	-	$90,800,000	8
2001	-	$91,100,000	-
2002	15	$58,900,000	-
2003	414	$85,400,000	1
2004	26	$157,600,000	2

The numbers in each of these countries demonstrate the point made by the senior members of Congress mentioned in the start of this chapter:

---

[14] Appropriated assistance and hearings convened are imperfect barometers of Congressional interest. In fact, Congress often times takes the Administration's lead on appropriations targets and hearings convened may reflect the interests of the Chairman himself rather than the rest of his committee, let alone the views of the entire Congress. Nonetheless, these two indicators are better than any other in terms of determining Congressional interest in a topic.

Congress has a difficult time sustaining attention to any one issue over time. For example in Somalia, attention and investment lagged dramatically after the redeployment of troops from that country in 1995. Relative lack of oversight from Congress which, according to one Africa specialist on Capitol Hill mainly consisted of the work of one person, Senator Russell Feingold (D-WI), contributed to a general policy vacuum on that country which has been the subject of considerable discussion since an Islamist movement took control of Mogadishu.

Kosovo is equally telling: in 1998 and 1999 Congress convened 29 hearings, but has held only seven hearings in the subsequent seven years. Haiti, which dominated many House debates in 1995 and 1996, fell off the map for all but a handful of members of Congress thereafter until troops were re-deployed there again in 2002 and 2003.

Bosnia-Herzegovina

Year	Troops	Appropriated Assistance	Hearings Convened
1993	-	$600,000	1
1994	-	$103,600,000	5
1995	1	$84,400,000	25
1996	15003	$284,500,000	17
1997	8170	$211,200,000	10
1998	6912	$337,500,000	3
1999	5800	$223,500,000	1
2000	5708	$121,700,000	2
2001	3116	$152,200,000	1
2002	3082	$71,600,000	-
2003	3041	$77,700,000	1
2004	951	$58,000,000	1
2005	263		1

Kosovo

Year	Troops	Appropriated Assistance	Hearings Convened
1997	13	$100,000	3
1998	37	$100,000	24
1999	6410	$14,500,000	5
2000	5427	$177,400,000	3
2001	5679	$176,100,000	-
2002	2804	$130,700,000	-
2003	319	$57,700,000	2
2004	1814	$110,000,000	1

The charts above also illustrate that Congress's engagement in a topic is related to how and at what levels Congress ratifies Administration requests for assistance. Generally speaking, Congress largely follows the Administration's lead in what assistance it provides for a given country or region. One former Appropriations Committee staffer calculates that Congress ratified Administration request levels about 90% of the time.[15]

While Congress generally confirms Administration request levels for assistance, it often seeks to fence off, limit or condition some or all of that money when it feels the Administration has not responded to Congress's recommendations for how the assistance is spent. Such efforts are known as Congressionally Directed Actions (CDAs), a term of art meaning legislative mandates for reports, administrative initiatives, and studies on specific pieces of larger programs. One long-time Intelligence Committee staffer said this about CDAs: "a debatable but fair generalization is that the quality of interaction between an oversight committee and an executive agency is in inverse proportion to the number of CDAs and reports."[16]

A good example of a CDA in a post-conflict effort was the so-called Dole Amendment on US assistance to Haiti. Section 583 of The Dole Amendment (P.L. 104-107), became law on January 26, 1996. It "prohibited assistance to the Government of Haiti unless the President reported to Congress that the Haitian government was conducting thorough investigations of political and extrajudicial killings and cooperating with US authorities in this respect."[17] While Congress basically ratified the Administration's overall assistance request level, the amendment effectively fenced off tens of millions of dollars while also eating up extensive time of senior level Administration policy makers as they sought to mollify Congressional concerns or meet Congressional demands.

Ultimately, therefore, it is in the long term interest of a successful foreign policy to keep Congress engaged. Doing so, given Congress's attention deficit disorder, is difficult, but refusing to try may have long term negative impacts on policy goals.

---

[15] Mark Lipert, conversation with author.

[16] Marvin C. Ott, "Partisanship and the Decline of Intelligence Oversight," *International Journal of Intelligence and Counterintelligence* 16 no.1 (Spring 2003): 69-94.

[17] *1996 Foreign Operations Appropriations Act* P.L. 104-107, 104th Cong., 2nd sess. (January 26, 1996) H12739-13175, section 583.

GETTING CONGRESS – AND THE ADMINISTRATION – TO KEEP AN EYE ON THE BALL

Taking for granted the contention that success in building a stable and unified Iraq will require US investment and assistance for years to come, American policymakers face the twin challenges of identifying the right policies for Iraq and building a coalition at home that will maintain support for those choices even as new challenges, from Iran to global warming to Medicare funding, present themselves.

Other chapters in this volume have identified the available policy choices for Iraq and the region. There are several steps this and subsequent Administrations will have to take to ensure a sustainable coalition at home to support those policies:

1. The Executive branch has to return to the regular budgeting process and move away from the reliance on emergency supplemental appropriations to fund ongoing military and reconstruction operations. Reliance on supplementals complicates internal Pentagon budgeting and planning while also deepening Congressional focus on short term challenges in Iraq without regard for longer term trade offs and funding challenges.

2. This and future Administrations need to focus on the sustainability of US reconstruction efforts in Iraq. While IRMO has established an Office of Sustainability as recommended by the SIGIR, that office still lacks the authority it needs from Ambasssador Khalilzad to demand that ongoing programs in Iraq meet sustainability requirements. Sustainability in reconstruction must be considered as important for stabilizing Iraq as providing security.

3. The Bush Administration must complete a transition to "cost to complete" reporting on ongoing reconstruction projects and begin providing that information to Congress on a regular basis. Calls from SIGIR to go to cost to complete reporting over the last two years have been ignored to date. Such reporting would make Congress—in addition to the Administration—responsible for seeing projects through to completion.

4. The Administration also ought to seek an updated World Bank assessment of Iraqi needs for reconstruction. Current development and reconstruction plans appear to be based largely on a rushed 2003 World Bank assessment prepared for the Madrid Donor Conference. An updated assessment will help contextualize the many remaining challenges—and increase pressure on other international donors who have not lived up to their initial pledges for direct assistance or debt relief.

5. Congress must strengthen its authorization committees, principally the House International Relations Committee and the Senate Foreign Relations Committee. For a number of reasons, including the reliance on supplementals and the Administration's refusal to engage those committees on a regular basis, neither has provided the kind of oversight of ongoing efforts in Iraq that would help lay out the size of the long term challenges in Iraq. Having an engaged set of authorizing committees creates for any Executive agency the kind of informed and committed constituency that it needs to fight for long-term policy challenges. Without engaged authorizing committees, the executive agencies involved in Iraq reconstruction will continue to be subject to the more narrow demands of the Appropriations Committees.

Lastly, and perhaps the most difficult in the near-term, the Administration and Congress must resist the urge to capitalize politically on the subject of Iraq generally and reconstruction specifically. The findings of this and other expert groups confirm that the challenges of Iraq will be here for this and subsequent Congresses and Administrations. Focus on the immediate political benefits of short term policy choices must be redirected toward long-term candor with the American people about the challenges we face and must defeat in Iraq.

A workable set of policy choices for the future of Iraq is possible, but not without the ongoing engagement of the Congress and the informed consent of the American people. Keeping Congress engaged and the American people informed is a challenge—but a worthwhile one without which success in Iraq will remain elusive, regardless of policy choices.

APPENDIX A

PREAMBLE, IRAQI CONSTITUTION[1]

In the name of God, the most merciful, the most compassionate. We have honored the sons of Adam We are the people of the land between two rivers, the homeland of the apostles and prophets, abode of the virtuous imams, pioneers of civilization, crafters of writing and cradle of numeration. Upon our land the first law made by man was passed, the most ancient just pact for homelands policy was inscribed, and upon our soil, companions of the Prophet and saints prayed, philosophers and scientists theorized and writers and poets excelled. Acknowledging God's right over us, and in fulfillment of the call of our homeland and citizens, and in response to the call of our religious and national leaderships and the determination of our great religious authorities and of our leaders and reformers, and in the midst of an international support from our friends and those who love us, marched for the first time in our history toward the ballot boxes by the millions, men and women, young and old, on the 30th of January, 2005, invoking the pains of sectarian oppression sufferings inflicted by the autocratic clique and inspired by the tragedies of Iraq's martyrs, Shiite and Sunni, Arabs and Kurds and Turkmen and from all the other components of the people and recollecting the darkness of the ravage of the holy cities and the South in the Sha'abaniyya uprising and burnt by the flames of grief of the mass graves, the marshes, Dujail and others and articulating the sufferings of racial oppression in the massacres of Halabja, Barzan, Anfal and the Fayli Kurds and inspired by the ordeals of the Turkmen in Bashir and as is the case in the remaining areas of Iraq where the people of the west suffered from the assassinations of their leaders, symbols and elderly and from the displacement of their skilled individuals and from the drying out of their cultural and intellectual wells, so we sought hand-in-hand and shoulder-to-shoulder to create our new Iraq, the Iraq of the future free from sectarianism, racism, locality complex, discrimination and exclusion. Accusations of being infidels, and terrorism did not stop us from marching forward to build a nation of law. Sectarianism and racism have not stopped us from marching together to strengthen our national unity, and to follow the path of peaceful transfer of power and adopt the course

---

[1] Iraqi Constitution, preamble, October 15, 2005,
http://portal.unesco.org/ci/en/files/20704/11332732681iraqi_constitution_en.pdf/iraqi_constitution_en.pdf (accessed July 17, 2006).

of the just distribution of resources and providing equal opportunity for all. We the people of Iraq who have just risen from our stumble, and who are looking with confidence to the future through a republican, federal, democratic, pluralistic system, have resolved with the determination of our men, women, the elderly and youth, to respect the rules of law, to establish justice and equality to cast aside the politics of aggression, and to tend to the concerns of women and their rights, and to the elderly and their concerns, and to children and their affairs and to spread a culture of diversity and defusing terrorism. We the people of Iraq of all components and shades have taken upon ourselves to decide freely and with our choice to unite our future and to take lessons from yesterday for tomorrow, to draft, through the values and ideals of the heavenly messages and the findings of science and man's civilization, this lasting constitution. The adherence to this constitution preserves for Iraq its free union, its people, its land and its sovereignty.

APPENDIX B

AUTHORS AND IRAQ WORKING GROUP PARTICIPANTS

AUTHORS [1]

Gordon Adams
Professor of the Practice of International Affairs (on leave), The Elliott School of International Affairs at George Washington University and Woodrow Wilson Fellow, Woodrow Wilson International Center for Scholars
Adams came to GW from the International Institute for Strategic Studies in London, where he held the position of Deputy Director. Before moving to London, he served as the Associate Director for National Security and International Affairs of the Office of Management and Budget in the White House. He was founder and director of the Defense Budget Project, and has held positions at the Council on Economic Priorities and the Social Science Research Council.

Barbara K. Bodine
Visiting Scholar with the Persian Gulf Initiative, Center for International Studies, MIT
Prior to her position at the Massachusetts Institute of Technology, Bodine was a Senior Fellow and Director of the Governance Initiative in the Middle East at the Kennedy School, Harvard. In her 30-year diplomatic career she served as US Ambassador to Yemen 1997-01, Coordinator for Counterterrorism at the Department of State, Director of East African Affairs, and as coordinator for post-conflict reconstruction for Baghdad and the central governorates of Iraq in 2003. In her last assignment, she served as Senior Advisor for International Security Negotiations in the Bureau of Political-Military Affairs at State.

Avis Bohlen
Adjunct Professor, Georgetown University
Bohlen is currently an adjunct Professor at Georgetown University. She retired from the US State Department in May 2002, after serving for 25 years as a career Foreign Service Officer. Her positions included: Assistant Secretary for Arms Control (1999-2002), Ambassador to Bulgaria (1996-1999), Deputy Chief of Mission at the US embassy in

---

[1] Most authors were part of the core working group, which convened in February and June, 2006. Other members of the working group are identified at the end of this appendix.

Paris (1991-1995). Before that, she held numerous assignments in the State Department's Bureau of European Affairs, including Deputy Assistant Secretary for Europe in charge of security issues.

David Edelstein
Assistant Professor, Georgetown University
David M. Edelstein is an assistant professor in Georgetown University's Department of Government, the Edmund A. Walsh School of Foreign Service and a member of the core faculty of Georgetown's Security Studies Program. He specializes in international security, international relations theory, and US foreign policy. Prior to arriving at Georgetown, he was a pre-doctoral fellow at Stanford University's Center for International Security and Cooperation and a post-doctoral fellow at Harvard University's Belfer Center for Science and International Affairs.

Michael Eisenstadt
Director, Military & Security Studies Program, Washington Institute for Near East Policy
Michael Eisenstadt is a senior fellow and director of The Washington Institute's Military and Security Studies Program. He is a specialist in Persian Gulf and Arab-Israeli security affairs and has published articles and monographs on US strategy in the Middle East; regional security; nonconventional proliferation in the Near East and Southwest Asia; and the armed forces of Iraq, Iran, Syria, Israel, and the Palestinian Authority. Prior to joining the Institute in 1989, Mr. Eisenstadt worked as a civilian military analyst with the US Army.

Michael Kraig
Director of Policy Analysis and Dialogue, The Stanley Foundation
Kraig is currently managing Stanley Foundation initiatives on Persian Gulf regional security strategies, US national security strategy, and weapons proliferation. He has presented talks on US national security strategy, WMD proliferation, and US nuclear policies at policy institutes in Germany and Italy and at the United Nations 2000 NPT Review Conference in New York. His current work on Gulf security strategies involves extensive travel and outreach in the greater Middle East.

Ellen Laipson
President and CEO, The Henry L. Stimson Center
Laipson joined the Stimson Center in 2002 after nearly 25 years of government service. Her previous positions in various foreign policy and national security institutions include: Vice Chairman of the National Intelligence Council (1997-02); Acting Assistant Director of Central Intelligence for Analysis and Production (2001-02); Special Assistant to

the US Permanent Representative to the UN (1995-97); National Security Council Director for Near East and South Asian Affairs (1993-95); and National Intelligence Officer for Near East and South Asia (1990-93).

Denis McDonough
Senior Fellow, Center for American Progress
McDonough is a Senior Fellow and Senior Adviser to Distinguished Senior Fellow Tom Daschle at the Center for American Progress. Previously, McDonough was Legislative Director for Senator Ken Salazar of Colorado. From July 2000 to December 2004, McDonough was Foreign Policy Adviser to Senate Democratic Leader Tom Daschle.

Paul Pillar
Visiting Professor, Georgetown University
Dr. Pillar is a Visiting Professor and member of the core faculty in the Security Studies Program. Dr. Pillar has twenty-eight years of experience in the US intelligence community. His most recent position was as National Intelligence Officer for the Near East and South Asia, before which he was a Federal Executive Fellow at the Brookings Institution.

Daniel Poneman
Principal, The Scowcroft Group
Before joining The Scowcroft Group, Poneman practiced law in Washington, D.C. for nine years, assisting clients in a wide variety of regulatory and policy matters, including export controls, trade policy, and sanctions issues. From 1993 through 1996, Poneman served as Special Assistant to the President and Senior Director for Nonproliferation and Export Controls at the National Security Council. He is the author of books on nuclear energy policy, Korea, and Argentina, and is a member of the Council of Foreign Relations.

Robin Raphel
Senior Advisor, Special Inspector General for Iraq Reconstruction
Raphel was Coordinator of Iraq Reconstruction at the US Department of State from 2003 to 2005, after serving in Baghdad as a member of the Coalition Provisional Authority. Her previous positions in the State Department include Ambassador to Tunisia and Assistant Secretary of State for South Asian Affairs from 1993 to 1998. Previously, Raphel served as Counselor for Political Affairs at the US embassy in New Delhi (1991-93), and at the US embassy in Pretoria (1988-91).

Nancy Soderberg

Senior Advisor, International Crisis Group

Soderberg is currently a Distinguished Visiting Scholar at the University of Northern Florida in Jacksonville and a Senior Advisor to the International Crisis Group. From 2001-2005, Ms. Soderberg ran the New York office of the International Crisis Group as Vice-President. Soderberg has also served as Alternate Representative to the United Nations; Deputy Assistant to the President for National Security Affairs (1993-97); Deputy Director of the Presidential Transition for National Security; and as the Foreign Policy Director for the 1992 Clinton/Gore Campaign.

Maureen S. Steinbruner

Distinguished Fellow in American Public Policy, Center for National Policy

Steinbruner served from 1993 to 2003 as president of the Center for National Policy, and then spent two years as Vice President and Senior Policy Advisor, responsible for overseeing the Center's programs in both domestic and foreign policy. Steinbruner is currently a candidate for the PhD in Political Theory at Georgetown University, with a focus on contemporary arguments about the role and purpose of government.

OTHER WORKING GROUP PARTICIPANTS

Raad Al-Kadiri
Director of Country Strategies Group, PFC Energy

Lincoln P. Bloomfield, Jr.
President, Palmer Coates LLC and Senior Advisor, Akin Gump Strauss Hauer & Feld LLP

Daniel Byman
Associate Professor and Director of the Security Studies Program and Center for Peace and Security Studies, Edmund A. Walsh School of Foreign Service, Georgetown University

James Dobbins
Director of the International Security and Defense Policy Center, RAND Corporation

Thomas Keaney
Executive Director of the Foreign Policy Institute, The Paul H. Nitze School of Advanced International Studies (SAIS)

Geoffrey Kemp
Director of Regional Strategic Programs, The Nixon Center

Steven Kull
Director of the Program on International Policy Attitudes (PIPA) and the Center on Policy Attitudes (COPA), University of Maryland

Robert Malley
Middle East and North Africa Program Director, International Crisis Group

Phebe Marr
Senior Fellow, Jennings Randolph Fellowship Program, US Institute of Peace (USIP)

Robert Satloff
Executive Director, The Washington Institute for Near East Policy

Jim Turner
Partner, Arnold & Porter LLP

Gen. Larry Welch (Ret.)
Senior Fellow, Institute for Defense Analyses (IDA)

Judith Yaphe
Senior Research Fellow and Middle East Project Director, Institute for National Strategic Studies (INSS), National Defense University

Dov Zakheim
Vice President, Booz Allen Hamilton